lou kelly
THE UNIVERSITY OF IOWA

from dialogue to discourse
an open approach
to competence and creativity

SCOTT, FORESMAN AND COMPANY
GLENVIEW, ILLINOIS   LONDON

ACKNOWLEDGMENTS

1	From "Spring." Reprinted from *Poems and Prose of Gerard Manley Hopkins,* edited by W. H. Gardner. Reprinted by permission of the publishers, Oxford University Press, by arrangement with the Society of Jesus.
7, 115	From *Freedom to Learn* by Carl Rogers. Copyright © 1969 by Charles E. Merrill Publishing Company. Reprinted by permission of the publishers, Charles E. Merrill Publishing Company.
27	© 1970 by The New York Times Company. Reprinted by permission.
51, 54-55	From "Awakening." Hermann Hesse, *Siddhartha,* translated by Hilda Rosner. Copyright 1951 by New Directions Publishing Corporation. Reprinted by permission of New Directions Publishing Corporation and by Peter Owen, Ltd., London.
56, 72	Reprinted from *Identity, Youth and Crisis* by Erik H. Erikson. By permission of W. W. Norton and Company, Inc., and Faber & Faber, Ltd., London. Copyright © 1968 by W. W. Norton and Company, Inc.
57, 136, 137	From "Letter to *The Amherst Student*" from *Selected Prose of Robert Frost* edited by Hyde Cox and Edward Connery Lathem, first appeared in *The Amherst Student.* Copyright © 1966 by Holt, Rinehart and Winston, Inc. Reprinted by permission of Holt, Rinehart and Winston, Inc.
70, 71	From pp. 399-401, 404-406 in *Europe and Elsewhere* by Mark Twain. Copyright, 1923, 1951 by Mark Twain Company. Reprinted by permission of Harper and Row, Publishers, Inc.
74	Reprinted from *The Prophet* by Kahlil Gibran, with permission of the publisher, Alfred A. Knopf, Inc. Copyright 1923 by Kahlil Gibran; renewal copyright 1951 by Administrators, C.T.A. of Kahlil Gibran Estate, and Mary G. Gibran.

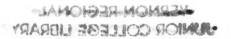

77, 241, 303	From *Teaching the Universe of Discourse* by James Moffett. Reprinted by permission of the publishers, Houghton Mifflin Company.
105	Copyright 1936 and renewed 1964 by Holly Stevens Stephenson. Reprinted from *The Collected Poems of Wallace Stevens,* by permission of Alfred A. Knopf, Inc.
111	From "A Short Dialogue on Some Aspects of That Which We Call Creative English" in *Creativity in English,* edited by Geoffrey Summerfield. Reprinted by permission of the National Council of Teachers of English.
150	Reprinted by permission of the publishers from *The Letters of Emily Dickinson,* edited by Thomas H. Johnson, Cambridge, Mass.: Harvard University Press, Copyright, 1958 by the President and Fellows of Harvard College.
150-152	Reprinted by permission of the publishers and the Trustees of Amherst College from Thomas H. Johnson, Editor, *The Poems of Emily Dickinson,* Cambridge, Mass.: The Belknap Press of Harvard University Press, Copyright, 1951, 1955, by the President and Fellows of Harvard College.
181, 194	Reprinted from *Language, Meaning and Maturity* by S. I. Hayakawa, published by Harper and Row, Publishers, Inc. By permission of S. I. Hayakawa.
300	Reprinted by permission of the publishers, Harcourt Brace Jovanovich, Inc., from *The Five Clocks* by Martin Joos.
Cover Photograph	*Oscillon 3* by Ben F. Laposky. Reproduced by permission.

to all the dialogues
          and
all the dear people
especially my dearest
sometimes wisest mentors
               Melissa Jo
               & Burgess
                    Katie

      without whom
this discourse could never be

to better understand
what an open classroom is
read pages 2-8

to know J O Y

in self
and in talking
and writing
for others

What is all this juice and all this joy.

Gerard Manley Hopkins

This book—your class—begins with you and what you already know, what you have already experienced.

Here you are free to talk and write in your own everyday language—to become more competent in using your language by using the competence you bring with you.

Here you are free to talk and write about your own ideas and opinions, your own knowledge and skills, your own feelings—whatever you want to share with teacher and classmates.

Here the *content* of the course develops from the diverse and unique concerns of all the diverse and unique human beings in the group. And the class finds its *structure* in the dialogues that occur as each person responds to what the other persons say.

For that is the primary purpose of language, the human purpose for which human speech evolved, *sharing experience* and *responding to others.*

When that purpose motivates a class, developing competence will not be drudgery. Instead, putting words together to say what you think and feel will be a joy, even as it was when first you learned to talk.

When that purpose motivates a class, it will become a *community of learners.* Where every learner teaches and every teacher learns. Not from academic requirements, but from human response. Not from passive listening, but from the free and lively exchange of ideas—between student and student, between student and teacher.

To begin with you is to affirm your existence. You are. Now. A thinking, feeling human being who brings to every experience, including college, a valuable background of previous experience.

That is the first assumption of this book—

> whether you are an uncertain freshman or a confident senior,
>
> whether you finished high school last June with honors or came to college with an equivalency certificate earned in night school,
>
> whether you've always made A's in English or "never been any good at writing or talking."

As a student you are exposed to many new ideas and experiences; you are asked to understand wide new areas of fact and philosophy; you are asked to develop new competence in using your language.

But you won't learn unless we who would teach you start where you are. You can't understand new ideas unless you can relate them to your old ideas. You can't develop new attitudes and skills unless you can fit them into the whole set of attitudes and skills that you bring with you.

Which is another way of saying that your ideas and attitudes and your language will change. Just as you will. Not only this year, in this course, but, I hope, each year for the rest of your life.

For living is not a sterile and static preservation of the person you now are. At eighteen or fifty-eight, living is becoming—whatever you *can* become—by responding to every new experience with the spontaneity and joy, the eagerness to discover and explore the world that you knew as a young child. Not only the natural world but the world of ideas and people, at large and in your own backyard.

Bringing the realities of your own life into the classroom may be for you a new concept of teaching and learning.

You have, most likely, spent most of your school days in classes where teachers make assignments and students do assignments. Thirteen years of that is a pretty thorough conditioning process, and, for most of us, change is not easy. You may be reluctant, if not unwilling, to take on the responsibility that comes with the freedom that comes with an open approach. You may want your teacher to always tell you what to do. To give you topics to write or talk about. To give you required assignments that tell you how to organize a theme or speech. You may think you need long chapters or lectures to teach you rhetoric and logic, or a book of rules and drills to teach you grammar.

But that is not the way you learned the language you bring with you, the language that expresses your *self*, the language that is *you*.

Like everybody else in the world, you learned to talk by living in a family of talkers. And you learned to use words in meaningful contexts, you learned to accomplish things with words, by using what you had already learned in personal encounters with your family—as a group and as individuals in that group.

These experiences prepared you to cope, with varying degrees of success, with the people and the situations you encountered in the world you discovered beyond your family. On playground and street and at planned and unplanned gatherings of friends and enemies, you related and interacted with others in various ways, but in almost every instance you also used words to convey what you were thinking and feeling. And each experience helped you develop more competence in using your language to connect with others.

That is learning through living. And I think composition and speech courses at all educational levels should be an extension of that living-learning process. For it is the only kind of learning that can become a significant addition to the continuum of experience that is a person, that is a life. It is certainly the kind of learning we value most. Because it changes us, our attitudes and our behaviors, in some significant way. And that change has a lasting effect upon us.

That is the kind of learning you can experience in an open class.

The teacher who accepts the ideas you bring with you recognizes the futility of attempting to pour into your head all that the professors "profess" to know.

The teacher who accepts the language you have been using all your life recognizes how difficult, if not how impossible, it is for you to make immediate and drastic changes in your language.

So in an open class we ask you to—

Talk and write freely, fluently and forcefully in your *own* language, about your *own* ideas.

Engage the linguistic and rhetorical skills you already have in *meaningful dialogues* with your teacher and your classmates.

Continue the exciting lifelong process of realizing all the possibilities for adapting and expanding your ideas, your language, your *self*.

A definition

Let me define the elements which are involved in such significant
or experiential learning. *It has a quality of personal involvement*—
the whole person in both his feeling and cognitive aspects being
in the learning event. *It is self-initiated.* Even when the impetus or
stimulus comes from the outside, the sense of discovery, of reaching out, of grasping and comprehending, comes from within. It is
pervasive. It makes a difference in the behavior, the attitudes,
perhaps even the personality of the learner. *It is evaluated by the
learner. Its essence is meaning.* When such learning takes place,
the element of meaning to the learner is built into the whole experience.

The dilemma

I believe that all teachers and educators prefer to facilitate experiential and meaningful learning. . . Yet in the vast majority of our
schools, at all educational levels, we are locked into a traditional
and conventional approach which makes significant learning im-
probable if not impossible. When we put together in one scheme
such elements as a *prescribed curriculum, similar assignments for
all students, lecturing* as almost the only mode of instruction,
standard tests by which all students are externally evaluated, and
instructor-chosen grades as the measure of learning, then we can
almost guarantee that meaningful learning will be at an absolute
minimum.

Carl Rogers
from *Freedom to Learn*

Nobody can tell you how to achieve that kind of learning. Nobody can tell you how to create and sustain an open class. The teacher must, of course, be committed to the idea, but he can not do it alone. Students and teacher together must work out the human relationships and the classroom situations that will help strangers become a *community of learners.*

This book offers suggestions. But I hope they will never become required assignments, imposed by teachers and hacked out by students because they are due on a date set by the teacher.

For I am trying to help you create a place where you will talk and write—not to fulfill a requirement—but because you have *something to say*; where you will learn to talk and write better—not to get a grade—but because you have *somebody to hear and respond* to what you say.

the Dialogue begins
between Student and Student

. . . being recognized and paid attention to
is . . . being *identifiable* from other people . . .
being known as a specific individual . . . having
a *particular identity* . . . To be understood
implies that someone is interested enough in a
person to find out his particular characteristics.

William C. Schutz

The joy in self that you can know through writing is incomplete without an audience. A community of writers—for sharing experiences, ideas and feelings with each other, for responding to what each person has shared with you.

For joy "requires . . . satisfying relations with others . . ." Seeing yourself as a "significant, competent, lovable" person is not possible unless others also see you.   (William C. Schutz)

First of all, as a physical body. But that is not possible if you sit in stiff and formal rows of chairs which, in the college classroom, are often bolted down.

So begin by rearranging the furniture. So you won't spend most of every hour staring at the back of somebody's head. I know hair is in, and beautiful, in a million lengths and styles. But faces are the medium for the message of community.

And faces *are* the message—

> closed faces—friendly faces,
> uptight faces—happy faces,
> lonely faces—together faces.

And eyes. That say what we think and feel before the mouth speaks.

Study each other's faces. And remember them.

Learn each other's names. There can be no sense of community without names.

If you wish, devise some little game for fixing names with faces. You may all feel a little silly playing it, but sometimes that is an easy first step into the vast distance that separates us from each other.

If you can't think of a better way of learning names, try this one—

Sit in a circle.

Have each person say the name he wants to be called by.

Then see if each person can name the two persons sitting next to him.

Maybe some potential public relations genius will name everybody on the first try. Maybe all of you will, because you will have heard each person's name three times.

The same day or the next, try this variation—

Sit in a circle.

Tell the person on your right one fact about you or one "particular characteristic."

The aim: to help make you "identifiable" from everybody else, to help establish your "particular identity" in the group.

You'll be hearing something from the "specific individual" on your left, of course.

Share what you have learned about each other with the group.

Read and *respond* to pages 14-16 just as soon as you can.

the Dialogue begins
between Student and Teacher

You remind me of my second grade teacher.
And that's not an insult. You're the first teacher
since second grade who gave a damn about me.

from a student-teacher dialogue

Most people don't like to write. Many say they can't write and their teachers, counselors and advisors agree.

They try to be kind, but the message always comes through brutal.

> You're in college now . . . a world of words . . . and ideas . . . where people are judged by the way they think . . . and write . . .
>
> paragraphs . . . themes . . . research papers . . . literary critiques . . . 200-page dissertations . . .
>
> on subjects to please teachers . . . on subjects to fit assignments . . . whether you care about them or not . . . whether you have anything to say about them or not . . .

And sometimes you feel like your mind turns off when there's a pencil in your hand. Many hapless years ago you checked into the system. An eager, curious, expressive child. Now feeling like a weary wordless adult. Now wondering if you can hack it. Not sure that you want to.

Or maybe you're one of the lucky ones. You've never had any trouble with writing. You say it's just a matter of good grammar and spelling and punctuation and psyching out the teachers, finding out what they want and giving it to 'em. In every paper.

So you struggle through or dash off the number of words required. Not caring if your words say nothing. To nobody. Because you are writing to fulfill an assignment. To get a grade. You rarely expect a human response from a teacher. Just corrections and criticisms. And good grades. And an occasional bit of bland praise.

The open class asks for a different kind of writing. For the open class serves the human purpose of language, the primary purpose for which human speech evolved. That is, *sharing experience* and *responding to others.*

Here you write about whatever thoughts and feelings you want to share—for your teacher to read and respond to, and, if you wish, for your classmates to read and respond to.

Here you respond, in writing, to something somebody—teacher or classmate—says in class. Or to what I say on the printed page to you.

Which means you simply *talk on paper*.

That may sound like a revolutionary idea. Students tell me that somewhere in somebody's English class they somehow got the notion that what they wrote was not supposed to sound like talking. They tell me that nobody *really* talks to English teachers. Not the way they talk at home. Or with friends. Even on perennial theme topics like tell-me-something-about-yourself or what-you-did-on-your-summer-vacation, you try to say what you think the teacher wants you to say, the way the teacher wants you to say it.

Before starting down that dead-end way again, let a student who has used this book point you in the right direction:

> The best thing that happened to me in this class was learning to respect my own writing.

That student had discovered that writing is not the mysterious thing he thought it was, that it's not an esoteric act limited only to English teachers and the gifted few, that it's not a painful, joyless academic grind.

Writing is human behavior. Like talking.

Talking to say whatever you are concerned about, whatever you feel strongly about, whatever you spend a lot of time thinking about—whatever you think is worth saying.

Even when your sense of failure is greater than your sense of self-worth, you are still the most important person in the world to you. Let that person speak in your writing. Turn on your *own* unique voice, use your *own* everyday language—the language you use in the corridors and at parties, the language that is a part of *being yourself.*

Whatever your style of talking, whatever the range of your vocabulary, feel completely free to say what you think, to express what you feel—as soon as you finish reading this page.

Don't pause to wonder what you *should* say or *how* you should say it. Let your pencil move as quickly as your tongue does when you are so pleased or angry that the words simply roll out. Be as open and fearless as when you know you are among friends.

Don't worry about spelling or punctuation or organization or "bad grammar." Don't delete the slang or the four-letter words you depend on to say what you feel. If you talk like that, write like that. Not all semester, but until you can write with some ease. And with much pride—in the sound of your own voice.

Put that *sound*, that *voice* on paper right now.

Your teacher will not be looking for errors when he reads what you have written. He'll be listening to the sound of your voice, he'll be looking for the *you* revealed to him in words.

There is no assigned subject for this writing. We ask only that you *talk on paper*—about what you are thinking and how you are feeling at this very moment. Say, as honestly as you can, what is going on inside your head *right now.*

Do it—for 20 or 30 minutes. Longer, if your mind and pencil are still spinning off words. Shorter, if you can't think of anything else to say.

the Dialogues continue
on paper and in class

... success comes—if it comes—by trust in our own poor skill, and by seeing at the start what we want to say; by confidence; by belief in ourselves ... back of all this, giving it power, is the inherent gift of something to say and of words to say it ...

Percival Hunt

Reading and responding to a page from
each of the following sections every
day for a week or so will help you keep
the class moving.

Talking on paper brings quick rewards for most people. They are delighted to discover that their minds don't really turn off when they pick up a pencil; that writing meaningful, coherent statements is much easier when they feel free to say what they think and feel. I hope it is the same for you. I hope you already feel a little bit of the joy I want you to know—in self and in writing. And I hope you keep on responding to the invitation to talk on paper—with your teacher.

He cannot, of course, give you the immediate response he would if you were sitting together in his home or yours or in the student lounge or in his office. But he will be responding to you as he reads what you write.

And not with the old red-pencil axe.

Even though "writing correctly" may be one of your main concerns, try to forget it for a while. *What* you say is far more important than whether or not it "measures up" to all the usual specifications. And you cannot do your best writing if you are uptight about "making errors" and "not sticking to the subject."

That's why we say just keep on talking—on paper.

Some other day, on other pages of this book, you'll find the help you need with the writing problems you may be worried about, the ones that keep you from *saying* your ideas as forcefully as you want to say them.

But if you are too worried to wait, if somebody has convinced you that you have more problems than ideas, if you're wondering if you'll ever be able to write well enough to get through college, let your instructor know how you feel.

If you insist, you may turn to other sections of this book before others in the class do. But for now, try to forget there's such a thing as an error.

Just hang loose and talk—on paper—as you continue the dialogue with your teacher.

Asking you to talk on paper—to use your *own* everyday language, to speak with your *own* voice—is an attempt to put some vitality into the dull and lifeless themes that students hate to write and teachers hate to read. It is an injunction against dullness. For student talk is full of special knowledge, vivid experience, and honest feelings. We hear life and beauty in the rhythms of your voices.

That's why every composition teacher can say what Theodore Baird of Amherst College has always said: "I think the student should entertain me."

And yet, many students are reluctant to share what they write. They think some pieces are too inept. Others, too personal. If that's how you feel, please say so, and your right *not* to be heard will be respected.

But since you are enrolled in a composition course, you will want your teacher to know that you *are* writing. Let him see the pages you have filled even though you don't want him to read them. Just mark each page with an obvious *please don't read*.

Ideally, your right to say when you want to share what you have written with a reader, including a teacher, should be inviolate. But the ideal is not always feasible. You cannot get the personal guidance you need unless your teacher knows what your particular needs are. And he cannot know that unless you show him what you write.

So bring what you have written to your teacher each class day. It will tell him how you are responding to him, the class, and this book. He in turn can be more responsive to you.

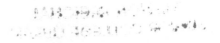

Please let your teacher know what you think of talking on paper. How is it like or different from the writing you have done before? Do you think you need more specific suggestions to get you started writing each time?

Do you think you can *really* talk on paper? And can you speak honestly, that is, say what you *really* think to your teacher?

No one can predict how you will answer. Certainly you will not merely respond to what I say to you here. Or to what your teacher says in class. Or to what he says in writing or in person as he responds to what you write. No matter how much we trust you, your initial attitude toward us will be determined primarily by the attitudes you bring with you, the attitudes that have been building up inside you through all your encounters with teachers since kindergarten. Especially English teachers.

Which ones did you talk to—with honesty and pleasure? How were they different from the ones you couldn't talk to?

What you have to say about all this is important to your teacher—*if* you have something to say.

But remember that the suggestions here are not required assignments.

If a question does not almost immediately set off an idea or a memory, forget the question.

Say what *you* want to say. Write about what *you* are most concerned about. At this very moment.

If talking on paper
has not brought
quick rewards for you—

    if you are feeling depressed
    because your mind still turns off
    when you pick up a pencil—

        if you simply can't imagine
        any kind of writing
        that would be easy—

don't let a temporary failure create despair

If the words won't come, if the pencil won't move, copy something from a favorite book or magazine. Then try to say why you like it.

Maybe something you heard on tv seems worth repeating. Or maybe a slogan tacked to a bulletin board or painted on a wall caught your eye today.

If you wish, write somebody else's words. Then say where you heard them and why you think you remember them.

If that sounds like a cop-out, fill the pages with the words you fill the air with when frustration reaches the desperate point.

Or write, *I can't think of anything to write*, until you do think of something.

Anything to get some words on the page.

Sometimes we have to loosen up the muscles that move the pencil before we can get our minds on the move. Filling a page or two several times a week is guaranteed to do both.

So try again. Right now. Fill a page, either with your own words or with somebody else's.

between student and student

To get the dialogue going, sit together in friendly little groups. Talk together about whatever you want to talk about.

Or let the class talk begin between two strangers, each asking the other some questions that will lead each of you to say something more personal, but less superficial and strained, than openings with strangers usually are.

Perhaps each of you can think of some questions that will help you achieve that goal. Your response to the other person's answer is, of course, an important part of the exchange.

After 10 or 20 minutes, one pair of talkers may wish to join another pair to find out what they have been talking about.

Next time, let the talk begin between two persons who have not talked with each other before. For starters, use the questions suggested below. Then continue by responding, just as you do outside of class, to what the other person says.

If you were a member of a self-sustaining community, what would you want to do for fun and games? What recreation would you recommend for other members of the community? What could you do to help plan and carry out your proposals? Assume no electricity.

If everybody had to contribute some manual labor each day, what would you choose to do? Assume no electricity, no plumbing.

What would you refuse to do?

What other contribution could you make in such a community?

Though you may not be sure that you could do it, what contribution from you would give you the most personal satisfaction?

After 10 or 20 minutes each pair of talkers may wish to join another pair to hear how they have been responding to these questions and to each other.

Where the class talk goes next in an open class cannot be predicted or prescribed—in book, syllabus or lesson plan.

Perhaps each small group will want to continue where you left off the day before. Or you may decide to share with the whole class what you learned about each other.

Some groups may have moved from the initial question considered to others that seemed more important or interesting.

For example, any mention of a self-sustaining community may start somebody talking about the communes which are now so widespread they are called an alternative life style. The movement is no longer limited to the young who are looking for freedom to live and grow the way they want to grow, but now includes some of the not-so-young who are looking for a way to break out of the "system" that has stunted their personal growth. If that is your interest, pursue it—in class talk, writing, reading, and, if possible, through first hand investigation.

Your ideas and concerns, long-held or newly-discovered, make up the list of subjects for class talk every day.

There are, however, on pages 28-31, some suggestions that will help your class move quickly toward becoming a community of learners.

Work in small "task" groups.

The task: to consider the questions asked here, to question the assertions made here.

And you can't do that without *responding* to each other's comments and questions.

the Dialogues continue
with the focus on Learning

. . . twelve years of dull, repressive, formal public schooling, four years of uninspired formal college teaching . . . The tragedy is that the great majority of students do not rebel; they accept . . . virtually every aspect of school life —As The Way Things Are.

Charles E. Silberman

This book is a response to the students who convinced me that The Way Things Are is not The Way Things Should Be.

But whether you are angry and hostile or meek and complacent, whether you are quite hopeful about your college education or full of despair, the open approach I here recommend will raise some questions about how and how much you can learn without traditional texts and assignments.

If you are wondering what to expect in your class, take a closer look at pages 2-8.

What are the theories of learning the open class is based on? Do you understand and accept the analogy I draw between the way you have been learning and using your language all your life and the way we expect you to learn to use your language more effectively in this course?

In large or small group—express your opinions. Talk about your previous learning experiences. Share your hopes and doubts about your open class.

Make sure that you understand what we mean by *experiential* learning. How is it different—

> from rote learning?
> from reading and memorizing facts and concepts?
> from doing assignments to get grades?
> from expecting someone *to teach* you what you
>   need to know?

To better understand the theories of language and the theories of learning this book is based on, read "Competence and Creativity" (105-111).

Then spend some time talking—in class and on paper—about your expectations in this class.

Do you think you can learn to talk and write more effectively by talking and writing?

What else will you need?

This book says you need an audience. A group of listening others. Readers. Fellow human beings to *hear and respond* to what you say—in person or on paper.

We call this ways and means of learning Feedback.

Read about it on pages 113-127.

Talk about it in class and on paper.

In the open class, each person must develop response-ability for his own learning.

Will you extend your language, your ideas, your *self* by responding to the feedback you receive from classmates and teacher?

Or do you need a required sequence of assignments designed *to teach* you what you need to know?

How often will you talk and write for this class if your teacher does not require the whole class to produce speeches or themes on certain fixed dates?

How often will you read, how perceptively and critically will you read, if you are not tested on your reading?

Is your class and each person in class willing to work out specific objectives or must they be imposed by the teacher?

Can you bring *experiential* learning into your classroom?

Are you response-able enough to ask *if* and *what* you are learning, or *why* you are not learning, throughout the term?

Will you respond to your teacher and this book by asking if you are achieving the goals you have set for yourself? by asking if you are contributing all that you can to the community of learners you are a part of?

the Dialogues continue
with the focus on Sharing

Reading and responding to the suggestions
that follow here can help you coordinate
your class talk and your talk on paper—
without giving up the freedom that
comes with the open class.

"publishing"

Some day soon your teacher may come to class eager to read excerpts from your writing. With your permission, of course. And with your cooperation, he may want to begin a "publishing" venture.

For writing is for reading. And reading student writing is not for teachers only.

Unless your teacher has a secretary with lots of supplies, he will need help with the typing of dittos, and money for a paper fund. Please give him both. Because your own writing can do more to keep the dialogues going and to turn class talk into thoughtful and extended discourse than anything teacher or text can tell you. In fact, publishing is essential to the joy you can know in writing, to the pride you can feel in the sound of your own voice.

Publish a page or two at least twice during the first month and then four or five pages as often as possible.

At first (and throughout the term) your teacher may want to select short excerpts from everybody's writing. Or all of what someone has handed in.

You are, of course, free to say when you want something distributed for discussion. Speed up publication by handing it in on a ditto master. Or by reading it to the class or a small group.

As your pagers get longer, you may wish to have a class notebook where anyone who wishes can leave a piece of his writing to be read by anyone who wishes to read it.

Near the end of the term each of you may wish to select the pieces you are proudest of and put them all together in an attractive class anthology.

If you don't want something you have written published, let your teacher know. Simply say so at the top of the page.

Even though you may feel what you have written says your thoughts and feelings as clearly and forcefully as you ever could, you're not sure how others will react to them. You're not ready to defend your ideas in case of attack. You don't want to risk being cut down. As you come to know and trust everybody in the class, that feeling will diminish. Disappear, I hope.

For publishing student writing in the open classroom is NOT for criticizing and correcting papers or pointing out what is wrong with them or saying how they can be improved. It is NOT to grade themes or persons from A to F or to label themes or persons superior, average or inferior.

Reading what your classmates write is to learn what they know. It is to start you thinking about their ideas. It is to make the student-teacher dialogue part of the student-student dialogue that fills your class hours. Reading each other's writing is another way for a group of strangers to become a community of learners.

But only you can say when you feel ready to be published.

"doing your thing" in writing

We often feel that classes and social encounters never provide the opportunity for us—me, you—to let people see how competent and clever we are or hope to become. The open class does.

Talk awhile—on paper—about what you know and do best. Or about something you enjoy doing.

When did you learn your special knowledge and skill? How did you learn it?

Why or how did it become a special thing for you? Why is it worth knowing?

If you have ever taught anybody else how to do it, write some shop talk about your "teaching methods" or your "educational philosophy."

Remember to use your *own* everyday language, to speak with your *own* voice.

Are there any jobs that require the same work, the same skills as your favorite pastime?

What makes work a drudge instead of a joy?

> It's hard to grow up when there isn't enough man's work. There is "nearly full employment" (with highly significant exceptions), but there seem to be fewer jobs that are necessary or unquestionably useful; that require energy and draw on some of one's best capacities; and that can be done keeping one's honor and dignity.
>
> Paul Goodman

Using Paul Goodman's criteria for man's or woman's work, evaluate the job opportunities available to you now; the career opportunities available to you in the future.

Why would Paul Goodman's statement not apply in a self-sustaining community?

Though some people are too modest or doubtful about their abilities to reveal them, there's a variety of knowledge and competence in every class. Plan some sessions early in the semester for sharing something you know or do, some part of yourself, with others.

Talk about it—on paper or in person—with your teacher. Consider other possibilities as you talk with classmates. Devise ways to discover what each person knows or does best. Or what he enjoys most.

If you are reluctant to face the class alone, ask someone to help with whatever you decide to do. Or talk two or three persons into making your turn a small group project.

Please allow me one demand: *mix a little joy* with whatever you share. Make the scene as happy, the vibes as good as you do in the world outside institutional walls. Bring that world into the classroom.

Maybe somebody will start things off with a little music—live or recorded—then talk awhile about the pleasure you derive from listening and performing.

Meanwhile another person or a small group may want to turn the chalk board into a graffiti board or a mural. Then let the class ask questions about what they see.

If you like some of the snapshots or photographs you have taken or some pictures you have painted, use the chalk tray to display your art. Tell how or why you like to do it.

Most college classroom walls are bare. Make yours a showcase for the poster art that began as a youthful fad and then became a part of our culture. If that sounds too expensive, bring some of your favorites to class for one day only. Talk about why they are popular. Are they aesthetically pleasing or is it the message that grabs you?

If you are an athlete, sandlot or varsity, male or female, you can demonstrate and explain the sport you excel in.

If poetry delights you, read and talk about a poem. If you can act, do a short scene from a favorite play.

And the blinds can always be closed for somebody's collection of color slides or light show or the film you made in another class.

It's a community of learners. And everybody has something of worth to contribute.

If none of the suggestions on the previous page appeal to you, perhaps you would enjoy talking about the work you do best. Demonstrate the skill it involves. Or display the products of your labors.

If you like to show off your expertise with food and household crafts, do it for the class.

And the lucky people who have mastered the machines we depend upon to make life more pleasant can show us how to keep them running.

Perhaps someone can explain what it's like to be a farmer these days. Or a builder of highways or houses. Or a policeman.

And can anybody say whether taxicab drivers and nurses really do know more about human nature than anyone else in town? If so, why?

If you are a salesman, try making your pitch and selling your wares to the class.

Perhaps children are your interest—from infancy to adolescence. Act out a little domestic scene on child care and training. Or show the class how you would discipline a problem child.

It's a community of learners. And everybody has something of worth to contribute.

the Dialogues continue
with the focus on *Self*
Self and Others
Values

Choose your own starting point—day by day—for the continuing dialogue with teacher and class.

Whatever is happening—to you, around you, inside you—may provide all the impetus you need. But if there are days when you can't get started, days when you don't want to talk or write about anything that you are thinking or feeling, maybe one of the following pages will suggest something that you are concerned about.

You may still be reluctant to share the interior you with teacher or classmate. But in the open class you don't have to "hand in" all that you write. So pursue your concerns with your silent composing voice. Then decide if you want others to read what you have said.

self

Sometimes we are anxious to share

    our troubles
        instead of our joys,

    our complaints
        instead of our thanks,

    our disappointments
        instead of our hopes.

That, too, is a time for talking on paper,
for saying our thoughts and feelings
for others to read and respond to.

If you're angry about being in this class, if you're here only because it's a requirement of your school, blast away, on paper,
about that.

Or blast away at the other bitter circumstances of your life and
hard times.

Or blast away at those who blast away.

Sometimes you may want to talk about the future. On paper. Whether or not you share what you write with teacher or classmates.

What personal goals have you set for your immediate and not-so-distant tomorrows?

Are they well-defined goals or still a bit hazy?

Are they realistic goals or still touched with a bit of fantasy?

Is college a good place to set or redefine or evaluate goals? Why or why not?

Perhaps today—or tomorrow—you may want to dream a little. To indulge your fantasies. To do a little wishing. Or share your real dreams—if all that fills our heads when we're asleep can be called real.

When someone is trying to awaken you, do you ever say,

"Please—let me finish my dream."

Finish your dreams—on paper. While wide awake. Even though you may think they are too beautiful or too crazy to share.

Love, he thought, *so that is love.* To dream a fool dream like that fool Bessie Guilfort, to dream a fool lie like that fool Cassie Spott-wood, to dream a lie and call it truth. And he thought of all the people moving over the land, moving in streets, standing in door-ways, lying in the darkness of houses, all in their monstrous de-lusion, and so he swept the picture from the mantel.

He heard only the tinkle as glass broke on the hearth, for he had turned away. He stood in the middle of that room of luxurious shadows, laughing.

Laughing, but only for a moment.

For the thought, like the sound of a slow bell, came into his head: *The dream is a lie, but the dreaming is truth.*

Robert Penn Warren
Meet Me in the Green Glen

If you enjoy dreaming on paper, maybe you would like to try one of Kenneth Koch's ideas for writing poetry. He thought it up especially for non-poets.

> Begin every line with I wish.
> Do not use rhyme.
> Make the wishes real or crazy.

Reading, poetry or fiction,

singing or listening to others sing

listening to the sound of a song or poem
that keeps running through your head

writing, memorizing, lines you've read or heard—

there are many ways of saying for self what you feel
but cannot say for others.

> So lonely am I my body is a floating weed,
> Severed at the roots.
> Were there water to entice me,
> I would follow it, I think.
>
> Amo No Komach—9th century

> Truly, nothing in the world has occupied my thoughts as
> much as the Self, this riddle, that I live, that I am one and
> am separated and different from everybody else, that I am
> Siddhartha; and about nothing in the world do I know less
> than about myself, about Siddhartha.
>
> Hermann Hesse—1929

And from a high school class will, 1971:

```
I, Liz Jensen
being of debatable existence
will very little
because I got very little
because I gave very little.
```

Sometimes we can understand what we feel today by recalling an earlier day that evoked the same feeling. Like the far away days of childhood when you went to a new school in the middle of the year and nobody knew you. They didn't talk to you on the playground and the teacher never called on you in class. And they didn't invite you to their parties. Or in the school you attended all your life they whispered and laughed every time you walked by. Because your family was very poor or your skin was a different color or you spoke with an accent or you attended a church that everybody made fun of. And you knew the desolation of always feeling like an outsider.

It's the lonely crowd and it gets lonelier. Agonizing by the time we reach the crucial adolescent years.

You cannot put all of it into words on a piece of paper. You can not convey all that you think and feel from your mind to the mind of another person. But when you find somebody you trust to hear what you say, the dialogue that then engages you is a comforting try. And though you may not want to share what goes on inside your head, if you can get some of all those thoughts and feelings on paper, the words you write may help you define and understand what you think and feel.

Some days we like ourselves very much. Feeling the warmth of somebody's love. Feeling more pride than we should perhaps in what we have achieved. Feeling what we hope is everybody's admiration instead of a touch of egomania. Or maybe just feeling lucky.

It's good to remember those days. And to talk about them if anybody will listen.

You've got a captive listener now. So tell him about the times you've felt at least a touch of pride in what you have achieved. Tell him about the talent or accomplishment that gives you the most satisfaction.

As Siddhartha left the grove in which the Buddha, the Perfect One, remained, in which Govinda [his friend] remained, he felt that he had also left his former life behind him in the grove. As he slowly went on his way, his head was full of this thought. He reflected deeply . . . he was no longer a youth; he was now a man . . . something had left him, like the old skin that a snake sheds.

Something was no longer in him, something that had accompanied him right through his youth and was part of him: this was the desire to have teachers and to listen to their teachings. He had left the last teacher he had met, even he, the greatest and wisest teacher . . .

Slowly the thinker went on his way and asked himself: What is it that you wanted to learn from teachings and teachers, and although they taught you much, what was it they could not teach you?

And he thought: It was the Self, the character and nature of which I wished to learn . . . Truly, nothing in the world has occupied my thoughts as much as the Self, this riddle, that I live, that I am one and am separated and different from everybody else, that I am Siddhartha; and about nothing in the world do I know less than about myself, about Siddhartha.

. . . The reason why I do not know anything about myself, the reason why Siddhartha has remained alien and unknown to myself is due to one thing, to one single thing—I was afraid of myself, I was fleeing from myself. I was seeking . . . to find in the unknown innermost, the nucleus of all things . . . But by doing so, I lost myself on the way.

Siddhartha looked up and around him, a smile crept over his face, and a strong feeling of awakening from a long dream spread right through his being. . .

I will no longer try to escape from Siddhartha . . . I will learn from myself, be my own pupil; I will learn from myself the secret of Siddhartha . . . I have awakened. I have indeed awakened and have only been born today.

But as these thoughts passed through Siddhartha's mind, he suddenly stood still, as if a snake lay in his path.

. . . When he left the Jetavana grove that morning, . . . it was his intention . . . to return to his home and his father. Now, however . . . . this thought also came to him: I am no longer what I was . . . .

What then shall I do at home with my father? . . .

Siddhartha stood still and for a moment an icy chill stole over him. He shivered inwardly like a small animal, like a bird or a hare, when he realized how alone he was . . . Nobody was so alone as he. He was no nobleman, belonging to any aristocracy, no artisan belonging to any guild and finding refuge in it, sharing its life and language. He was no Brahmin, sharing the life of the Brahmins, no ascetic belonging to the Samanas. Even the most secluded hermit in the woods was not one and alone; he also belonged to a class of people. Govinda had become a monk and thousands of monks were his brothers, wore the same gown, shared his beliefs and spoke his language. But he, Siddhartha, where did he belong? Whose life would he share? Whose language would he speak?

At that moment, when the world around him melted away, when he stood alone like a star in the heavens, he was overwhelmed by a feeling of icy despair, but he was more firmly himself than ever. That was the last shudder of his awakening, the last pains of birth. Immediately he moved on again and began to walk quickly and impatiently, no longer homewards, no longer to his father, no longer looking backwards.

Hermann Hesse
from *Siddhartha*

The evidence in young lives of the search for something and some-body to be true to can be seen in a variety of pursuits more or less sanctioned by society . . . Yet in all youth's seeming shiftiness, a seeking after some durability in change can be detected . . . This search is easily misunderstood, and often it is only dimly per-ceived by the individual himself, because youth . . . must often test extremes before settling on a considered course.

These extremes, particularly in times of ideological confusion and widespread marginality of identity, may include not only rebel-lious but also deviant, delinquent, and self-destructive tendencies. However, all this can be in the nature of a moratorium, a period of delay in which to test the rock-bottom of some truth before committing the powers of body and mind to a segment of the existing (or a coming) order . . .

. . . fidelity is that virtue and quality of adolescent ego strength which . . . can arise only in the interplay . . . with the individuals and the forces of a true community . . .

Identity: Youth and Crisis

Fidelity is the ability to sustain loyalties freely pledged in spite of the inevitable contradictions of value systems.

. . . it is the cornerstone of identity . . .

Insight and Responsibility

. . . it is the center of your most passionate and most erratic striv-ing . . . the vital strength which you need to have an opportunity to develop, to employ, to evoke . . .

Identity: Youth and Crisis

All ages of the world are bad—a great deal worse anyway than Heaven. If they weren't the world might just as well be Heaven at once and have it over with. One can safely say after from six to thirty thousand years of experience that the evident design is a situation here in which it will always be about equally hard to save your soul. Whatever progress may be taken to mean, it can't mean making the world any easier a place in which to save your soul—or if you dislike hearing your soul mentioned in open meeting, say your decency, your integrity.

Robert Frost
Letter to *The Amherst Student*

self and others

To be nobody—but yourself—in a world which is doing its best, night and day, to make you everybody else—means to fight the hardest battle any human being can fight; and **never** stop fighting.

e e cummings

If those words express your attitude toward the world, toward the problems and questions that beset you today, they'll make a good starting point for talking on paper.

What cultural forces, what mores and traditions, what institutions —family, mass media, church, school—seek to control your ideas and to mold you into *their* kind of person? What is it like to be always coping, with or without success, with the seemingly impossible standards set by others?

Why do/did you resist? How do/did you fight back?

One student changed "and never stop fighting" to "and never stop writing." What do you think of that?

Long before we reach college, we learn to play the roles expected of us and to judge others by the roles we expect them to play.

And the roles they assign to us, the roles we assign to them, can become rigid. Hard to break out of. Eventually impossible to escape.

What role has always been expected of you—at home? in school?

What happens when you don't live up to the expectations of parents or sibling or spouse? of teachers and friends?

If you feel you are playing a role instead of being yourself most of the time—at home, on the job, in this class—what can you do about it?

Does our culture offer any inviting alternatives? Or would all the popular life styles be for you another phony role instead of a way to find or express self?

I am an invisible man. No, I am not a spook like those who haunted Edgar Allan Poe; nor am I one of your Hollywood-movie ectoplasms. I am a man of substance, of flesh and bone, fiber and liquids—and I might even be said to possess a mind. I am invisible, understand, simply because people refuse to see me.

Ralph Ellison speaks not only for black people; "on the lower frequencies" he is speaking for all of us.

. . . That invisibility to which I refer occurs because of a peculiar disposition of the eyes of those with whom I come in contact. A matter of the construction of their *inner* eyes, those eyes with which they look through their physical eyes upon reality . . .

. . . you often doubt if you really exist. You wonder whether you aren't simply a phantom in other people's minds. Say, a figure in a nightmare which the sleeper tries with all his strength to destroy . . . You ache with the need to convince yourself that you do exist in the real world, that you're a part of all the sound and anguish . . .

If the passage from Ralph Ellison's Prologue to *The Invisible Man* moves you as it moves me, silence may be your only response.

How can any white person respond to the voice of the black man who is speaking in the novel? How can we respond to all the hostile, hopeless voices of black men and women?

How can I respond to the young people, black and white, my students and my children, whose despairing voices I hear in the final paragraph?

What can I say to myself on the days when I hear my own voice in *The Invisible Man*?

Does the alienation we feel when people refuse to see us help us see others as they *really* are?

Who among us can go beyond the quick and easy generalizations of first impressions to *see* the person he is encountering?

Can anyone in your class, anyone at your college, perceive with his inner eyes the *reality* that is you?

If human interaction is to move beyond the social and academic games people play, then we must ask if we are perceiving persons instead of merely recognizing stereotypes; we must ask if we are encountering individual human beings instead of receiving representative members of a group, even though we may think we have great empathy for that group.

An unusual experience may sometimes help us break through a stereotype so that we can at last see the person who has been invisible. If you've had such an experience, please share it with the class.

Perhaps it will help others examine their attitudes toward some of the persons they have known for years. Or toward someone they have met this school year. Or toward someone in this class.

Are you beginning to *see* your teacher and classmates?

How can we let a person know that we are aware of his existence? his worth?

Without being condescending.

How it feels or what it means to be _____.

Can you fill that blank with a word or a group of words that is an important part of you—

> as a person—the *self* you've got to live with (for better or worse, with no possibility of divorce in case it's worse) all your life,

> and/or

> in relation to others—the aspects of the outward and visible *you* that people react to first, the part of you that leads them to put you in the little mental box they've constructed for people like you, the part of you that makes it impossible to be known as you really are.

When you have filled the blank space you'll have a starting point for a dialogue—in class or on paper.

If you can't think of any words to say what you think and feel about self and others, check out the possibilities on the next page.

Say how it feels to be or what it means to be in one of the situations listed here—

the quiet one, sitting on the back row in every class,
not mixing at every dorm mixer

the only square at a swinging party

a first generation college student

a person living in poverty, surrounded by affluence

farmers and small town folks in a dorm full of city jerks

a devout Christian in a room full of scholars who've just
discovered atheism

a jock in a class full of brainy students and a prof
who hates football

a conservative in a liberal prof's class

a radical in the reactionary's class

a veteran or a rotcy surrounded by peaceniks

a competent, ambitious woman in a man's world

anyone perceived as a sexual object

an "old maid" or a young or old divorcee in a world of couples

a homosexual person in a heterosexual world

a black person in white America or on a white campus
or in a white class

a white person in a situation where one black face is surrounded
by white faces and white silence

a white person at a dining table, in a corridor or on a city street
where blacks outnumber whites

anything that is an important part of your concept of self as an
individual, or anything that has a significant effect on the way
you fit or fail to fit into groups

Take a second look at the list of human situations on the previous page.

This time, try to imagine what it means to be what you are not.

Begin by saying—at least to yourself—how you feel when you encounter people who are in one or many ways extremely different from you and your family and friends.

Do you perceive them as unique human beings or do you judge them because they deviate too much from your way of life?

Ask your teacher to suggest some books or articles by writers whose lives have been extremely different from yours.

Listen to their voices. Try to understand how the world looks from their point of view.

What would they think of you?

As we think and talk about self and others our dialogues move beyond an easy and superficial exchange of pleasantries, and we talk about what we value.

Take a quick backward look at the class talk you have engaged in and jot down the topics of discussion you remember. Scan the pages you have filled with words.

We can assume, I suppose, that even a passing mention of an idea indicates at least a passing interest. But is that interest reflected

> in the beliefs and opinions you mean to hang on to?

> in the goals and aspirations you have set for yourself?

> in the things you now possess or expect to acquire?

Do you speak with great confidence or much uncertainty about whatever you consider important? Or do you fluctuate between believing and doubting all the concepts and objectives you are "supposed to" accept?

If you kept a detailed diary for a week,

> how much of what you *do* would confirm what you *say* you value?

A serious consideration of our values entails more questions.

If each member of your family listed his values, how would each list be different from the others?

How do your values now differ from the values you lived by 5 years ago? 2 years ago?

As you talk in class about what you value, what basic differences became apparent?

How do we arrive at a personal hierarchy of values? How do we come to value specific ideas, a certain kind of person, particular activities, particular things?

How have your values been influenced by mass media?

A look at the way we react to a new family that moves in next door may tell us something about the values we live by.

Do general appearances, like clothes and cars and boats and television in living color, make a difference? Is the level of family income, or the occupation that is the source of that income, your measuring stick for new neighbors?

And what about manners, good or bad? And moral standards? And good taste?

How much education does it take to be "in" in your neighborhood?

Are people judged by the way they talk?

Are people of some religions more welcome than others?

Are families without fathers, women without husbands, fully accepted in your neighborhood?

Does the color of a person's skin make a difference to the people of your home town?

If you spoke for a generation of parents when you answered the questions just asked, speak now for your generation. For yourself.

After meeting a person for the first time, or the ninety-first time, do you base your opinion of him on external "facts" or human qualities?

What facts and qualities determine status among the young? Is there more than one kind of people-hierarchy in your high school? How is the situation the same or different now that you are in college?

How much is your opinion of another person influenced by what you think of a particular group which he apparently or obviously belongs to?

How much of what we call getting acquainted is actually assigning people to the stereotyped compartments within our own minds?

Are male and female humans judged by the same criteria?

How do the boys size up the girls, the girls the boys, at a party? in this class?

What does our perception of others say about the values we live by?

How many of our values are freely chosen after considering all the available alternatives?

You tell me whar a man gits his corn pone, en I'll tell you what his 'pinions is.

A "gay and impudent and satirical and delightful young man—a slave—who daily preached sermons from the top of his master's woodpile," expressed that opinion about opinions to young Sam Clemens in 1850. Fifty years later, as Mark Twain, he agrees that

a man conforms to the majority view of his locality
by calculation and intention.

Then he disagrees with the .

. . . idea that there is such a thing as a first-hand opinion, an original opinion, an opinion which is coldly reasoned out in a man's head, by a searching analysis of the facts involved, with the heart unconsulted, and the jury room closed against outside influences. It may be that such an opinion has been born somewhere, at some time or other, but I suppose it got away before they could catch it and stuff it and put it in the museum.

I am persuaded that a coldly-thought-out and independent verdict upon a fashion in clothes, or manners, or literature, or politics, or religion, or any other matter that is projected into the field of our notice and interest, is a most rare thing—if it has indeed ever existed.

A new thing in costume appears—the flaring hoopskirt, for example—and the passers-by are shocked, and the irreverent laugh. Six months later everybody is reconciled; the fashion has established itself; it is admired, now, and no one laughs. Public opinion resented it before, public opinion accepts it now, and is happy in it. Why? Was the resentment reasoned out? No. The instinct that moves to conformity did the work. It is our nature to conform; it is a force which not many can successfully resist. What is its seat? The inborn requirement of self-approval . . . But as a rule our self-approval has its source in but one place and not elsewhere —the approval of other people . . .

A political emergency brings out the corn-pone opinion in fine force in its two chief varieties—the pocketbook variety, which has its origin in self-interest, and the bigger variety, the sentimental variety—the one which can't bear to be outside the pale; can't bear to be in disfavor; can't endure the averted face and the cold shoulder; wants to stand well with his friends, wants to be smiled upon, wants to be welcome, wants to hear the precious words, "He's on the right track!" Uttered, perhaps by an ass, but still an ass of high degree, an ass whose approval is gold and diamonds to a smaller ass, and confers glory and honor and happiness, and membership in the herd. For these gauds many a man will dump his life-long principles into the street, and his conscience along with them.

Men think they think upon great political questions, and they do; but they think with their party, not independently; they read its literature, but not that of the other side; they arrive at convictions . . . drawn from a partial view of the matter in hand . . . They swarm with their party, they feel with their party, they are happy in their party's approval; and where the party leads they will follow, whether for right and honor, or through blood and dirt and a mush of mutilated morals.

In our late canvass half of the nation passionately believed that in silver lay salvation, the other half as passionately believed that that way lay destruction. Do you believe that a tenth part of the people, on either side, had any rational excuse for having an opinion about the matter at all? I studied that mighty question to the bottom—came out empty. Half of our people passionately believe in high tariff, the other half believe otherwise. Does this mean study and examination, or only feeling? The latter, I think. I have deeply studied that question, too—and didn't arrive. We all do no end of feeling, and we mistake it for thinking. And out of it we get an aggregation which we consider a boon. Its name is Public Opinion. It is held in reverence. It settles everything. Some think it the Voice of God.

To talk of values
is to talk
of what our culture is
and
is becoming

In youth the tables of childhood dependence begin slowly to turn: no longer is it merely for the old to teach the young the meaning of life. It is the young who, by their responses and actions, tell the old whether life as represented to them has some vital promise, and it is the young who carry in them the power to confirm those who confirm them, to renew and regenerate, to disavow what is rotten, to reform and rebel.

Erik Erikson

The thing with kids is, if they want to grab for the gold ring, you have to let them do it, and not say anything. If they fall off, they fall off, but it's bad if you say anything to them.

Holden in *The Catcher in the Rye*

There is a revolution coming. It will not be like revolutions of the past. It will originate with the individual and with culture . . . It will not require violence to succeed . . . It promises a higher reason, a more human community, and a new and liberated individual. Its ultimate creation will be a new and enduring wholeness and beauty—a renewed relationship of man to himself, to other men, to society, to nature, and to the land.

This is the revolution of the new generation. Their . . . ways of thought and liberated life-style are not a passing fad or a form of dissent and refusal . . . The whole emerging pattern . . . makes sense and is part of a consistent philosophy. It is both necessary and inevitable, and in time it will include not only youth, but all people in America.

Charles A. Reich

Your children are not your children.
They are the sons and daughters of
            Life's longing for itself.
They come through you but not from you,
And though they are with you
            yet they belong not to you.
You may give them your love but not your thoughts,
For they have their own thoughts.
You may house their bodies but not their souls,
For their souls dwell in the house of tomorrow,
            which you cannot visit, not even
            in your dreams.
You may strive to be like them, but
            seek not to make them like you.
For life goes not backward nor tarries
            with yesterday.
You are the bows from which your children
            as living arrows are sent forth.
The archer sees the mark upon the path of
            the infinite, and He bends you
            with His might that His arrows
            may go swift and far.
Let your bending in the archer's hand be
            for gladness;
For even as he loves the arrow that flies,
            so he also loves the bow that is
            stable.

                                    Kahlil Gibran

If I try to bend that far, I will break.

Tevye in *Fiddler on the Roof*

Find out who your parents are.
Show them your love.
Save them from involutional depression.

from *The Organizer's Manual*

Perhaps love is the process of my
leading you gently back to yourself.

Antoine de Saint-Exupéry

the Dialogues continue
with the focus on Interaction

Discussion is a dramatic method of developing intellectual powers. The main purpose is to promote the social art of conversing, the intellectual art of qualifying, and the linguistic art of elaborating.

James Moffett

From the moment the dialogue begins between student and student in the classroom, the *content* of the course expands. It is no longer only you and the ideas you brought with you. Each of you now has other rich resources for your writing. That is, your reactions to the ideas and opinions, the special knowledge and skills of every other person in the class.

But a community of learners is impossible unless we are willing to abandon the old ways of class discussion.

Going from neat, straight rows-of-students with the teacher-at-center-front to teacher-sitting-with-students in a circle of chairs or around a ring of tables is an improvement *only* if all the people sitting in those chairs are really talking and listening to each other.

How many persons (or what proportion) participate, frequently and extensively, in your class discussions?　How many participate only when directly invited to?　How many do not participate at all?　How many really get involved?

Does the teacher talk more than anybody else? more than everybody else?

Do most students address most of their comments during class discussion to the teacher?

Does the teacher *direct* the discussion? That is, does he ask the questions and make the responses that take the class in the direction he wants it to go? to the conclusion he wants it to reach?

Can students talk freely when the teacher is the discussion leader?

After considering the questions just asked, you will, I hope, want more interaction and involvement than is usually achieved in discussions that attempt to include the whole class.

Where we sit in relation to each other in a classroom can initiate or cut off communication. The distance across a circle of chairs can be just as wide as the distance from the podium to the back row. And the ring of tables in a seminar room can feel like, and therefore *be*, a barrier between us. Either arrangement can also become as inhibiting to spontaneity and freedom as anything that is based on unchanging routine.

Small group work is one way to deal with these problems.

I hope you will spend a lot of class time talking with each other face-to-face in small groups. For only in a small group can you give and get the feedback that all of us need when we try to say what we think and feel.

Sometimes, while exploring a question or seeking a solution to a problem, you may want to pair-off. But I think it takes three to make a group. And please—no more than five. In fact, five may be too many.

Most classes have only fifty minutes together, three or four times a week. Obviously, as the small group gets larger, each person has less time to express his ideas and to discuss the ideas of others.

But even more important, the reluctance to talk that many students bring with them increases as the size of the group increases. And we don't need to look for deep psychological reasons to explain this behavior. It's a matter of proximity. We don't talk to everybody in the bus or plane we're riding on—only the person we sit next to. And when eating or drinking alone in a crowded dining room or tavern, we get into a discussion only with the stranger who asks to share our table or booth.

So keep the small groups small enough for person-to-person communication.

Sometimes, of course, we seek the comfortable feeling we find in the familiar place or activity. Have any of you staked out your little space against the back wall, or in a corner by the door, or on some other spot where you wait each day for the teacher or the class to come to you? Are you literally "keeping your distance," always making sure that nobody comes too close, even when you're sitting with a small group?

Obviously, talk is not the only sign of involvement in or withdrawal from whatever is going on. The feelings expressed on our faces, the attitudes revealed as we sit, rigid or relaxed, the whole body talks even when our voices remain silent.

Read all the signs. Talk about them—in class or on paper.

Human communication is more than words.

Respond to all the nonverbal messages you are sending out to each other. Respond with sensitivity and concern for the person you are trying to communicate with.

You can accomplish that best, I think, in small groups. But only *you* can say what works best in your class. Not only how many persons in a group, but the combination of persons that turns on the most talk for everybody.

Not talk merely to turn off the silence. But talk that is *human sharing* and *responding*. Talk that takes place where each listener can look into the eyes of each speaker. To ask, as we do in one-to-one conversation, if the nonverbal message reinforces what the man is saying.

The small group, like any other academic innovation, can, of course, become a sterile unproductive thing. Like rap sessions where nobody raps. Though everyone may at first enjoy the freedom to simply talk, if the talk becomes repetitious, if you are not learning anything, small groups can become as boring as a dry fifty-minute lecture.

The small group is an improvement only if the persons in it become involved in talking about something they find intellectually stimulating. Which means you may not want to spend all your time with the same small group. You will want the freedom to consider moving to another group if you feel you can not accomplish what you want to accomplish with the group you're in.

And sometimes you will want some feedback from the whole class. Then you can ask for full class discussion.

When a small group or the whole class really gets into a subject, you will not be satisfied with what you are learning through discussion. Somebody will raise questions that nobody can answer, and you will want other sources of information.

Then anybody who learns anything new about the subject will share it. First, perhaps, with the small group, then with the whole class. For when we think something is important and exciting we want everybody to learn enough about it to become as involved as we are. And we want feedback—from anybody who will listen and respond.

So, quite naturally, the small group talking together can become a panel talking to the rest of the class. Perhaps each person will then speak for a longer time without stopping for a response from other members of the group. But the panel will be more interesting to the audience and more natural for the speakers if they continue to talk together, spontaneously, instead of regarding the presentation as a series of public speeches.

The response of the class to the panel, their questions and comments, may lead to a day or two of full class discussion on the same or related subjects.

To assess the effectiveness of your small groups again ask *who* is talking.

> Does one person talk more than anyone else no matter who else is in a group with him?

> Do some of you never speak except when directly questioned?

> How much or how little talk comes from the people in between the two extremes?

Before talking together about your answers, take a long look at your own involvement, your own contribution to the community of learners you are a part of.

Sometimes we talk a lot but contribute very little. Sometimes we talk a lot but never say what we'd like to say. Sometimes we merely say what we think we are expected to say. Sometimes our facile talk is a facade to hide some feeling of inadequacy; sometimes, an attempt to prove to self and others that we are as great as we'd like to be; sometimes, a fulfilling ego trip that those who love us share or condone.

> How would you evaluate your talk in this class? Has anybody learned anything from listening to you?

> Have you learned from the talk you've listened to?

If your answers to these questions do not please you, what are you going to do about it?

Please, as often as possible, put onto paper what you sit and think but don't say as the talk goes on around you in class.

Some of the best student writing I have ever read comes from the people who don't ever talk much in class. And from the ones who on a particular day do not say what they are thinking.

But when you say what you think on paper, you or your teacher, with your consent, can read it to the class. Or it can be "published" for the class to read. You then will have made your contribution to the discussion.

If you feel what you are thinking is too personal or too inept to share, or more critical of another person than you want to be in public, write it down anyway. You may change your mind while writing or while reading what you have written. Or you may see how you can revise it, or your teacher can help you revise it, so that you will want to share it. If not, your right *not* to share is inviolate.

Though we want everybody to become involved in the class talk, to know the joy of interacting with others, we acknowledge your right *not* to be heard.

As one student put it, isn't silence also a response?

What are we saying when our only response is silence?

Are we saying that we lack confidence in the sound of our own voices? Are we saying that we fear how others will react when we speak? Have we been put down by teachers or peers, bosses and colleagues so many times that we feel intimidated and threatened?

Perhaps you feel somehow removed from all that goes on here. Bored or indifferent. Somewhat or very superior.

Or would you say nothing and nobody is gonna shake you up, make you lose your beautiful cool?

Perhaps you don't talk because you still doubt that class talk can be for sharing and responding, not judging and grading.

It is also possible that your reluctance to talk began at home. For in some homes, talk is limited. Language functions primarily as an instrument of basic physical needs. There is no exchange of thoughts and feelings, no lively discussion of events or ideas. In other homes, there's constant talk. On many provocative subjects. But nobody asks the young folks what they think and feel. How was it at your house?

If you can't talk in class about *not* talking, please continue the dialogue that I here begin by putting *your* lines on paper—for your teacher to read and respond to.

What you talk about—in small group or full class discussion—at the beginning of an hour cannot always be predicted.

Sometimes you will simply carry on where you left off the day before. But what do you do if nobody returns with the enthusiasm for talking that he had the day before? Many times it seems that the subject has turned stale overnight.

Is it then the teacher's responsibility to come up with instant excitement? Is he supposed to take over the minute the talk in a small group slows down or stops?

How long should he let you struggle to get something going before he steps in to help?

Not too long, of course. And yet, will you have an open class if most of your talk is teacher-initiated?

This book could supply topics for much class talk. In fact, I hope you will explore further the subjects introduced here. Talking about them. Asking your instructor for more information. Finding books and articles that will tell you more. But only if you are interested enough to *want* to learn more. For your class will not be open if you try to go through this book page by page, slavishly following somebody else's suggestions.

An open class means everyone—students and teacher—is always free to make, and responsible for making, suggestions. Not only to get things moving again when nothing is happening. But to keep the good days going.

Some days the class may begin with someone saying he would like to read a paper that is a response to what happened in class the day before.

Many times the hour ends just as you are getting into the discussion. Or the next class is knocking at the door as you wait impatiently for a chance to make *the* cogent statement of the day. Or as the discussion goes on inside your head after the class is over, you begin to see what they were all talking about. Or after mulling it over for awhile, the fuzzy thought you expressed seems clearer and you want to explain it further. Or you think of ways you could support the opinion everybody questioned when you expressed it. Or you think of something really brilliant you wish you had said.

In many classes you don't get a second chance to contribute to a discussion; in the open class you do. So put on paper the thoughts that occur after you leave class. Then, if you wish, read them to a small group of your classmates or to the whole class next day. Or "publish" them for everybody to read.

Some other day you may want to read a statement or talk because something is troubling you. Or you need some help in making a decision. Or in dealing with a problem—academic or personal.

Or you want to respond to a classmate's "published" statement. Or you have read a book or an article that you want to discuss with somebody.

Or something is happening on campus or elsewhere that you feel must be discussed.

Most likely you will prefer talking first with a small group. Which means the work of the larger group or several small groups could still go on. But the open class must always be flexible enough to meet the needs of each individual without permitting anyone or any group to dominate the class.

The small groups advocated here are not for turning the class into encounter groups where all or most of the emphasis is on discovering and expanding self through *intensive* group experience. Fifty minutes a day, three or four times a week for one or two semesters gives us *ex*tensive time, not the kind needed for a group brought together solely for psychosocial purposes.

Though I am obviously committed to the emphasis placed on self and others in this book, though I believe your best writing will come from intense awareness of self and a highly developed sensitivity to others, I think *that* emphasis must always be coordinated with the writing and talking you do in response to your class and to this book. Writing and talking are very special ways to define, to discover, to know yourself—and others.

The small groups here recommended are not for the purpose of *studying* group performance or interaction. All the research that has been completed and all the scholarly and popular books that have been published on group dynamics, communications theory and interpersonal relations are certainly relevant. But if that became the content of the course, the emphasis could no longer be on you, talking, in class and on paper, about your own ideas and concerns.

Breaking the class into small groups is only a means for releasing more talk, from everybody, and for giving each person maximum feedback on the ideas he expresses.

Analyzing and evaluating group interaction is only a means of asking why we are not achieving what we are trying to achieve.

Mastering all the popular techniques of group interaction might make me a better composition teacher, it might make you a better composer. But whether or not we pursue that interest, we can go on interacting with each other. The relating, communicating psychological being called teacher spends a lot of time trying to relate to and communicate with a lot of relating, communicating psychological beings called students. Which means, I hope, that we have learned to *ask each other why* when we feel we are not getting through to each other, as persons or as a group; *to ask each other how* we can break through the barriers that separate us from each other.

the Dialogues continue
with the focus on Reading

Man reading should be man intensely alive.
The book should be the ball of light in one's hand.

Ezra Pound

Many composition texts and teachers imply or explicitly declare that you write college level essays only when your "content" or "subject matter" comes not from personal experience but from reading. They make a sharp distinction between the insignificance of the ideas you bring to a class and the significance of the ideas they want to introduce you to.

If you've been with me since page one, you know I don't see that distinction. For I say nothing is more complex, nothing is so full of significant content as human experience—*your* human experience.

A *required* collection of essays or fiction or poetry or a *required* reading list would be, I think, a contradiction of the basic concepts of an open class. But the group that does not read may bog down in boredom if not ignorance.

So plan to do some reading—for this class and for the rest of your life.

Read voraciously—

in all the subject areas your dialogues with your teacher and your classmates lead you into,

in all the directions your own curiosity takes you.

Read to understand—

who you are, who you are becoming.

Read to understand the world you live in—

to ask about public decisions that change your world,

to ask how you can have a say in those decisions.

Read to make your opinions, long-held or now in the making, *informed* opinions—

to test your opinions against the opinions of others,

to test your opinions against the information that may strengthen or modify them, against the facts that may support or refute them.

Reading, like writing, is not worth the time it consumes unless it is human experience. Unless you see some connection between the academic act and your own concept of self and the world you live in.

You may cover many pages and complete many assignments, you may recognize the words and pick up a few facts, you may even pour back the bits and pieces in an essay exam, a book report, a 500-word argumentative theme, or a library paper. But you haven't really read a book or an essay or a poem unless the act of reading is a *self-involving* experience. You are not reading unless you are responding to the person who is talking on the printed page to you.

As your eyes take in the words, your mind—*you* must talk back. Just as you listen and talk back in class in response to the ideas of classmates and teacher.

If you don't respond as you read, then reading is a boring mono-logue, just as conversation is when someone drones on after every-body has stopped listening. But when you do respond, reading be-comes an exciting dialogue with the writer, an encounter with the voice of another human being who is sharing his ideas and experi-ences with you.

You make reading a dialogue, of course, every time you turn to a printed source for the information you really want or need. Then, nobody has to tell you to concentrate on what the writer is saying. And you need no warning against missing his most important ideas. You know what you are looking for and you look until you find it.

If it's a book of instructions you've picked up to learn how to do something, you visualize the equipment the writer describes and your mind goes through all the steps that he includes as a part of the process.

When you are reading about something you wish you could have experienced, you reconstruct the action in the most concrete images you can imagine. The sports story may not give all the details of the game, but as the faithful fan reads, he is on the field with the team he admires. He sees the backs in precise formation; he follows the complicated, deceptive plays and the brilliant running and passing; he feels the brutal punishment the offensive linemen give and take; he moves downfield with the sharp and furious blocking that led to the touchdowns the news story is all about.

Comprehending the complex political and economic factors and decisions that led to the revolution or the stalemate recorded in a history book requires the same urgent need to know. The same willingness to try to understand—to try to reconstruct what happened and why.

The writer's meaning is in the words visible on the page. But you don't "get the meaning" the instant the physical images of those words are reflected on the retinas of your eyes. You "get the meaning" in your own mind—when you respond to what you read.

Perceptive reading is your side of the dialogue that gives new life to a writer's words. Without you, the responsive reader, those words would remain inanimate symbols on a piece of paper.

Responding to what you read, engaging in a dialogue with the writer, is essential to becoming a competent person in any subject area you are attempting to master.

Let your teacher know if you cannot get a dialogue going with the writers you have met in this or your other courses. Together you may decide that your basic reading skills are not yet sufficiently developed for you to approach a book with any hope of finding the meaning the writer hopes you will find.

If so, use whatever special services your school provides to help you develop more skill.

In addition to talking together in large or small groups about the reading you are doing for this class, a small group, or the entire class, may decide to spend some time analyzing the required texts from other courses that seem to be too difficult. I suppose you could call it sharing your frustrations.

Bring the books you are having trouble with to class. Ask why they are so difficult. Ask how you can cope with a writer who gives you nothing familiar to grab onto, nothing that you can talk back to him about.

Don't ask classmate or teacher to explain *what* he means. Instead ask *how* you can find the meaning, *how* you can turn another man's words into some action inside your own head.

The avid reader does not need a special course for building up his vocabulary. Instead, he is alert to the unfamiliar word as he reads, and he immediately asks himself what it means.

If the answer is not readily apparent from the context, from the way the writer has used it in relation to other words, then we must turn to the dictionary for help.

If, in this book, you are finding a lot of words that prevent you from comprehending what you read, make marginal notes to help you remember the meanings you find in context and dictionary. Or set up your own word list. Learn the words by sight, sound, and definition.

Then—*assimilate* them. Take them from the printed page and make them a part of your thinking. Use them in your speaking and writing—absorb, incorporate, and digest them, as the body assimilates food. Make them a part of your language and your *self*.

You may sometimes want your classmates and your teacher to read a selection you have read, not because you are having difficulty reading it, but simply because you want to talk with somebody about it.

You're pretty sure you understand what the writer is talking about. You enjoyed talking back as you were reading. The ideas are still buzzing around in your head.

What you want is a response to *your* response. You want to share your new ideas and get somebody's reaction to them.

You may also want to put some questions to other readers. The ones you'd like to ask the writer. About the passages that puzzle you. Or perhaps you are not at all sure that you really grasp the full meaning the writer is trying to convey.

Do others interpret the selection as you do? Have they found some meaning you have missed?

Assemble a small group and compare your reactions to what the writer is saying. Explore the reasons that the reading was a unique experience for each of you.

You may also want to assemble in a small group to look at the way a writer puts his ideas together to make an essay. How is his writing different from the textbooks you use in other courses? Is it more difficult or easier to read? Why?

Is the writer's purpose explicitly stated? Are his main ideas summarized at beginning and end? Or does he use more subtle means to say his thoughts and feelings?

Is there some relationship between the content of the selection and the form the writer has chosen for that content?

I hope your school has a library so full of so many exciting resources that you'll discover something new every time you spend
an hour there. I hope you'll give yourself time to browse. To enjoy
the feel of all those books. And to learn how to find what you
want and need.

Don't be shy about asking questions. Somebody is (or should be)
there for the sole purpose of giving you the help you need to
make the library a vital part of your college life.

Ask for any printed guides that may be available. And if you can't
do it on your own, don't be reluctant to ask a librarian or an upper classman to help you locate:

> general reference works
> specialized reference works
>
> general and special sources of bibliographical information

Play around with the

> periodical indexes and the card catalogue

until you think you can find what you are looking for without
too much frustration.

Explore the stacks if they are open to students a your school.

Get a dialogue going with all the voices in all these books.

Let your teacher know what you are reading.

Keep a list and hand it in every week or so. In addition to the usual bibliographical entry, say, very candidly, how and how much of each source you have read.

I hope you will become so engrossed that you will read a whole book. Or a collection of articles on one subject. Or perhaps a lively curiosity will take you through a wide range of subjects.

Respond to what you read by talking a while on paper about each piece that you read. What you write will be your lines in the dialogue with the writer who turns you on.

Share your ideas about what you read with the class. Persuade others to pursue your interests by reading the same piece you have. Or by finding and reading other sources on the same subject.

Sometimes, of course, you will merely scan some selections or find them so boring you will fall asleep, or so difficult you will give up on them. That's the time to ask *why*.

Why are you not responding to the voice on the printed page? Why is your reading not a *self-involving experience*?

And, most important, what can you do about it?

If reading is for you a dreary attempt "to cover" the content of an academic requirement, writing about what you read will be drearier. For you will not be composing *your* ideas. You will be trying to restate somebody else's ideas.

Sometimes that means trying to say what you do not understand. You write incoherently because you do not *know* what you are trying to explain.

Even when we feel quite sure that we understand what we have read, we often cannot talk or write about it with ease and confidence. Because—we are encountering all or most aspects of the subject for the first time; or we encounter so many new words we cannot grasp the concepts that are basic to meaning; or we find the concepts so complex we cannot see the relationships and implications that are basic to understanding.

But these are not writing problems. They are reading problems.

No composition text or teacher can give you writing techniques that will apply in another course unless you can analyze and classify the mass of confusing and disorganized experience you encounter in that course. You cannot organize a paper for another course unless you can organize the concepts and facts and opinions gathered from your reading and listening. And that means *knowing* the content of the course. It means figuring out relationships and implications.

Begin, I say, by getting to know some of the people in the class. Find out if they have any answers for the questions that are plaguing you. Talk about the course. Not in all-night cram sessions just before an exam. But right after class if you have a free period, a bit later if you don't. Do it frequently. Maybe regularly.

And open up all your classes with questions.

Don't be reluctant to speak out.

> I'm not here to show off what I know. I'm here to learn what I don't know. These questions say what I don't know and want to learn today. I've tried to read the assignments and listen to the lectures and discussions but I'm confused. And I need some help.

Then read off a few well-stated questions.

If you don't have enough confidence or courage or whatever it takes to do that during class, have a question ready for your professor as the class ends. Tell him, tactfully, without laying the blame on him or you, that you don't understand him or the text on several specific points. Tell him you've talked with other students who have the same problem. Ask him for the help you need to clarify your confusion, to organize and categorize what you are trying to learn.

You can write for other classes as we ask you to write, only if you *know* the subject. And that takes becoming involved enough in the subject to ask some questions.

Like what does it all mean?

How are all the concepts in the course related to each other?

How is each concept related to what you already know? what you have already experienced?

What implications does each concept have for you? for others?

How will this new knowledge help you better understand yourself and the world you live in?

What do you *think* about what you *know* about the subject?

Anticipate some essay questions you may have on midterm or final exams in other courses. Write out a few of them.

What arrangement of ideas, what logical order is suggested by the question? What relationships determine that order?

How can you develop and extend the topic you are asked to write about? Do you need to—

define key words?

clarify the implications of the question?

cite supporting facts and statistics? specific details and examples?

What kind of question on an exam calls for an answer that is different from a personal essay?

What kind asks you to express and support your opinions?

If you wish, talk together in small groups about writing essay exams. Together you may decide to write and discuss some answers.

If your reading for other courses is an involving experience—if you respond as you read, if you talk back to the person who is talking on the printed page to you—then your writing about reading is like writing about any other experience. You see "the subject" as a realistic situation. And you say what you think about that situation. You express a specific, perhaps a strong, attitude or opinion about it.

Then, if you want others to hear and accept your opinions on a subject, you analyze that opinion.

What implications does the situation you are talking about have for you? For the other people involved in it?

Have you tried to consider the total situation or is your attitude based on limited experience? Do you need to restate your opinion so that it will not exceed the scope of your experience?

Can you explain *why* or *how* you came to hold a particular opinion? Begin by listing specific reasons or ways.

Can you explain the "truth" of your opinion? *In what ways* (list them) is the assertion you make true for you? for others?

Answering these questions—in writing—before you attempt to explain your opinion is always helpful. On a complex subject, such an analysis is essential.

It provides a sense of direction in the confusing mass of new concepts you are trying to understand. It provides tentative form for your own ideas about what you are learning, what you are experiencing through reading. It helps you clarify and amplify your ideas. It helps you present, in logical order, the supporting facts, statistics, details and examples you have gathered from reading and from other experiences.

the Dialogues continue
with the focus on Competence
and
Creativity

And when she sang, the sea,
Whatever self it had, became the self
That was her song, for she was the maker. Then we,
As we beheld her striding there alone,
Knew that there never was a world for her
Except the one she sang and, singing, made.

Wallace Stevens

To speak of creativity in a composition or rhetoric course is to raise the hackles of curriculum builders and teachers and students and parents who are dedicated only to the development of competence. The ones who think competence cannot develop side by side with creativity.

That view is also held by many of the students and teachers who want to be and let others be creative. They seem to think being creative means that anything goes, that everything comes easy. They seem to hope that the impulse to write is all that's needed, that all the joy is always in easy writing, never in the struggle to perfect what we are trying to say, never in the contemplation of the thing well said.

And so we have some writers who only want to become competent; others who only want to be creative.

If you could ask all your teachers, from kindergarten to college, what competent writing is, you would, I think, get some agreement. All of them would probably say that student writing should be clear and coherent, and most of them would, most likely, add "correct."

In the schools you have attended creative writing probably has a pretty definite meaning, too. It happens at a certain hour on a certain day every week in the lower grades, or in a two-week unit a few times between fifth and eighth grade. Everybody writes poems or attempts to imitate somebody else's poems. And in high school there is a special course in creative writing—for students with special talent.

The separation of competence and creativity in our schools developed, I think, from a larger attitude toward public education. Most of us think of school, from kindergarten through college, not as a place for creative living but a place to prepare children and young adults for life. In a *practical* world. Language Arts or English or Rhetoric class is not a place to continue the creative processes of language you have been participating in since first you learned to talk, but a place to learn to read and write in order to get along—comfortably if not affluently—in a highly competitive economic world.

Give them linguistic *tools* some educators say. And that may be a good word for what gets taught when the most human part of you is reduced to a useful but mechanistic *lever*. That lever may help you get what you want—in other courses, on the job, even in verbal exchanges with other people. But if you use your language only as a tool you shall never know the joy, the power of language that opened up for you when first you learned to talk.

This book begins with the assertion that language evolved because early men, like all of us, felt the need to communicate with each other. And the first and final aim of this book is to initiate an exchange of ideas in an open class. There is, however, a second though not secondary, purpose of language.

That purpose derives from the whole complex relationship between language and *self*, between language and your capacity to understand the inner you, to create some order from the chaos of inner experience that is just as real and just as important to you as the practical external world.

Competence and creativity emerge and grow, not separately but as one, during those early years when most of the young child's talk is not for others but for self. At first his talk is only the repeating of the names he has learned for the objects that make up his external world. The names that help him define and understand that world. The names that help him classify the things he experiences in that world.

But soon from the room where he plays alone or where he is supposed to be taking a nap, we hear a voice that is obviously carrying on an earnest conversation. He is talking to himself about whatever he is doing. Though partly unintelligible to others, that talk is very meaningful to the little person who is explaining to himself the external world he is experiencing. He is making that external experience a part of his inner self. His mind and emotions are responding to all that his senses are taking in.

A little later he begins to see and explain what he is doing in the light of what he told himself the day before. The names he learned for the objects of yesterday's world provide the basis for understanding whatever happens today.

Intuitively, the child has made the language learned from others his own symbolic expression of experience. He has created the meaning of his experience with language. And every new experience, every new word and concept, becomes a way of understanding and classifying future experience.

And he knows, as you and I knew, through intuitive awareness of self in the world, that using language to say what we are thinking and feeling is a creative act.

The child's creative use of language continues—a delightful audible monologue that fills his days—until someone makes him feel self-conscious about talking to himself. (You're talking to the devil when you talk to yourself is how they teased in my day.) Then the child's most creative use of language becomes the undercurrent of private thoughts, the interior monologue, the silent talking to self that we all know.

The need to understand the external world, the need to create our own internal reality, does not diminish while we're growing up or while we're growing old. Finding words to say, if only for self, what is going on inside us, is a basic human need, a fundamental process of being human.

From that human need, language evolved. With his creative, cognitive power man developed a symbol-making process to define and give meaning to human experience.

To define and give meaning to our particular experience, we talk to ourselves about what's happening. And if you *really* want to hear what you are saying, you try to put your interior monologue on paper.

That which happens outside you is not *your* experience until you have "taken it in"—literally. You see, hear, taste, smell and touch the world that is outside you. Then your mind and emotions respond. You tell yourself what you are experiencing. You tell yourself the meaning of what you are experiencing. You tell yourself with words that symbolize the external world as *your* senses perceive it, as *your* mind and emotions shape that world.

Through vague and undefined ideas, you search for clarity and completeness. Modifying and rejecting ideas. Combining and synthesizing ideas. That is how you form your *own* concepts, your *own* view of human experience.

And that makes living a creative process—of thought and feeling and symbol-making. Using the words we already know, putting those words together in combinations old and new, we define, we create our own inner reality.

This book is not devoted to making every man a poet to be read and acclaimed by his fellow poets. It does claim that every man can become his own poet—trying to say, if only for self, what human experience is. And what it can become.

That kind of creativity is certainly an inherent part of competence.

Neither can be developed by teacher or text telling you what to do. Or by giving you drills in the fundamentals of grammar or prosody or rhetoric. Or by requiring you to follow prescribed models for your sentences or your poems or your themes.

But creativity and competence can develop simultaneously in an open class.

Creativity as here defined is not only for the lonely hours when you face the empty pages you are trying to fill. It is also for the hours of talk and interaction.

> "Creative English" is not a matter of simply eliciting verse or worse, but rather of establishing a relationship and an ethos which will promote experiment, talk, enquiry, amusement, vivacity, bouts of intense concentration, seriousness, collaboration, and a clearer and more adequate self knowledge. This will involve us in talk about our selves, our language, our behavior, our attitudes and beliefs, and, when appropriate, in recording such things in writing.
>
> Geoffrey Summerfield

You may never create a poem or novella that the critics will praise or the public will buy, but you can know the satisfaction that comes from trying to explain your *self* and your world to you. You can know the joy that comes when your words reach out and touch another human being.

the Dialogues continue
with the focus on Feedback

Today responsibility is often meant to denote
duty, something imposed upon one from the
outside. But responsibility, in its true sense, is
an entirely voluntary act; it is my response to
the needs, expressed or unexpressed, of another
human being. To be "responsible" means to be
able and ready to "respond."

Erich Fromm

Looking to others, a group of others, for protection and support is universal, extending beyond the family of man to the monkeys swinging through the jungle and the ants building their little hills.

But in most schools, in most classes, competition is the force that keeps things moving.

Your future place in society is mirrored, if not destined, by the place assigned to you on the bell-shaped grade curve. There the elite are separated from the failures by all the mediocre people in between. With impressive grades or scores you dream realistically of entering a prestigious profession, of assuming an influential role in the community. But if you are at the bottom of the rating scale, you spend a lot of time hoping you are not headed for a job of low esteem, hoping you, too, can attain one of the "successful" roles in our society.

It's the American Dream built into an educational hierarchy.

But a lot of people are asking if keeping both eyes on your GPA is the best way to learn. In the wide C-range the competitive action is slow, the learning limited. And if you fall below a C, you learn only what it means to fail. And to live with the fear of failing again.

To become a community of learners is to ask if education can become non-competitive in a competitive culture. It is to seek alternatives. Instead of reading books to ace exams, instead of writing papers to win a teacher's esteem, you are asked to find better ways of helping each other learn.

To become a community of learners is to become response-able as Erich Fromm defines the word. It is to learn by responding. To others. The others who are your classmates. The other who is your teacher. Here we call it feedback. It is, I believe, the best way to experience meaningful learning as you attempt to extend your linguistic and rhetorical skills.

If you *watch* the reactions of others as you speak or as they read or listen to what you have written, if you *hear* what people say in response to your ideas, you do not need a grade to tell you how great or how rotten your performance is; you do not need an official "instrument of evaluation" to point out the ways you should improve. The reactions of your audience will tell you whether you delighted or bored them, whether you informed or confused them, whether you persuaded or alienated them.

Feeding that information back to the *interior* you, where your mind and emotions can act upon it, using that information to help you develop new skills and insights, is your best source for self-correction and growth. Learning from that kind of feedback, from classmates and teacher, is one of the most involving and pervasive ways to learn.

But it may not be the easiest way. Sometimes it may be quite painful. Negative reactions from classmates can seem far more devastating than a low grade from a teacher.

That is why an open class cannot *be* without respect. Not the kind traditionally bestowed upon those among us who enjoy the social status that "merits" respect. Nor those who "deserve" honor and esteem because of their achievements. Nor those in authority over us who "demand" our respect because we fear what they can do to us.

But the kind described in another Erich Fromm definition:

> ... [respect] denotes, in accordance with the root of the word (respicere—to look at), the ability to see a person as he is, to be aware of his individuality and uniqueness.

Carl Rogers brings the Erich Fromm concept of respect into the classroom.

> ... it is hard to know what term to put to it ... I think of it as prizing the learner, prizing his feelings, his opinions, his person ... It is an acceptance of this other individual as a separate person, having worth in his own right. It is a basic trust—a belief that this other person is somehow fundamentally trustworthy ... Prizing, acceptance, trust ... accepting the fear and hesitation of the student as he approaches a new problem as well as accepting his satisfaction in achievement ... accepting his occasional apathy, his erratic desires to explore by-roads of knowledge, as well as his disciplined efforts to achieve major goals ... accepting

personal feelings which both disturb and promote learning—rivalry with a sibling, hatred of authority, concern about personal adequacy. What we are describing is a prizing of the learner as an imperfect human being with many feelings, many potentialities.

In an open class that kind of respect, that kind of *seeing*, is not the sole response-ability of the teacher. For the open class is a community of learners.

To be aware of another person as a separate person, worthy of our trust, to see him as he is—imperfect—means, first of all, listening. Hearing what he is saying. Then trying to let him know we are receiving the message he is trying to send us. It means trying to understand the meaning that message has for him.

It means reacting *without* judging. That is, asking questions so he can clarify what we don't understand. Then sharing our opinions even though we disagree *and* sharing the experiences that explain our disagreement.

It means giving non-threatening feedback. Which is feedback that never makes the other person feel defensive. For if we want to learn, we must *feel free to reveal our weaknesses and ask for the help we need to overcome them.*

That kind of learning brings confidence in self and a sense of community with the people from whom the feedback derives. And it generates response-ability.

What you do with the feedback received from classmates and teacher determines what you will learn, what you will become in the open class.

So listen to their responses. Ask how you can use their responses to help you convey your thoughts as best you can from your mind to the minds of others, to help you use more effectively the language and the rhetorical skills you already have, to help you realize all the possibilities for developing your ideas, your language, your *self*.

Respond to the feedback received by asking *why* whenever teacher or classmate says he does not understand the idea you are trying to express, or whenever someone seems to misunderstand what you have tried to say. Ask how you can attempt to explain the meaning you find in experiences your listeners have not shared. Ask how you can express your ideas more forcefully, how you can recreate your experiences more fully.

Ask how you can persuade others to understand the truth as you see it, even though they may not be able to accept *your* truth as their own. Ask how you can understand why *their* truth is not the same as yours.

You will find the answers to those questions in your dialogues with classmates and teacher. And you will learn how to expand and support your ideas, you will learn how to turn dialogue into discourse, because you will be listening and responding to their response to you.

But learning from non-threatening feedback is for realists only. Romantic and sentimental dreamers are bound to be disillusioned if they try it.

Because we are all human, our responses to each other are often erratic and inconsistent. Sometimes unkind. Sometimes, even though we want to respond, it is impossible to feel the generosity that others are enjoying.

Some days nothing can make us turn on the enthusiasm for learning that everybody else arrives with. Some days nobody arrives with any enthusiasm. The subject that seemed so exciting yesterday has turned stale overnight. All the goals and objectives we set up last week no longer seem important.

The question for all those days is *why*.

The task: to explore the possibilities of changing the direction the class is taking; to evaluate any procedures that are becoming dull routines—for everybody or for one individual.

From beginning to end of the term, and, I hope, for the rest of your life, you'll be asking *if* and *what* you are learning. Or *why* you are not learning. And I hope your answers will be as honest as the ones that follow here are. I hope your answers will lead to as much lively talk, as many good essays as these responses to teacher or text did.

To know joy is to write for others . . . Some
things you see and they don't. Break it down
for them, write of the joy in the object or
the feeling. Just let it flow out to everyone. Let them share your happenings. Let them
participate in some wonderful thing you're
grooving on. Like walking along the river
just digging the air and the birds and the
sights. You're there, right there, on the
riverside, walking along, blocking out everything else from life. Your mind begins to
wander, you feel the wind talk, sing, whatever. The birds sing out to you and the grass
tickles your toes. This is joy. The feeling,
the wonderful feeling that you get when you
get into the swing of things.

Don't just sit there. Jump in, put your whole
mind and soul into it. Don't just do it, live
it.

> Billy Williams

If you really expect my reaction to all these
ideas to be one of great joy, you might as
well hang it up. There's been a lot of guys
with a lot of great ideas that didn't make it.
The basic idea for your open class is great
but getting it to work after your students
have been brainwashed for 12-13 years of school
will be a real chore. People clam up easy and
refrain from free and open speech because it's
never really been allowed. Let the students
case into the situation don't just push 'em off
a cliff and expect them to fly. If you want to
try, and really mean it, you'll make it, but if
you're not going to give it everything you've
got let me know and I'll forget it too . . .
I'd like to hear what your ideas are. Show us
you're a person, not an idealistic freak.

> Brian Barrett

The ideas expressed here are something of a shock to me. I graduated from high school in 1960, and have had almost no classroom experience since then. The only classes I ever had were guessing games. Now I think it could be fun to play those games, but I seriously doubt that I ever learned anything of real lasting value. I have never been able to function in a strictly rigid atmosphere.

Lonnie L. Lee

It appears to me that a course of this type is too idealistic. Speech and writing inhibitions, which have developed over a period of 18 years or more, cannot be eliminated by merely being told to do so. Confidence and self-pride have to be developed to a fine degree in order to "throw off" the oppression of inhibitions, especially in speech. Also, the entire class has to be thoroughly honest with themselves, each other and their instructor. In my opinion, this condition cannot exist.

It is therefore necessary to have a rigidly planned class with the instructor being the omnipotent authority. Perhaps this cramps the style of the more creative students, but considering the class as a whole it is the best policy. This type of class allows the methodical development of the average student.

Richard Van Amerongen

What I don't understand is where does the learning come in? Most people come to class expecting to learn. They come to class expecting a teacher to stand before the class giving a most boring lecture and giving an assignment at the end of class. I'll admit that becomes a drag. The teacher and student play guessing games about what each wants. But this class is no guessing game. The teacher and student feel they are on the same level of understanding.

As I said before, though, I don't understand
what we are supposed to be learning. How does
the association in class help us to learn about
comprehensive English? You haven't told us yet
how all of this association will help us learn
English B.

Doug Paris

The environment you are trying to induce is
good—if the students get involved. I prefer it
over any other English course by far. Because I
don't feel like the teacher's pawn.

Dennis Vandel

feedback about experiential learning

Class was easy in grade school and high school.
I hated class. Some teacher was always leading
you around and saying, "See that." And you'd
say, "Isee that." And she'd smile smugly and
say, "You have great potential." You'd wonder
why. Then she'd give you a test and you'd say
"I see that" again. You'd get an A and everyone would say you were smart, you had great
potential, and you'd wonder why.

So now I'm very down on public education. I
spent a lot of time in it, I was exposed to a
lot, but I sure as hell didn't learn much. I
mean as far as understanding. I learned a lot
of words and concepts, but what was behind
them? I learned to do many things I didn't like
to do. Superficially learning techniques, being
told or shown how. Then I'd do it without both-
ering to understand. And every one thought
their way was the best way, that there was only
one way. If that were so, nothing would ever
improve or develop or change. And things do
change.

We change when we learn to do things we enjoy.
We watch something being done or we read or
listen to descriptions of a process. Then we
try to do it. Then we step back, watch again,
thinking about how we did it. Then we try
again. Thinking, trying. Building on experi-

ences and example. And adapting. We learn not
by being told but by exploring and discovering.
Like children—who have no preconceptions.
Nothing is right or wrong, only new and different. Not to be accepted, but to be wondered
about.

Lee Grover

The class has set me thinking again about Zen
Buddhism and an article I read about Synanon.
Basically what Synanon teaches about Zen is that
every endeavor is not to beat someone else or To
Win, but to get better at what you are trying.
Like a ping pong game where the people playing
are not competing but helping each other get
technically better at the game.

Lee Grover

You can learn by being helped—shown another
way. But you must have the freedom to accept
or reject that other way, or to modify it to
fit your own style.

When I was learning to ride and race a motorcycle, a friend of mine showed me a better way
to hold the clutch lever while starting the
cycle. I was holding it back with my whole
hand, at least the full four fingers. That
made starting awkward, because as soon as the
starting flag drops you must accelerate as
quickly as you can and still keep the bike
under control. Which means hanging on with
both hands. And that's hard to do if you have
a good grip in only one hand. My friend showed me that it was better to grip with three
fingers and use my index finger to encircle
the hand grip. I tried that way and it was
better. But then I tried it using just two
fingers on the clutch lever. That was better
—for me. But not for him—because he had
shorter fingers.

My friend helped me even though I already
had my own way. A poor way, but it was a
place to be helped from. He showed me a way
which was better. I tried it, found it better,
adopted *and* adapted it. Then it was my way.

Can that kind of learning take place in this classroom?

I, too, am skeptical. But hopeful. Of exploring and discovering. With a child's sense of wonder.

I just came back from the Air Force where you don't wonder about something but accept it. Because if you don't accept it, there are 138 articles in the UCMJ and someone will use one of them to lock you up.

Authority exists to preserve the development of humility.

Lee Grover

feedback from midsemester

I don't claim to be a good writer but I have always been a good student. Now I'm not sure. Am I capable of deciding what to read and write about? Will I ever work for this class if there are no *required* assignments that must be completed and handed in to be graded on a certain day?

Everything that I am concerned about is so personal. I can't believe you are interested in what goes on inside my head. And sometimes it's not easy to put it into words that would make sense to anybody else. Sometimes what I think doesn't even make sense to me.

unsigned

You say you are wondering what I'm getting out of the class. And you seem to be unhappy about what I'm putting in.

Remember that big sigh of relief you heard when you announced there would be no *required* assignments in this class? Well, I'd say at least 93.64% of it came from me. So I hope you will not be offended if I say I'm beginning to question your credibility. But I'm leveling with you.

I've always been taught to take the easy way
out. From kindergarten on I guess I've
thought of school work as something to be
avoided. And usually I got by with a C even
in the toughest courses with the meanest
teachers. I expect to do the same in college
if I can figure out what the minimum requirements are in this class. At first it sounded
easy but now I'm not so sure.

unsigned

You ask why I have not responded to your
response to my last paper and why I never
write about the subjects being discussed in
class. This will be a very short answer.

I'm lazy, lazy, lazy, lazy, lazy.

Breaking old habits ain't easy. The pool
tables in the union always seem more inviting
than the desk in my room.

unsigned

Respond, Respond, Respond.

If you don't teach us a new term to use occa-
sionally I'm going to lose my mind!

I Responded, I Responded, I Responded.

John Kennedy

dumb, dumb English
students sit with teacher rapping about what
     is of no interest to them
they act perceptive
they show false anticipation
they're getting by

Why shouldn't they?
Certainly no one sitting in this room is
     working for a degree related to this crap!

John Kennedy

Explaining why I often miss class is very
difficult if not impossible. When I'm present,

I do learn; when I'm writing, I do enjoy it; and when I'm thinking about the paper I'm working on, I do enjoy reliving the past or analyzing the present. However, I sometimes think the very reasons I enjoy writing for this class could be the reasons I shy away from it.

Throughout my school days I have been told what to write. So it became not only possible but necessary for me to adopt the teacher's views, not only as an easy way out, but as the only way out. Except, of course, failing the course.

Your class presented me with a radical change. No longer can I hide behind the skirts of a schoolmistress. Instead I have to stand beside her, sharing with her the formation of my ideas.

This is not only the first class I was ever allowed to write freely in; it will become the first class wnere I will be criticized for my *own* work. Before, I could blame the teacher for a putrid subject or even suppression of my natural talents with mandatory motifs. But now I come face to face with my *own* capabilities and my *own* inadequacies. Perhaps it is fear that has made me retreat. Perhaps I am not writing because I am apprehensive of losing my pride and self esteem.

If this is true, I could be likened to someone with a mysterious disease that is slowly destroying the movability of his limbs. But he is afraid to let a surgeon cut into his insides to remove the cause of his trouble. He is afraid of learning something more frightening than what he already knows. I fear the knife of the critic that might reveal even more writing ills than I am now aware of. But if I do not enlist the critic's help, I may suffer a paralysis of the mind.

Perhaps this paper will be the first step toward my recovery.

Pat Hogan

We emphasize the joy and spontaneity of talking as a way to make writing an easier and a happier act, a way to give your writing the touch of life, the voice, that makes good reading.

But that is not to say that "talk on paper" is an incantation that casts a magic spell upon pencil or typewriter. We must always know what we are talking about. Which means we must go on learning. We must learn new words and new competence with words whenever we want to talk about new knowledge and new processes. That's how the work of the world gets done. From toasting a slice of bread for breakfast to taking a walk on the moon, our world depends on dependable verbal directives and exchanges.

And yet, any attempt to clarify concepts, old and new, presents a different problem. Does anyone ever learn to convey what is in *his* mind to the mind of another person without some misunderstanding, some loss of meaning, or some change in meaning?

And when we turn to describing human experience or expressing human feeling, the question becomes even more perplexing. Can we ever say *exactly* what an experience was like? Can words ever express *precisely* how we feel?

This book does not promise that you will ever develop enough linguistic competence to glibly or precisely express the monologue that fills your head.

Instead, I would say that writing is sometimes difficult for all of us, and always difficult for some of us, because each person's unique experience is inexpressible. All the words you know plus all the words you don't know will always be inadequate to say what is going on inside you, inadequate to say what you mean.

If you wish to explore this "pessimistic, hard-to-live-with" attitude toward life and language, this "tragic view of language," read Walker Gibson's *The Limits of Language.* And find comfort in his optimistic conclusion:

> The very point is that language will never *say* our experience "as is," and recognizing this truth, we have immense freedom of possibility to make, create, form what we can out of words or out of anything else.

That is the freedom waiting *for you* in the open class—as you express the ideas and feelings you bring with you; as you express your reactions to whatever happens *for you* in that class.

turning Dialogue into Discourse

All dialogue could be called discourse. But here the word is used for bigger pieces of talk—like the compositions, themes or essays generally expected in rhetoric or English classes.

If you are already participating in the free and lively exchange of ideas we have urged for your class, you have, most likely, already turned some dialogue into discourse. You have already responded to something said in class or on a page of this book with such singleness of purpose, such clarity and force, that you have a few or many pieces of writing that could be called good paragraphs or essays. And if you do not usually achieve that in your initial remarks on a subject, you do when classmate or teacher asks *why* or *how* or *what do you mean*. As you answer questions like those, you are composing one paragraph or several paragraphs that fit together to form an essay.

But that is not to say that talking on paper is an easy way out every time you need or want to put words onto paper. To tell you that would be a lie—or a romantic myth. And we already have enough writing-made-easy myths.

Perhaps our oldest, most honored myth is the one that says you can learn to write by writing a certain number of papers that meet the usual specifications for the 500-word theme. It begins, of course, with a beginning—called an Introduction. And the Introduction begins with an attention-getting device and culminates in a thesis statement. Then it goes on—to list the three points coming up in the middle which is called the Body. The Body has at least three paragraphs, each paragraph has a topic sentence, each topic sentence restates, preferably at the beginning of the paragraph, one of the three points already stated in the Introduction. And in between the paragraphs there are neat little mechanical devices called transitions. They help hold the parts of the Body together. And to tie it all up in a tight little knot at the end, there is an ending called a Conclusion which sums up or restates the thesis statement, then goes on to sum up or restate the three topic sentences already stated in the Intro and the Body.

It's a "tried and true" and trite old form, imitated by millions of students every year. With some success, no doubt, but how much competent, creative writing? How much joy in writing?

This book rejects the traditional 500-word theme because it leads to too much writing that is too much like the 600-word theme that follows here.

The assignment asked the young man to choose one of the subjects suggested and write a 500 word theme. He chose: Possible Causes of Success in College. Then he wrote for two hours.

The reasons a college student is successful are numerous. Success is not acquired in one night. It is acquired gradually over a long period of time. The first stepping stone up the ladder of success is the individual's family background. The parents of the child must exhibit correct leadership. They must be good examples so the child will be exposed to the proper ways of life. The parents should show great interest in education. The child should be convinced that obtaining a good education is a necessary part of life. The only way a child can see that education is an important part of his life is through the interest expressed by his parents. By being good parents, and trying to direct their child in the best possible direction, the parents are showing the child they are interested in his future. The first step in being a successful college student is to have a good family background.

The second step up the ladder of success is to develop good or excellent study habits in grade school and in high school. The child will not realize how important and how helpful this will be to him whenever he reaches college. If a person has good study habits, then college will not be too difficult; but if a person lacks proper study habits, college will be very difficult and time consuming. The individual must take a personal interest in bettering himself. The student must study hard but also have an interest in what he is doing. A student may attend class every time it meets but his mind is in a different place. What good does this do? The student may be causing himself more harm by going to class and daydreaming than he would if he missed the class altogether. The teacher might resent a student coming to class and not paying attention more than if the student did not attend the class. Therefore, the stu-

dent must have a real interest in obtaining a
good college education. The student must also
realize the value a good education will mean
to him in the future. The student must think
of the future, not the present. The present
will last for three or four years, but the
future will last the rest of the student's
lifetime.

As we continue up the ladder of success, we
find that the individual student must have the
right mental attitude and a great desire to be
a success. The student must be willing to
learn. He can not think or feel that he knows
all there is to know. He must have an open
mind and a desire to learn as much as he possibly can. The student should realize he came
to college for the sole purpose of obtaining
an education that will better prepare him for
the future. He must dedicate himself to studying. This is where a person's mental attitude
is involved. He must have the correct attitude
and must maintain it throughout his years in
school. A person can't be a success in college
if he never studies and is always on the
streets. In other words, he can not be a play-
boy if he has any desire to be a success.

The final step up the ladder is probably the
most important of all. It is a person's pride.
Pride is a driving force behind all individuals
who are successful. The student must have pride
in himself and in his ability. Without pride a
person is nothing. The student must have enough
pride in his ability to be the best so that he
will not embarrass himself or his parents. The
individuals which have the highest amount of
pride in themselves and in their work are the
individuals who have the greatest amount of
success.

College is a difficult task. The successful
college student is always visible above the
average student because he has a good family
background, good study habits, correct mental
attitude, the desire to be a success, and the
pride to drive him to success.

The man who wrote that paper has obviously had some lessons on "organization." He forgot that the Introduction is supposed to be a separate paragraph. But he has a thesis statement, his Body is structured around four topic sentences, and for transitions between paragraphs he takes us up four steps of a "ladder of success." Finally, to sum it all up in a Conclusion, he takes us up those four steps again.

But what does he say about his or anybody else's particular experience? Can his life really be as dull and full of cliches, can his days be as void of particular meaning as his writing is?

Having known this writer, I know the answer for him was *no*. And I believe it is *no* for every other human being—if we find someone we can trust to hear and respond to what we want to say.

To insist that you talk on paper about your own ideas is not a rejection of the timeless principles of unity and logical order essential to good writing. It *is* a rejection of any approach to teaching composition that makes the required forms sound more important than what you have to say. It *is* a rejection of all the rigid little rhetorical boxes student writers are generally expected to fill.

Like the traditional patterns of organization—Time sequence, Space sequence, Cause and Effect sequence, Comparison-Contrast sequence, Extended Definition sequence. All have a place in our attempts to convey information and ideas But never first place. Never in rigid week by week sequences. For they may indeed offer even less possibility than does the 500-word theme for writing that is alive with the sound of you.

In fact, any assignment that requires a whole class to follow a specified organizational pattern may produce more frustration than inspiration. And writing that must fit into a box designed by teacher or text is often as dull as all of you would be if you were all cut from a single pattern and mass produced.

Requiring you on certain days during certain weeks to write narration or description or exposition or argument, each pure and unadulterated, can be equally inhibiting and deadening. Coming up with a subject to fit into the specified box often eliminates what you really want to say. And the box may always seem more important than any ideas you can think of to pour into it.

This book attempts to reverse that approach to learning by beginning with your ideas and by making our natural way with ideas and language the way of the composition class. When we give you the freedom to choose your own subject, we also give you the freedom to build the box that fits your subject.

Organizing ideas does not mean deciding on the most appropriate textbook pattern for developing a topic. Organizing ideas is seeing relationships. And you do that every day. Intuitively. Without thinking about how you are doing it.

When you want to share an experience just as it happened, you place the details in chronological order, you write a little narrative. Just as you did when you rushed home from first grade and greeted your momma with an excited "Guess what happened today?"

If you think you understand *why* something happened, you not only say that one act or remark was followed by another. You also try to show that the effects produced by the first act or re-mark led to the second one. That's how you've explained every unpleasant incident you've ever been asked to explain.

When you engage in the kind of discussion that goes on in a community of learners, you define the words that cause misunderstanding and the words that are the keys to talking about and understanding the ideas and opinions of other people. Which is our natural way with language until we grow up enough to feel too prejudiced or too threatened to be open and honest with each other.

How did it happen? Why did it happen? What do you mean? are not academic questions. You did not first hear them in a school book. You have been using them, in and out of school, all your life.

When you know the answer to the question, you simply answer. Without worrying about organization. The structure of your writing evolves from the relationships you perceive. And those relationships are an inherent part of your answer. A part of your *knowing.* The form of your answer and the content of your answer do not pop out of your head in separate little pieces. They are one. Each a part of the other.

When you *know* what you want to say, it comes out coherently. When you're not sure, it doesn't. And that is what everybody's struggle with organization is all about.

Writing is not always easy because seeing the relationships is not always easy. Seeing the relationships is not always easy because the relationships do not make a simple and isolated time or space sequence. Or any other simple and isolated little sequence.

Incidents occur in time *and* space—simultaneously. And the temporal and spatial factors are all mixed up with causal factors. And while you are trying to explain how the causes produced the effects, you wonder if it wouldn't be best to compare the incident with something that has happened many times before. But when you start to do that, the differences seem more striking than the similarities. Then you wonder what's wrong with your mind.

It's a drag and a puzzle. I can't get my thoughts together on paper. In high school I won honors in other subjects that require a quick mind. But I can't write a simple paper like the ones a lot of simple people I know can. Please tell me that the problem is not in my mind.

from a student-teacher Dialogue

This book is to tell you it isn't.

The origin of the problems we face when trying to get our thoughts together on paper is not in our minds but in the nature of human experience.

It's a problem we share with every other kind of writer:

a poet,

> The background in hugeness and confusion, shading away from where we stand into black and utter chaos . . .

Robert Frost

a novelist and short story writer,

> The life of reality is confused, disorderly, almost always without purpose . . .

Sherwood Anderson

a professor of philosophy,

> The most obvious aspect of this field of actual experience is its disorderly character. It is for each person a continuum . . . with elements not clearly differentiated.

Alfred North Whitehead

The confusion and disorder, the chaos of actual experience these men are talking about, the flux and disorder of our thoughts is certainly more like life than the orderly existence suggested by the traditional approach to the teaching of organization.

For life does not come packaged in neat and tidy topic sentences and 500-word themes.

But like all men, whether by nature or culture or divine inspiration, we long to change and control the chaos. In Genesis it sounds easy—God created a well-ordered earth from a formless void. But for us, even the best writers among us, creating a logical world with words is more often than not a struggle.

> Form! I kept saying the word to myself, striking the table as I worked; this chaos of life must be reduced, somehow, to form.
>
> Sean O'Faolain

Student writers cannot express their confusion as eloquently as the pros can. But perhaps you feel it even more intensely.

That is why this book offers no easy answers, no oversimplified patterns of organization, no prescribed assignments intended to produce a set of papers structured to fit the assignments. Such an approach could help you fulfill one academic requirement. But would it prepare you to organize the mass of new knowledge and ideas, the continuum of actual experience that is your college education? Would it help you assert a little form upon the flux and disorder of thought and feeling inside you?

For most of you, I think, the answer is no. Oversimplified forms imposed upon you from the outside may remain external forms—to be used as strategies in the academic games you play for the chips called grades, to be used as substitutes for thought and insight. They may never become a part of your *inner* experience.

But when you begin with the unending, uneven flow of thought and feeling inside you, when you try to move the interior monologue that fills your head to an empty sheet of paper, your writing is an encounter with reality. Then you are using your language, oral and written, to categorize and organize your own experience. Which is one of the main reasons man first created language.

Fortunately we don't need to know how bad the age [we live in] is. There is something we can always be doing without reference to how good or how bad the age is. There is at least so much good in the world that it admits of form and the making of form. And not only admits of it, but calls for it. We people are thrust forward out of the suggestions of form in the rolling clouds of nature. In us nature reaches its height of form and through us exceeds itself. When in doubt there is always form for us to go on with . . . The artist, the poet, might be expected to be the most aware of such assurance. But it is really everybody's sanity to feel it and live by it. Fortunately, too, no forms are more engrossing, gratifying, comforting, staying than those lesser ones we throw off, like vortex rings of smoke, all our individual enterprise and needing nobody's cooperation; a basket, a letter, a garden, a room, an idea, a picture, a poem. For these we haven't to get a team together before we can play.

The background in hugeness and confusion, shading away from where we stand into black and utter chaos; and against the background any small manmade figure of order and concentration. What pleasanter than that this should be so?

Robert Frost
Letter to *The Amherst Student*

Much of our dialogue with each other—in person and on paper—is a search for form that will give meaning to our particular human experience.

Talking on paper makes the search a little easier. It gives you the freedom that is essential to all creative work. It gives you the loose and easy feeling you need—to play with all the possibilities.

You do not have to question each idea as you verbalize it—asking if it is too general or abstract, wondering why you keep coming up with ideas not directly related to the preceding sentence or the topic sentence or the assignment, finally striking it all out and sitting there—disgusted—mind blank or full of thoughts far removed from what you are *supposed* to be thinking about.

Instead, as one student put it,

```
When I think I talk to myself. Now I write
what I think and talk (to self and teacher)
on paper.
```

You can say the same about your side of the dialogue with your teacher.

Some days, with little conscious effort, a short passage or several pages may sparkle out of you. Your silent composing voice is creating form as well as substance. Putting words together to say ideas. Putting words together in meaningful order. Composing ideas with words. Composing verbal structures of your thought and feeling.

On other days everything comes out in fragmented bits and pieces—

the first slight beginning of an idea, incomplete, like an embryo—but, like an embryo, alive with the promise of full development—

vague, undefined reactions—a few sketchy details that make up a moment of experience—

a groping for words to interpret what happened to you in the past, what is happening to you now—

a questioning of your own attitudes, the ones fixed in childhood (are they coming unfixed?) and the ones you are now moving toward—

a looking out to the world beyond your immediate experience for more understanding of your own identity, your own life—

Your teacher does not need to tell you it's not a unified paragraph or theme, with clearly stated main ideas and subordinate ideas. He does not need to say that none of the ideas are developed, none of the generalizations supported with specifics.

You know that. You know you are only attempting to record the jumble inside you. Thinking on paper. Searching for meaning. In the confusions of your own mind. In the complexities of your own heart. Searching for verbal forms to give meaning to your own experience.

through thought alone
feelings become knowledge and are not lost,
[through thought alone]
feelings become real and begin to mature.

Hermann Hesse

You can, of course, find meaning without trying to put what goes on inside you onto paper. And you can compose—a poem, a plan for essay or short story, perhaps something much longer—before picking up a pencil to jot it down.

But most of us need to play with the possibilities first. We need to make the complexity a little clearer by making our thoughts and feelings *visible*—in words—on a piece of paper.

How do I know what I think until I *see* what I say?

E. M. Forster

This book assumes that we *don't* know what we think—not when we are trying to organize and categorize our own complex experience, not when we are trying to explain an insight we have just perceived about a complex situation, not when we are trying to form a new concept by putting together and reshaping our old ideas about a complex subject.

Then the mind—the imagination—must not be boxed in. For when we are *really* composing, we are constantly making choices. And the choice we make determines the direction and the form that our ideas take at that moment.

That's why we say talk about it first—on paper.

When we *see* what we think, we can react more fully and decisively—and more critically—to our own ideas. And that reaction generates more ideas. And questions. It's like the feedback we get from another person in a lively discussion. You are telling yourself what you think about what you just said. You are asking yourself if the words you just wrote say what you are trying to say. Sometimes that means elaborating on what you just said. Sometimes it means changing it.

And that's how a vague and undefined idea can grow—and develop—from its confused and fragmentary beginnings to a single meaningful statement, then to a well-developed paragraph or essay.

The finished form is not predetermined by formula or model. Using somebody else's plan may help you repeat somebody else's ideas. It may provide a ready-made solution for hacking out assignments—in class or on the job. But when you are putting words together to compose your own ideas, the form and substance of those ideas is growing—together—as you play with all the possibilities. The form and substance—together—is what you discover as you write and rewrite your talking and thinking on paper.

When you *see* what you think, you *see* the potentialities and the limitations of your ideas. Then you can decide if you want to turn your talk on paper or in class into a longer, more fully developed statement. If you do, ask how you can clarify, expand and support your ideas. Ask how you can speak with your own voice in a competent, creative essay.

Michel de Montaigne, a Frenchman of the sixteenth century, first used the word *essay* to name a piece of writing. Before that, and even now, in his language and ours, *essay* is also a verb. It means *to try*

Writing an essay means trying. Not trying to turn out a finished product to meet a list of specifications. But trying to say what we think and feel.

Writing an essay is a creative process, a human process, that is self-fulfilling because it is a sharing of self with others.

with your own voice

... the human mind was born free, or at any
rate born to be free, but everywhere it is in
chains; and now at the end of its tether ... it
will take a miracle to free the human mind ...
We are in bondage to authority outside ourselves; most obviously—here in a great university it must be said—in bondage to the authority
of books.

Norman O. Brown

You've been around quite a while now.

You've done a lot, seen a lot, heard a lot.
And you've done a lot of thinking and feeling
about all that you've lived through.

Some days your little world is a beautiful and loving place.
Some days everything is ugly and dull, everybody indifferent.

Some days you feel like a person of great worth.
Some days your capacity for joy in self seems quite depleted.

That's the way it is for most of us—
while growing up and while growing old.

But can you show the many faces of you to the people in this
class? Can you let them *hear* all the voices of you that fill *your*
ears?

Long before college we learn to play the roles expected of us. The
lines, the stage directions are fixed and nice kids, like nice adults,
make good actors. But if you're not sure of your role in a given
situation, if you don't know the lines that go with the part you
are supposed to play, you feel uneasy, sometimes quite afraid of
doing or saying the "wrong" thing.

That's the way it is for most of us—while growing up and while
growing old.

But in a class motivated by the human purpose of language, where
people share experience and respond to each other, the old familiar roles change. You are no longer the good little student. Putting
on a good little performance. Saying what you think or hope the
teacher wants to hear with just the tone of voice he expects from
you. You are no longer competing against your classmates for the
A's and B's everybody wants. Or resigned to getting C's or lower
because you are too far behind or too lazy to compete.

Instead you are here to bring *your* reality into *this* classroom. The
beautiful and loving. The ugly and dull and indifferent. The joy
in self and others. The emptiness and self doubt and anxiety that
often displaces joy. All that you have seen and heard and lived
through. All that is a part of you. You are here to speak to others

about the little world of experience that is the vital center of the universe for you.

If you do that when you write, your writing will not be dull and lifeless. For your readers will encounter *you* as they read. They will feel the presence of a living person, one not unlike themselves, at the other end of the pencil or on the other side of the type-writer. They will hear a *voice*—carried from speaker to listener by inanimate symbols, carried by words on a piece of paper. But it will be a very audible voice. A voice that is alive with the sound of you.

Close your eyes for a moment and try to visualize everybody in your composition class.

Can you see them coming through the door? Each in his own in-dividual way—bouncing or dragging or slinking in. With the smile or scowl that is their usual greeting.

Count off the Gillette-clean cheeks and bushy sideburns, the Afros and Prince Valiant bangs. The little corkscrew curls or shags or buns. The sweep and pride of hair that reaches to their waists.

Then watch them push or bluster or ease their way into a group. Or sit alone. With sassy or sullen eyes staring you down, or fright-ened and timid eyes that never meet yours.

And when they start talking—could you recognize any of their voices if you sat in class blindfolded?

Who speaks with reticence? who with audacity? who with some-thing in between?

Do you remember something each person has said? Which can you recall more vividly, the words spoken or the unique sound of a person's *voice*? an idea expressed or a *personality* revealed?

Recall and relate an incident that occurred in class or elsewhere—

> When a person's tone of voice helped determine your first impression of that person.

> When a person's tone of voice has caused you to change your opinion of him, your feeling toward him?

> When a person's tone of voice had a significant effect on the meaning of his words.

When a change in a person's tone of voice seemed to have a happy or unhappy effect on what happened next.

When the meaning of a person's words and his tone of voice were unmistakably the same.

When the meaning of a person's words and his tone of voice had opposite meanings.

In thinking or writing or talking about the incidents recalled, what words have you used to describe tone of voice? to describe persons?

Do you know anyone who is usually described with words that also describe his habitual tone of voice?

When does a person's tone of voice change without conscious effort?

When do we consciously attempt to change our tone of voice?

Talking about the tone we hear when a speaker's voice expresses the emotion he feels is easy. We have all heard somebody's love—or cold indifference—or contempt—or hostility. Sometimes in a one-word greeting. We have often detected a speaker's attitude toward us or the subject he was talking about though he never put that attitude into words.

It's not a one way thing, of course. Before you learned to talk, you learned that the "right" tone of voice can sometimes get you what you want, and in your first dialogues with your family, you discovered that your voice, with or without words, could alternately charm or terrorize the household. And the force of all the other physical manifestations of your personality—the pleading look in your eyes, the sad droop of your mouth, the easy loving touch of your whole body—at four and fourteen, it was, as it is now, as it is for all people of all ages, an essential part of effective communication. Much that is not verbal is a part of every verbal exchange.

But when you face those empty pages that have to be filled, whether for a class or some other purpose, you cannot rely on the persuasive tone of your speaking voice or your forceful personality. You've got to do it with words.

Read aloud what you have written.

Do your words express the *personality* you want to project? the *you* you want others to hear?

Would someone who does not know you, someone who is not already concerned about you and your ideas, read what you write with interest? or boredom?

Or ask about your writing as you would ask about your speaking—

What about your *voice*?

Have you put words together so that you hear yourself talking as you read what you have written? would you ever *say* those sentences?

What tone of voice would you use in a conversation to help you convey the meaning, the feeling you want to convey in each piece you have written?

Do your written words convey that tone?

"The times they are a-changin' . . ." but it's still an adult's world where neither child nor college student begins his day by searching for answers to his own questions. Instead he must learn the facts and moral codes that provide the answers to the questions the adults in his life are asking. About what is best and what is true. About survival techniques that may be outmoded before he takes his place as a well-trained adult in a world controlled by adults.

So the student masses arrive and leave college without discovering the sound of their own voices. It's always easier (and frequently more pleasing to the only person who reads an academic paper) to ape a bookish tone of authority. Even when you know you're not an authority. It's even easier (and sometimes more rewarding when grades are handed down) to dutifully repeat the professor's point of view. Even when you don't understand or believe what you write.

Perhaps that is why some of you rarely attempt to express, by talking or writing, what is going on inside you. You don't want to lose your cool. Confrontations are bad manners—at family dinners, at parties and in the classroom. Nice kids, like nice adults, don't raise their voices to express devout commitment to an idea or a cause, or to protest some person's inhumanity to another person.

To keep the class discussions and the students' papers above all that, some teachers provide a content that is Solid and Objective—to be read, digested, then restated in acceptable forms. And students fall into a writing style that is a dull and labored imitation of what they think correct and impressive teacher-talk is. And academic papers are a warmed-over, tasteless mix of what book or professor has served up or what book or professor has directed student to mix and serve.

Unless what you hear and read and write becomes a pervasive part of you—a part of your thinking *and* feeling—unless it makes at least a little bit of difference in your attitudes and your behaviors, you have not *really* learned, you have not *really* composed. You have not created out of your own experience a theme or an essay or a research paper that is *really* yours. You have not spoken with your own voice.

Your teacher is probably the only person, besides you, who has read everything you have written for this course. Ask him this little favor—

> Assume for a moment that you know me only through my writing. What have I told you about my attitude toward myself? Do I speak with confidence about my own ideas? Do I ever sound too confident?

Maybe you'd like to exchange all your writing with someone in the class and ask and answer those questions for each other.

If you want to achieve a voice that you are proud of in everything you write, you must begin by asking what your tone says about *what you think of you.*

> One of the things that is a very interesting thing to know is how you are feeling inside you to the words that are coming out to be outside of you.

> Gertrude Stein

In a culture noted for an absence of open motives and honest talk, a book that asks students to speak honestly about their own thoughts and feelings may immediately be labeled naive—touchingly naive if the critic is a kind man. I hope they are all kind men.

> Truth is so rare a thing
> It is delightful to tell it.

> Candor is the only wile.

> Emily Dickinson

No poet of any country, of any time, has a more distinctive voice than the woman who wrote those words. Her candid voice speaks in 1,775 poems—about the world she saw from the windows of the house where she lived in Amherst, Massachusetts, and the world of interior monologue that filled her days.

The chronology of Emily Dickinson's life (1830-1886) lists only four out-of-town "visits" and one trip to Boston for an eye examination. And during her last years, when she was still writing poems unlike any anyone had ever written before, she left the house on Main Street only after dark, slipping through the garden to the house next door where her brother's family lived.

The quality of her genius is rare and unique—born of her particular awareness of the world and of self in the world. And in all her poems we hear Emily talking—sharing with us the truth of her particular experience.

> I can wade Grief—
> Whole Pools of it—
> I'm used to that—
> But the least push of Joy
> Breaks up my feet—
> And I tip—drunken—   252

So We must meet apart—
You there—I—here
With just the Door ajar
That Oceans are—and Prayer—
And that White Sustenance—
Despair—   640

The Birds begun at Four o'clock—
Their period for Dawn—
A music numerous as space—
But neighboring as Noon—

I could not count their Force—
Their Voices did expend
As Brook by Brook bestows itself
To magnify the Pond.

Their Witnesses were not—
Except occasional man—
In homely industry arrayed—
To overtake the Morn—

Nor was it for applause—
That I could ascertain—
But independent Ecstasy
Of Deity and Men—

By Six, the Flood had done—
No Tumult there had been
Of Dressing, or Departure—
And yet the band was gone—

The Sun engrossed the East—
The day controlled the World—
The Miracle that introduced
Forgotten, as fulfilled.   783

Emily Dickinson

I like a look of Agony,
Because I know it's true—
Men do not sham Convulsion,
Nor simulate, a Throe—   241

Much Madness is divinest Sense—
To a discerning Eye—
Much Sense—the starkest Madness—
'Tis the Majority
In this, as All, prevail—
Assent—and you are sane—
Demur—you're straightway dangerous—
And handled with a Chain—   435

To write poetry like Emily Dickinson is impossible—even for
other poets. But I hope you can all find some words to say what
human experience looks like through the windows of the houses
you live in.

To know joy in writing is not possible unless, with your "own way of telling, you attempt to put *your* "vision of life" onto paper. Which means the joy promised in this book does not come in instant-mix packages. No matter how elated you are with the success you achieve by talking on paper, you will, sooner or later, realize that is not the answer to all the questions you must consider as you write and all the questions your readers may ask as they read.

Sometimes talking on paper is talking to self. It releases the hidden pressures of our emotions. It becomes a pouring out of feelings we have never shared with another person. And as we read what we have written, we hear more of self than we want to reveal to teacher or classmates.

Take another long look at what you have written.

Do you think you could ever express in public (even the friendly public place an open classroom is) all the thoughts you have written in private? What determines whether you do or don't wish to share what you have written? Which pieces of your writing would you read to the class with no reluctance or embarrassment?

Why couldn't you read the others to your class? Could you read them to some other group? to some individual?

Every writer faces similar questions.

How can we create with words the "perfect" balance between telling all and telling nothing of our strong feelings and firm convictions? How can we find the distance that seems just right—between self and reader, between self and what we are saying?

How can we avoid the excess of feeling called sentimentality that a reader may reject? How can we keep an angry voice from turning into an abusive verbal attack that will further alienate us from our audience?

How can we turn an intense and gushing diary or a bitter harangue into a statement that will cause a person to feel something of what we feel, or lead him to look at a situation from our point of view?

On thinking back over the books I have written, I can only say:

Ladies and gentlemen, this has been my vision of life. This is what living in my time has seemed to be like—life with its romance and cruelty, its pity and terror, its joys and anxiety, its peace and conflict. You may not like my vision, ladies and gentlemen, but it is the only one I have seen and felt, therefore, it is the only one I can give you.

Theodore Dreiser

Yet only from his life—indirectly; by some contagion; unconsciously almost always—has come the substance and center of what [a person] writes, and the unity of it, and its details. Under the light by which he sees his whole world, with his own way of telling, he expresses a meaning he sees in the acts and purposes of men.

Percival Hunt

Many times before, you've been through the same hassle. With the same "audience." The audience of two that talks more than it listens. All your life they—he—she's been telling you they know what's best for you. Because they know and love you best. Even when they say no, it's because they love you.

And they haven't budged an inch—probably never will—from their fixed abode over there on the other side of the famous gap you leaped across many years ago or only last year.

You can predict what they will say if you say what you'd *like* to say on the subject you must again discuss with them. So you resolve to present a respectful statement of your point of view. To try to tell them what you think and feel. Then it happens again. They don't hear a word you say and you blow your well-planned cool. Or in sullen "respectful" silence, you admit you've lost again. And they know they haven't won.

Family discussions sometimes bear little resemblance to an open class. And from both sides of the vast distance that separates us, we ask why. Why do our words fail to say what we are trying to say? Why are we so often misunderstood or ignored?

There is no simple or singular answer, of course. When human feelings and relationships are involved, there are no single causes. All just and loving explanations are full of complexities. And ambiguities. We see all human experience, including our own, as "through a glass darkly." But the words we use in our attempt to penetrate the darkness can make a difference. Sometimes a big difference.

List some of the strong words you depend on to express your negative feelings when engaged in a verbal fight with someone with whom you do not have to "watch your language."

List some of the words you turn to when you want to express strong feeling or firm conviction on a happy day.

Now question the possible effects of the words you use to express strong feeling or firm conviction.

If you have listed words like *horrible* and *rotten* and *crappy*, you have most likely discovered that your vocabulary contains a weakness you can spot in almost everybody's every day language. Even the "obscene" and "profane" words that feel so powerful on our lips convey only the intensity of our feeling, not the feeling itself. They do not explain or clarify *what* we are experiencing. They only say and resay *how much* we feel whatever it is we are feeling.

We face the same problem when trying to say our happier thoughts and feelings. Words like *great* and *marvelous* and *fantastic* and *super* and *far-out* do not move another person to accept what we believe in. They do not say why we are committed to an idea or a movement. They do not explain or clarify the experience our opinions or feelings are based on.

A reader may respond to words that say only the intensity of your emotions—if he has had an experience very similar to yours. If he hasn't, he cannot feel and think as you do. And your strong words are for him only an angry or joyful noise, not a reading experience that conveys to him some part of what you are living through.

No matter how much we want to understand another human being, no matter how much we try to see a situation from another person's point of view, we can't—unless we know what his point of view is. Which means we must know something of the experience that shaped that point of view, the experience that led to the opinions and emotions that make up that point of view. We cannot *really* hear and respond to each other unless we reveal to each other at least a little glimpse of the psychic reality, the complex interior self that is me, that is you.

Every writer faces the same problem. We must create out of our experiences of thought and feeling an experience that a reader can respond to.

How and out of what can you create such an experience for your reader?

What kinds of words will give him a sense of living through what you have lived through? How and with what can you evoke in him a response like the one you knew during the actual experience?

The answer can be very short—

  With Your Own Perceptions.

Or 14 pages long. That is, pages 157-170 of this book.

There I hope you will discover what every good writer must discover: how to put words together to create your *voice* on paper— the *voice* that will become your reader's *eyes*.

with your own Perceptions

Experience is the reaction to what
happens, not the happening itself.

Elizabeth Bowen

As a young child you explored your world with all your senses. You saw blades of grass, not well-trimmed lawns, and you grabbed a handful of the green stuff and put it in your mouth. The grassy slope was to roll down and the mud puddle was to wade in, barefooted. Playpens and fences were to climb out of—because you wanted to see and hear more of the world beyond. Your first name for a thing often resembled the sound that thing makes. And your first question was Why?

Once upon a time that's how it was—but now—

What do you *see* as you walk to class each day? Has something along that street or in this building changed since yesterday? Is there anything different or new since you walked that way for the first time a month ago or last year? Do you see individual human faces in the crowd or only the student masses?

And yesterday, downtown—how many distinct sounds did you *hear* as you stood with the crowds at the curb, waiting for the green light, or as you hurried from counter to counter in a department store full of harried customers and inefficient clerks, or as you pushed your way through the happy bodies around the flashing, noisy pinball machines in your favorite after-class place?

And the last time you cut across a grassy lawn—did you *feel* the soft earth under your feet? did you *smell* the green life you were sharing?

The sensory delight the young child feels in all that his senses take in and the inquisitive mind he turns on the world is each a part of his sense of *self* in the world. So it seems important to ask what happens to our sensitivity and curiosity as we grow up and as we grow old.

Does our capacity for joy in self simply become jaded? Is our intuitive desire to know used up as we learn?

Is there a steady loss of sharpness in our sensory and intellectual perception, or do we simply turn off because we can't take in all the stimuli that surround us?

How often do you feel that you are taking it all in—all that you see, hear, smell and taste, all that the tactile cells throughout your body feel? How often do you ask why?

If we remained keenly aware of all that we perceive, would a

nation or a village ever permit environmental problems to reach
the crisis point? Would cities, large or small, grow filthy and ugly?
Would people destroy seascape, wilderness and countryside?

What does our lack of awareness tell us about our hangups—

> with self?
> with others?
> with alcohol and drugs?

For most of us, the day's schedule has already been determined,
by necessity or by previous choices, and it can not be drastically
changed. But the quality of our daily lives *can* be changed—if only
we keep the sensory perceptors busy, if only we load up the con-
veyor belts (nerve fibers) that supply the brain. If only—and this
is the way to really live—if only the brain does all that it can with
all that our senses take in.

Labeling and storing, of course, is part of the job, but if that is
all, your mind is just a warehouse. And warehouses are dull places.
And you will be a dull person, you will write and talk dull talk, if
living and learning is for you a passive thing, if your brain receives
without responding, if you look and listen to the action without
*re*acting.

How you interpret what you see and hear is far more significant
than *what* you see and hear. To paraphrase Elizabeth Bowen—
what you think and how you feel about what's happening *is*
what's happening.

And good writing is putting your perceptions into words so that
others can share what you have experienced.

Here are some word pictures of a writing "lab." Each was written by a student required to attend the lab because he had flunked a departmental theme exam.

Train passing, building shaking.   1

    Hideous square pillars hold up the   2
    warped and cracking ceiling.

There's a hole in the door where the   3
knob should be. Like somebody took a
shotgun and blew it open one night.

    A crack on the wall looks like an   4
    ancient fossil the Smithsonian would
    pay thousands for.

The ancient radiators clang out their woes 5
to the enormous pipes overhead. Sounds
like an engine that's run by rushing,
boiling water and raging steam. The small-
est leak, and the whole system would explode.

    The warm pipes feel like a girl's   6
    warm arm.

There's an art student's cubist style   7
painting in cool blues and greens--a
sharp contrast to the drab greys and
black and the blazing parching orange of
another student's attempt at surrealism.

    The modern paintings speak with elo-   8
    quence about this decrepit old shack.
    The black girl knows she's still in
    the ghetto. The gaunt and troubled
    woman dressed in blue is looking for
    a way out. And the sickly, green
    fellow, highlighted with violent
    splotches of red--he's had it, man!

Students cocooned in thought. Pens plod-   9
ding or skimming across yellow pads. Then
a crumpled, crackling sound of rejection,
failure. A wad of yellow paper is tossed
against the dingy wall. Another lies on a
table notched and gouged by hands more
deft with pen knife than with pen.

"Incompetent" writers achieved competence and creativity when they turned their senses on the here and now.

Each gives us a little glimpse of what an hour in a particular room was like for him, a particular person. That person draws a little picture with concrete details that help us see and hear that room, that help us experience it as he did.

These writers engage our attention, not by attempting to enumerate all the observable physical characteristics of the room, not by describing the spatial arrangement of all the objects in the room, but by giving us graphic representations of their sensory perceptions. The experience each writer shares is not merely what he was seeing and hearing, but how his mind and emotions were reacting to what his senses were taking in.

Even the first sentence, though it states a verifiable fact, seems to suggest more than it says. Could the writer be as cynical as he is cryptic? Maybe so, maybe not.

But about *hideous* in the next sentence there can be no doubt. The writer is no longer merely reporting what he sees. He is also judging. The external experience has moved inside. And in the third sentence, the mind that receives the picture of the hole in the door tells its *self*, then the reader, how the hole could have come to be.

These two writers are no longer saying, "This is what I see." But, "What I now see is like something I have seen before or like something I now imagine."

Which did the writer of the fourth sentence think of first—the museum of ancient artifacts the old building was obviously ready for, or the ancient fossil the crack in the wall reminded him of?

The writer of sentence five reacted first to what he heard. With words, spoken first to self, then on paper to a reader. With words to say that the sound he heard reminded him of something raging and explosive.

But another person doesn't hear the dangerous sound because the monologue going on inside him is more important. Today anything warm to him is loving.

Compare the reactions (that is, the sentences) of the persons who noticed and wrote about the paintings. How does one writer go beyond description to an interpretation of experience?

How does the writer of sentence nine use visual details to say what he thinks and feels about his "lab" experience?

When our writing is an attempt to share our reaction to the happening, not the happening itself, we can suggest—even in a single sentence—the tone (of voice) we might use if we were speaking about the experience.

Point out the two sentences in which the writers achieve a light humorous touch by the way the descriptive detail is presented.

Which sentences seem to be ridiculing the place by using what sounds like an exaggerated comparison?

Which writer sounds the most critical of such a classroom building? Point out the words he uses to build up the critical tone.

What is the writer's tone in the sentence that focuses on the students? What kind of details does he use to achieve that tone?

The sentences below were written about the "same" lab experience.

> It's a depressing white cavern,   1
> choked with the sight, the sound,
> and the taste of Rhetoric.

> It has a quaint, comfortable feeling   2
> reminiscent of my old parochial
> school.

> It's like a coffee house, full of   3
> busy people sounds. There's even a
> mad Greek dashing around.

> Good writing is a lot like gourmet   4
> cooking and the Writing Lab is like
> a master chef's kitchen. Not a
> bright and shining stainless steel
> domain, but an old and cluttered
> temporary arrangement that became
> permanent because it was highly
> functional.

> The dirty old windows remind me of   5
> my cell in the dorm, and the hard
> straight-backed chairs have slats
> like prison bars.

> The grey filing cabinet, like a grey   6
> coffin, inters our dead words.

These sentences contain only four concrete details or "facts"— dirty old windows, hard straight-backed chairs, the mad Greek, and the grey filing cabinet. And yet, in a very important way they are more forceful, they evoke a stronger response from most readers than the other group. Why?

What is each writer really talking about as he "describes" the lab?

What is his attitude toward himself and toward being in the lab?

What is the tone of each sentence?

What determines that tone?

None of the young writers quoted could have written even one page full of sentences about the Writing Lab like the ones I have shared with you. And why should they? Trying to say more when we have put so much into one or a few sentences usually only weakens and distracts. Listing a hundred specific ways that a decrepit old shack is decrepit or a dirty old shack is dirty would evoke nothing but boredom in a reader.

Depend instead upon a few or even a single significant detail. The *telling* facts that strike you immediately. The salient feature that leaps out at you at a distinct moment of experience.

Pass on to your reader the image that says how your mind and emotions react to all that your senses take in, the image in which you find the meaning of an experience.

The last sentence quoted is by a young man who had not written a passing paper since coming to college. He was on probation. His university life would end if he failed rhetoric. And there were many things he wanted to say about that. And about many other things. His eyes took in a gray filing cabinet full of student folders. And to him it was a grey coffin full of dead words. *His* dead words.

We can never know precisely what another person feels, but we can imagine what an experience is like for him if he says what it is like with an image that we can perceive and respond to.

If you want your words to come alive for your reader, you must not only give him sensory details to *visualize*. You must interpret the details. You must give him images that he can *perceive* as feeling. For no one can know what you feel unless he can *imagine* what your inner psychic reality is like.

Which means a reader's capacity to understand you is determined not by *his* imagination but by *yours*. That is, by your ability to create the *images* that at least suggest what an experience is like for you.

Much of what we live through is common to man. But each man's experience is unique. One man hears the noise and danger of raging steam, while another, at the same moment, hears only the crumpled sound of rejection and failure. A warm pipe becomes a human touch and a crack in the wall is a valuable museum piece.

The "same" place for different persons was a parochial school, a master chef's kitchen and a busy coffee house—a pleasant reminder of a happy time and place. But for students demoralized by failure, it was a ghetto, a prison cell, and a depressing white cavern —"choked with the sight, the sound and the taste of Rhetoric."

Experience for all these writers was not what their senses took in. It was not what was happening. That class hour in the Writing Lab was what their creative minds did with what was happening— *to* them, *around* them, *inside* them. It was sensory perception turned into thought and feeling. It was thought and feeling expressed in images called metaphors.

Obviously, the sentences quoted *are not offered as models for you to imitate.*

Forceful sentences come only from your reaction to and your interpretation of your own experience.

But I hope the writers quoted will help you see how you can give your writing the sound of you, how you can say your wry amusement or the depth of your despair with concrete details and metaphors.

Perhaps some of you will become so interested in metaphor that you will want to study some of the other possibilities that it holds for the serious writer.

Or a group of you may wish to study the metaphorical nature of all language and report your findings to the class.

Sometimes the situation we perceive is so baffling, everything about it looks so bleak or ridiculous, there seems to be no way, no tone of voice, to express what we feel. Our dilemma is not new of course. And the way out may lie in an ancient tradition—man's inclination to see the humor, and to laugh at the absurdity, in his dreariest failures and in his noblest endeavors.

If you can't turn off the gloom you feel about current disappointments, major or minor, look back to the ones diminished by time, the ones turned funny by distance. If we laugh enough—not at somebody else's well-rehearsed jokes or everyday flashes of wit—but if our futile efforts to deal with the realities that confront us sometimes seem amusing, if we can laugh at the crazy world we live in, maybe the effort will become a personal inclination, then a personal habit.

And from the droll or bitter little jokes you tell about you, out of the confusing reality and the conflicting opinions bombarding you, maybe a sense of irony will grow. Then your perceptive eye will become an ironic eye. Then you will see that sometimes a subtle or colossal put on is the only way to deal with the stupidity—even the tragedy—you must live with.

Then your voice will become an ironic voice. A voice that achieves honesty in a special kind of dishonesty. A voice that conveys your strong or mild aversion to a situation by expressing opinions and emotions that are exactly the opposite of what you think and feel. And maybe that will make it easier to live with what *is* as you wish and work for what ought to be—for you and for others.

Perhaps some of you will become so interested in irony that you will explore the possibilities it offers the serious writer.

Ask your teacher to suggest some essays, poems or stories, or some cartoons and comic strips that provide examples of the ironic voice. Look for your own examples as you browse through the offerings at library, book store and newsstand. In art exhibits, poster collections, and the music you make and listen to, you'll discover artists who perceive the world with an ironic eye, people who speak to us with an ironic voice.

Create whatever you can from your sensory perceptions.

Share your experiences with a vivid metaphor, a few lines of poetry, a single sentence that says, as well as words *can* say, your feelings of joy or dismay. Let the reader see what you see and hear what you hear. Let him see and hear how you react to all that your senses take in.

For he cannot *see* what you mean unless the details of your experience—external and internal—become his reading experience. Unless *the sound of your voice* on paper evokes a reaction—of thought or feeling—in him.

Work again in small task groups. Focus on the *here and now*.

Go together to some corner of your little world. A block of urban blight or suburban elegance or some place in between. Find a junk yard or a park on a river bank. A place familiar and loved, or a place you've never been to before. An empty place or a place filled with people.

Put all your senses to work. What do you see, hear, smell, taste? what do the tactile cells throughout your body feel?

Find out how alive the dull days can be, how full the empty hours—if you are aware of every sensory impression that is a part of your sense of being.

Ask what's happening— *to* you, *around* you, *inside* you.

Record whatever you perceive.

Don't attempt a paragraph of connected sentences.

Record a single striking impression.

Take notes on specific objects, people, sounds and actions—the particulars that make up the situation.

Don't compile a lifeless inventory.

What do you think about the situation you are observing or participating in? How are you reacting—feeling—toward all that your senses are taking in?

What are your attitudes toward the particulars and toward the total experience that is, at this moment, your life?

Ask what it all means—to you, and to the other human beings who are a part of the situation.

Compare your notations about your perceptions with the notations made by the others in your group. The differences may amaze you.

Word pictures, like photographs, are limited by the position and focus of the camera. Which, in this instance, is you. The point at which you start looking, how and where you move about, determines the starting point and the continuing order of your perceptions. But would any two persons sitting or standing or walking side by side ever come up with the same list of perceptions?

Every photographer gets a different picture of the same place, the same news story. And each can explain how he achieves the differences he wants. He moves his camera about to catch the scene from various angles, and he plays with the endless mechanical possibilities his camera provides to produce meaningful effects.

But for us, the important question is why.

Why does one man see and photograph one aspect of the place, the person, or the action, while another takes a slightly or completely different picture? What determines what each man sees, and what he recreates for us to see?

Nobody sees every detail of the situation he observes or participates in. Why do particular objects or persons, particular sounds or movements claim your attention?

The easy answer lies in the physical properties of your surroundings. You see a row of red spot lights before noticing the soft, indirect lighting in a room. But that does not explain why you perceived the things you did. Or why, even while trying to include everything, you may have missed much that seems obvious when somebody else points it out.

Why did the person right beside you see things that you missed? Why is everybody's reactions different from everybody else's?

To answer the whys about sensory perception you must assume a new role in our analogy with picture-taking. You are no longer the photographer, but the camera. With one *big* difference. Cameras record images on blank film; you don't. You bring to every new experience a lifetime of past experiences, beginning with your immediate past and the state of mind it left you in.

As you try to become involved in a situation, you may be thinking about what happened an hour before. Or the night before. Perhaps months or years ago. So you see the scene as gray or as cheerful as your passing mood. Or as hopeful or pessimistic as you habitually start another day.

The particulars that make up an experience for you are also determined by what you choose, consciously or unconsciously, to perceive. That choice is sometimes a matter of personal taste. While remaining indifferent to all other stimuli, you may be aware only of what you like or dislike; you may see and hear only what delights or irritates you. Or a value judgment may be the decisive factor. That which offends your moral sense or your sense of justice makes a distinct impression upon you, while you remain untouched by everything else.

Perception involves far more than the physiological functions called seeing, hearing, smelling, tasting and touching. The sensory stimuli that fill a given moment may reach your brain with no conscious effort from you and no visible effects upon you. The part of the moment that you *really* perceive is determined by what you bring to that moment. Which is: the *whole set of personal attitudes and values* that have evolved from your past experience.

That is why the "same" experience can be vastly different for different individuals.

That is why there may be wide variation in the tone (of voice) we hear as different people talk or write about the "same" experience.

with the Values you live by

As far as I could detect he never really approved any statement I made. He would ask a question, make a noncommittal observation, test my assertion by supplying additional data, ask if I had considered a different alternative.

Kimball Wiles on Louis Rath

Only you can say what an experience means to you, for no one else sees what happened from your point of view. No one else brings your set of values to the situation that you and others are caught up in.

But if we hope to become a community of learners, in this class or anywhere else, we attempt to explain and understand the differences in the values we live by. We listen and respond to each other as we explore and compare our divergent attitudes and opinions.

We attempt to define and understand our own value judgments—always weighing our "truth" against our prejudice before attempting to explain our "truth," before attempting to persuade others to accept it as *the* truth. We try to understand the other man's "truth."

If we do that, we give no time to old-fashioned pro-and-con debate and argumentation. Neither do we engage in the more modern and devious means of bending the minds and wills of other people to suit our fancy or design.

Instead, when controversy arises, we form small task groups of *un*liked-minded persons to consider all aspects of the situation.

The first task—to formulate statements of the most opposite views you can imagine on the controversial subject you wish to explore. Brace yourself for the hassles that are sure to arise as you try to find the words that everybody can agree on. But if you've learned to listen to each other, you can do it.

Next, each person in the group should try to explain his position in relation to the two extremes. A brief written statement is more effective than an oral one for two reasons: writing means thinking through your position more carefully, and it's easier to question each person's opinion if it is in writing.

But please accept me as the authority for this one moment—

Questions are to *clarify* what each person has said—NOT to "correct" the papers or to point out what is "wrong" with them or to say how they can be "improved."

Focus on the writer's ideas—NOT on your notion of the criteria for rating a theme from A to F or labeling it good or bad, great or lousy, fantastic or crappy.

Remember the purpose is *to clarify opinions*, not to win an argument or to cut each other down or to make anybody feel stupid.

Willingly submitting to questions from people who want to know more about what you have said means rethinking and going beyond what you have said—not only for your questioners but also for yourself. In fact, there has been no dialogue until that has happened.

When you are discussing a controversial subject, *wha'd' y' mean?* is sometimes a good question because it gets a good answer. But sometimes it gets a mere repetition of a person's original statement.

To avoid the unproductive exchange, focus on specific words that keep you from understanding the other person's statement.

Which words do not have a clear, precise or definite meaning for you?

Do the words that should convey the main idea fail to do so because they suggest nothing specific or concrete for you to relate them to?

Do some words suggest more than one meaning?

Do some words convey such strong feeling that for you they obscure meaning?

Don't be reluctant to answer your questioners with a candid *I don't know* or *I can't* whenever you don't or can't.

Maybe somebody else will see a possibility you have overlooked or an implication that would never occur to you. Or one person may see through the confusion that baffles everybody else.

Remember that the open class is not for showing off what you know or for competing for grades or any other kind of status. Instead, it's a community of learners. And we can't learn if we try to convince everybody that we already know everything there is to know, or if we get uptight and defensive when someone questions our opinions.

But if nobody feels threatened or intimidated, if nobody considers the questioning of his ideas a personal attack on his competence or integrity, everybody will learn.

Sometimes we can best understand our differences, and often diminish them, by trying to discover points—even areas—of agreement. For the range of opinion in a group is usually a continuum of overlapping opinions. Even the two persons who are furthest apart in a controversy may find some similarities that come through as clearly as their differences do. We can sometimes work our way out of an ideological deadlock by actually listing the statements everyone is willing to accept.

But the purpose is to hear and understand. I am certainly not suggesting that you compromise all that you believe, or that you conform to whatever ideas the majority or a loud minority is pushing. That would be unthinking acceptance. A bland existence. Which you know by now I'm not for. Instead I hope each of you will help all the rest of you feel free to say what you think, without fear of being labeled provincial or freaky.

If each of you can approach controversy with your ultimate cool and your most rational stance, you will probably decide, more often than not I suspect, that nobody is adequately informed to explain what he believes. That's when you should either shut up or open up some sources of reliable information.

Your teacher, of course, is your most accessible resource person. But use all the knowledge and skill within your small group before turning to your teacher for information or directions. He will, of course, check the progress of each small group regularly and help you work your way out of the muddles and dead ends you work yourself into.

But what a teacher can tell you will have lasting value only when you become involved enough and concerned enough to work on your own before asking for help.

In a community of learners the teacher does not have all the answers. Instead you are free to gather information and opinion in every department of your school, in every building on your campus.

All that we have said about reading and the library applies here, of course. But don't limit yourself to books.

Make your college newspaper a regular source, talk to upperclassmen in corridors and dorms, roam the student union listening as you go, eavesdrop or table-hop in cafeteria and snack spots. Take another look at the schedule of courses and request permission to visit the classes of the professors who sound interesting. Anything to help you find out who and where the best resource people are.

But your world of ideas and action is not limited by the boundaries, the property lines, between campus and community. Read the local papers. Explore the small town or city that now is or for many years has been your home. Comb the countryside—or the inner city and suburban sprawl for the people who know what you want to know, the people who hold or control what you want to question.

Encounter as many significant others as you can. Collect all the information, all the opinions you can.

Interview or invite resource people to your class. The directors of the institutions—public and private, cultural and economic—that make up the local community. Question them about their work and their values. And don't forget to hear the point of view of the people who say their lives are in large part controlled by others or by cultural or institutional forces beyond their control.

As you learn from all the resources available to you, keep in mind what may be the crucial question:

> What are the *implications* of the situation you are exploring?

What does it mean—to you and others? What consequences, immediate or long range, may develop from such a situation—for you and for others?

Are you experiencing the situation as an insider or an outsider?

Sometimes the lines are not so sharply drawn. Perhaps we should ask how the implications differ for all the people invovled—in various ways and in varying degrees.

Can you be "objective" enough to separate the implications the situation has for you from the implications it has for the other human beings involved in it?

Do you understand the specific reasons their reactions to the situation are different from yours?

To ask you to approach every encounter with another human being with an "open" mind or complete "objectivity," to say that you should be, or that I am, devoid of expectations based on past experiences would be gross dishonesty.

I bring to every human encounter what I now am—what I have become as I have lived through and been shaped by thousands of previous encounters. But I hope my relations with other human beings shall never be boxed in by what has been or what is. I hope what I am, shall always be what I am becoming.

To achieve that goal is to question old values in the light of new experience.

It is to acknowledge that we bring our biases with us to all our dealings with other human beings.

It is to know that every generalization we make about groups of people, no matter how well supported by our own experience, may be untrue for some person in the group; that every generalization we make about a person may seem unfair from his point of view.

It is to experience the joy and agony of freely choosing from all the available alternatives before declaring what we value and what we believe.

with the Questions you ask and are asked

You cannot write writing . . . Unless the emphasis is placed upon writing as a form of communication and directed very definitely to an actual, live reader, the importance of clarity, organization, and validity is not likely to become very apparent. Their importance becomes obvious, and the means of achieving them . . . (can be discovered) the moment one begins seriously to write-about-something-for-someone.

Wendell Johnson

You can write-about-something-for-someone by turning your dialogues into discourse, by extending class talk in essays that say more fully what you think and feel. Or, to use the more traditional terms, you can learn to organize and develop your ideas. You can learn—experientially—by talking in class and on paper—to analyze your reactions to a particular concrete situation or to a particular abstract concept. You can learn because classmate or teacher will ask questions that you cannot answer.

Then you must decide if you are *concerned enough* to rethink what you already know and learn what you don't know about the subject. You must decide if you *want* to make a vague, undefined thought or feeling clear to yourself, then to others. You must decide if you want to explain why you hold a particular opinion.

Answering the questions you are asked usually means asking more questions.

Begin with your grasp of the idea or the situation you are talking about. Have you perceived enough, do you know enough to make what you think and feel meaningful to others? Do you have the facts you need?

Did the idea occur to you while living through some particular situation? Or did you learn what you know about it through some other kind of self-involving experience—like reading? Should you supplement one kind of experience with another kind before you attempt a well-developed essay?

If your idea gets through that round of self-questioning, you are ready for the second round.

Have you tried to see all the aspects of the situation your idea grew out of? Either personal or political, historical, etc.

What is the nature of each part of that situation? How does each function as part of the whole?

How important is each part to the total situation? Is one part more important than any other part? than all the other parts?

Do you see and can you say how each part is related to each of the other parts? How each is related to the whole situation?

The open class is, of course, a natural setting for finding the answers to all those questions. As you talk—in class or on paper—classmates and teacher supplement the feedback you give yourself. Their responses to what you say can help you figure out the meaning that has eluded you. They can help you discover the relationships you have not been able to see.

For in a community of learners you can discuss the subjects that baffle you as well as the subjects you have already mastered. You can share not only what you know but also what you don't know.

Whenever you're concerned but uncertain about an idea or a situation, you can ask one or several persons if you are seeing things as they are, if they see some things you don't. You can ask them for facts that you don't have. You can ask how they interpret those facts. You can ask how they interpret the facts that you have but don't understand. Sharing our insights about complex ideas, subjects and situations helps us see and analyze things from different points of view.

Small group work is usually more productive than tackling a job alone. The task groups suggested in "with your own Perceptions" (157-170) and "with the Values you live by" (171-179) lead to much talk that can be turned into competent, creative essays.

When we *think* we know what we are talking about but really don't, when we make a statement, long or short, that is not coherent or logical or well-developed, somebody in the open class will let us know it isn't. Somebody will ask us to clarify the vague ideas or make the relationships between ideas clearer. And somebody will ask us to support the generalizations we are making.

If we can, then their questions have helped us organize or compose our ideas. If we can't and somebody else supplies the answer, the questions have served the same purpose.

Even when nobody comes up with an answer, when you leave class with a head full of questions, you are still getting the help you need. For you leave unsatisfied. The questions keep worrying around inside you and you keep picking at them—looking at them from different angles, listening for new clues to meaning. If some of your classmates and your teacher engage in the same silent talking to self about your questions, your next class meeting can be a sharing of insights.

Understanding the complexities of human experience is, for most of us, impossible without asking questions. And even when we think we know, we cannot be sure that we have all the meaning, perhaps not even the crucial part of the meaning, until we have tested our insights by sharing them.

After talking at length—with self and others—about an idea or a situation you are concerned about, you will, I think, be able to see and express some of the meaning it holds for you. You will be able to explain some of the implications.

You will consider the consequences a situation holds for the people caught up in it. You will take a backward look to ask how it has shaped some important aspect of their past, you will try to determine how it affects their lives now, and you will try to predict how it could influence what will happen for them or to them in the future.

When you've asked all the questions you can think of and answered them as fully and as honestly as you can, your next decision about the form and order of your discourse is one that every writer faces—*how much* of what you know should you include?

If we try to share all of our ideas on any subject or all the details of a particular or some general experience, we soon wish we hadn't. For we keep remembering something we have omitted. And we talk on and on, wondering if anybody is listening. And because nobody likes to be ignored, we wonder if there is not a better way of telling.

When you greet somebody with "guess what happened" you have intuitively found a better way. You have chosen one incident, sometimes a single moment from a long day—*because that moment has special significance for you.*

The brief or long "composition" you then tell may not include all the descriptive and narrative details or all your specific reactions to the experience. You may not arrange the details of thought or action in the precise order they occurred. But you include enough, you are coherent enough, to say *why* or *how* the moment was significant—for you.

And your happy or disappointed words and voice convey your attitude toward what happened. And the combination of words and voice and details helps your listener understand *how you feel* and *what you think* about yourself and the experience you are sharing.

It's the natural way of human communication.

Composing on paper can seem just as natural—if you make the choices that lead to the natural forms of human thought, if you choose to talk on paper about what you naturally talk about when you feel no social inhibitions and no threats to your ego.

And that means you talk about an idea you are involved in, intellectually or emotionally; you talk about a situation you are already reacting to. Then you not only try to make your attitude toward that idea or situation clear. Your attitude will control *what* you say and *how* you say it. Your attitude will determine the *content* and the *form* of the words you put together to compose your ideas.

Turning dialogue into discourse is as simple or as complex as the implications of the concept or situation you are talking about. But if you are sure about your grasp of the subject, if you have no doubts about your attitude toward it, you have already found a way to change the chaos of experience into a coherent verbal form

When you ask *why* or *how* you arrived at a particular point of view, you can answer your question with the specific reasons or ways that are a part of your own experience.

You can explain the "truth" of a particular opinion by asking *in what ways* the assertion you are making is true—for you, for others. Then you can list the answers drawn from actual experience—including reading about and discussing the subject.

You do not need textbook patterns of organization or model outlines because you use your own natural thought processes to arrive at the guidelines for a logical and coherent statement.

Call it an outline if you wish. But perhaps *experiential* plan would be more descriptive. For it evolves from your reactions to your own experience and your questions about that experience. Developing your plan is not a routine academic chore but a *self-involving experience*.

When a strong and well-defined attitude is the *raison d'etre* of composition, you choose the words and the details to make that attitude the tone of voice your listener or reader hears. And that attitude naturally leads you to focus on the perceptions that produced it—the people and things observed or read about and your reactions to them.

If you have perceived a happy situation, then you write with a happy voice and include happy details. If you think the happy place with its happy people is in any kind of danger, your voice becomes insistent as you talk about why it should be protected. If you have perceived a situation that appalls you, then you attempt to create an appalling effect with the sound and content of your talk on paper.

Your voice and the attitude it expresses help your reader *see* what you saw—from *your* point of view. As you focus his attention on your perceptions and insights, he feels some of the impact the experience had on you. For you have given him a verbal form of that experience.

We may not achieve that much when we first pour our thoughts and feelings onto the page. But if that is what you want your reader to see and feel and think, you will listen very critically as you *read aloud* what you have written.

When you write to explain a singular and strong attitude, your talk on paper usually comes out unified and forceful. But sometimes we do not sustain the same tone throughout a speech or paper. Sometimes we begin with a hostile or unhappy voice, then gradually change as we talk or write, because saying what or how we feel eases the tensions and calms the emotions we feel. Other times a change in our tone of voice indicates a change that is directly related to the dialogue we are engaged in.

As you read what you have written, what tone (of voice) do you hear? Does it come through distinctly from beginning to end?

If not, try to decide why the tone changes.

Does your tone of voice ever change as you talk with someone about the "same" experience that was vastly different for each of you? Or as you talk with someone whose views on a particular controversial issue seem directly opposed to yours?

If your change of voice does not indicate a change in your attitude toward the subject being discussed, what attitude of yours has changed?

Your tone of voice conveys much meaning and emphasis as you talk—in person or on paper—about something you have strong and well-defind feelings about. And your readers hear and respond as you hope they will if your words help them understand how you perceived and reacted to the situation you are writing about.

But if you are talking to people for whom the "same" situation has a vastly different meaning, communicating the meaning of your particular experience becomes more difficult. Your tone of voice must still convey confidence in self and confidence in your ability to speak with some authority about the knowledge or experience you want to share. But audience and readers listen first for something else. They want your voice to express an awareness of them as human beings who also think and feel. Human beings with as many opinions and tender sensibilities as you have.

In fact, your attitude toward your audience may come through before anything else you say does. And if they are displeased by what your tone of voice says you think about them, they may not stay with you long enough to hear what you came to say.

Our involvement in a situation, our commitment to a cause or an idea can always use a little detachment. And that sounds like a paradox—if we are *really* involved.

How can you separate yourself from something and still remain "all wrapped up" in it—emotionally *or* intellectually? How can you see what the other person sees unless you bring to the situation the same background of experience, the same set of attitudes and values that he brings?

Learning to handle that paradox is one of the expectations of the open class. There each person is trying to hear and respond to every other person, and each gradually becomes aware of the other's point of view. And though he may never accept that view as his own, he comes to accept the inevitable fact that every question has at least two and sometimes two hundred different "sides."

Which is, of course, the attitude we need in all our dialogues outside the open classroom. Many times when working with other groups, there seems to be little time and no opportunity to build up the relationships we have encouraged you to try to sustain in your class. But the voice our readers and listeners hear can convey our willingness to listen to others as we hope they will listen to us. Our attitude toward audience and reader can say that we are not only eager to share what we know, but hopeful of making the encounter a learning experience for self.

Then, as in the open class, we will hear opinions far removed from our own, we will get a few glimpses of what the world is like from other points of view. And if we look, even momentarily, without our biased-colored glasses, we will see things we've never seen before.

Our involvement with the situation and all the ideas it encompasses need not diminish, but we may be able to detach ourselves from our limited point of view.

And maybe that's what getting an education really means.

So talking is a way of learning—the facts of another person's experience and how to understand our own experience. And when we understand, then we can build a coherent verbal structure out of what we know and understand. We can show how the various aspects of a subject fit together, we can present a unified word picture of it, we can make a well-organized statement about it— because somebody helped us see the relationships we overlooked. We can say what it means because somebody helped us find the meaning. And we can explain the significance of an experience by conveying with voice and details our attitude toward subject and audience.

Sometimes, of course, you may want and need to sketch out a plan that indicates the shape your ideas may take as you let your attitude toward subject and reader control your writing.

But don't use somebody else's detailed blueprint that tells you how to write each paragraph. And don't think of your own plan for a paper as the *finished* framework for the verbal structure you hope to build. No outline should be like the structural steel that fixes the shape of a building.

When we are really composing—when we are creating with words— our ideas grow and develop as we write, sometimes taking unexpected forms, sometimes changing quite drastically.

For in all our telling, there is choice.

The choices you make as you write may lead to new insights. And new insights may lead to a new attitude. And a new attitude may change the tone and the structure and the substance of what you say.

The choices you make as you write may suggest a more forceful way to order and develop your ideas than the one you planned. In fact, within the logical patterns of thought we all engage in, the range of possibilities is as wide as your own creative imagination. Try other arrangements whenever your ideas do not move as you want them to. Play with the possibilities until you find the form and order that pleases you.

Read aloud what you have written.

Will the progression of ideas and the sound of your voice on paper carry your reader from paragraph to paragraph, creating a continuum of thought and feeling—a reading experience that he will respond to?

Before sharing what you have written with a wider audience, ask teacher or classmate or friend to respond to the version you like best. Ask what effect your arrangement of ideas produces on him.

Talk about the changes you need to make so that your ideas will reach the people you want to reach.

And that's how "organization" is "taught" as we turn dialogue into discourse.

This book says it's the best way because it is based—not on school book principles and terminology—but on your own search for coherence and meaning in your own confusing experience (including reading and listening).

But sometimes, no matter how many questions we ask or how many answers we find—no matter how many people we talk to about a particular idea or situation—we find ourselves still searching for meaning in confusion.

For that, we need a voice that continues to question even as it attempts to explain the little snatches of reality we think we understand.

For that, we need a sense of detachment. A special kind of cool. So we can stand apart from our own confusion to turn a keen analytical eye upon self and the world we live in.

So keep on talking about it all—in person and on paper. Then turn that talk into competent, creative essays.

Let your readers hear the sound of *your* voice. Let them feel the presence of another human being as they read what you write. Challenge them to respond to you and your ideas.

. . clearness depends upon, and can be measured in terms of, the degree of agreement between the writer and his readers as to what the words of the writer represent. Simply by striving for a high degree of such agreement, the writer discovers, in some measure, his ingenuity in achieving it. He discovers the usefulness of conditional and quantifying terms, the confusion created by leaving out significantly differentiating details, the degree to which the meaning of a term varies from context to context, and the kinds of differences he must allow for among his readers' habits of interpreting words. He learns to rely less on the dictionary and more on the linguistic habits of the people for whom he writes . . . . He discovers that there are various levels of abstraction, and that if he goes systematically from lower to higher levels he can use so-called abstract words and still be reasonably clear.

Above all, perhaps, he discovers the basic significance of order, or relations, or structure, or organization. This matter of structural relationships has wide ramifications, and no writer ever exhausts it, but the student quickly grasps some of its more obvious aspects, if he is striving for agreement between himself and his reader. It does not take him long to understand that the organization of what he writes should correspond to the organization of what he is writing about if the reader is to follow him readily . . .

. . . The ability to move from one sentence or paragraph or chapter to the next, in such a way as to blend them into a unified whole, is largely dependent upon an understanding of the reasons for going from one to the next, of why one statement should follow another instead of the reverse, of why one should say, "It follows, then," rather than "But." And these reasons are found in the character of the relations existing among the details of that about which the writing is being done. This becomes obvious to one who is not trying to write writing, but who is attempting, rather, to write-about-something-for-someone.

Wendell Johnson

Voices from the open classroom

I seem to be a verb,
an evolutionary process—
an integral function of the universe.

Buckminster Fuller

Treating students as adults has a lot to do
with whether or not they enjoy the course. I
like to be treated as an adult. When the person in charge treats me as a child I resent
it. When I talk about myself, I am a kid. I
always want to stay a kid, but this kid has
done his time and thinks he ought to be treated as an adult.

David Tallant

When I was sitting in class I could not express my feelings clearly. I just wasn't at
ease. I felt trapped in a cage, afraid to respond to anything around. It is so different
from what I am used to. Living out in the
country, a person can get away and be by himself and be more independent. Not being in
what you really call the wide open spaces,
but just down between the hills with the vis-
ibility not more than a quarter of a mile.
Out there I seem to be much more involved
with the environment. There is so much going
on in each field . . .

Ken Meisner

You know that self-sustaining community we
were talking about today? Well, I decided I'm
gonna live something like that some summer.
I'm gonna take my motorcycle and some clothes
and stuff and take off up into Canada somewhere and build some kind of a shack. Or maybe if all that isn't any fun, then I'll try
to be a forest ranger and work out in the
middle of nowhere watching for fires. I love
to be outdoors in a forest or just anywhere
secluded. Like maybe on an island.

Bob Wessels

When you say farmer to the people who live in
cities (big or little), they immediately see

"American Gothic", the old man and woman with pitchfork that Grant Wood painted. This might have been the right view for the 19th and early 20th century but today the Iowa farmer probably has more money invested in modern machinery than many of the upper class urban money-makers. But we still rely heavily on the pitchfork. We like to keep our buildings neat, clean and healthful, and we haven't trained our animals to shoot the craps outside. The only difference between our town friends' animals and ours is that ours come in larger sizes and make money for us. Theirs just raise a big stink and a lot of family fights over "Who takes it out today?"

Pat Furlong

I've got to go to work. I need money right now, and I've got ways of getting it if I ever get out of here. I don't mind working hard out in the fields irrigating or picking watermelons. I like to be in the open air with mama nature humming through me all the long day. If I had my way, I'd like to live alone in an open field of clover on some countryside. I hate crowds. People can be so deceiving. I'd just as soon lock myself away from them sometimes.

Gayle Jarvis

I'm really bothered with having to write things down and letting someone else read them . . . I feel that what I have written isn't good enough . . . I've had the feeling that if I say something wrong I will be laughed at. I don't want to be laughed at, so I try to act like someone else and not be myself.

unsigned

I like to see and hear what other people have to say before I show myself to them. I like to

know where another person stands so that I
might act in a way that would keep me up and
even with that person. This I find is sometimes very hard to do.

Murphy Anderson

You can never really know a person. A person
can put on all kinds of fronts for you. You
can dig a person for a lengthy time and still
never know him. A person puts forth what he
wants to put forth in any manner he chooses
and at any time . . .

A lot of the kids in the class give me the
impression that I'm in that little crushable
box they'd like to step on. I don't give a
damn 'cause I treat people the way they treat
me. Step on me and I'll step on you if I can.
I really dug what Jane said about not accept-
ing her parents' prejudices towards Blacks.
She made a friend quick. I hope she never
changes her ideas.

Billy Williams

Why do people have so much trouble communicating? Many people in close daily contact
with each other never really communicate. If
people would only tear down their walls--the
so-called protective barriers that everybody
has built around their personal lives. I a-
gree we can't always let our personal feelings and beliefs show. But most people can't
tear down the walls when they really need or
want to . . . By not truly communicating with
anybody whose beliefs differ from their own,
these people begin to live so much in their
own world that they fail to recognize, or
even come close to understanding, another
person's values. What a terrible way to go
through life!

Dwight Glenny

A Man's Mind one day
closed its steel barriers
to the world, never to
reappear. And thereby
became a fortress of
thoughts that would
never be stated or
expressed to the good
people of the universe.

A Man's Mind
     lay idle
for many years
letting the world
        and its madmen
pass it by.

No one ever inquired about
        the Man's Mind.
The Man's Mind
     never inquired about anyone.
The Man's Mind was
Given up
       For dead.

                          Lee Plagman

loving

Mary Skinner's mother died Monday.
Now it's just Mary, Daddy Clarence,
   and 26 year old brother Dick.

It's not cool.
A fifty-five year old man
   doesn't always understand
A fifteen year old girl.

Girl, hell, she has to be a woman now.
A little bit a mother, taking care
   of her brother,
Cooking, cleaning--a housewife
Dutiful as daughter
Still having to be his child.

Never can she be a teen-age girl
   full of giggles
        and childish love.

                          Lisa Haller

This is the first poetry I've ever attempted
to write so I'd like to tell you about a
member of my family who I really love--my
brother.

He is a mountain
   tall and stable
   a certainty in my life
but he is also a tree
   bending in the wind
   unsure of which way is better
He is the sun
   bright when all others are not
but he is also a cloud
   overshadowing a good day
He is an ocean
   his ideas changing with the tide
but he is also a rock
   never changing position
You think that he doesn't know
   himself very well
No . . . . . He is just very young

                    Shirley Peterson

My best friend
is growing tired
of hearing your name . . .
   perhaps if I had something to say,
   she'd be more willing to listen,
   but as it is, I can only repeat
   and repeat the same old things
   and be thankful she's still around at all.
Is it that talking of you
brings you here again
in a sense?
   Does the utterance of your name
   make you more believable and real;
   and is it perhaps a poor attempt
   to cover the inward, frantic fear
   that you won't come back to me after all,
   when the waiting period is over?
One thousand miles is a great distance
to lie between any two people . . .
even those, unlike us,
who've made a spoken bond.

                    Claudia Diggs

```
Joy is being alive
knowing you belong . . .
to many, many people
          Meaning many, many things
Most of all
          JOY is a girl
          I love this fall.
```

Fuzzy Thompson

I am so confused about sex. I have talked to
so many people and they have told me so many
different things and it's all floating around
in my head and I feel that all I have to do
is fit it all together, all in one list, and
maybe I'll have some of the answers. Ever
since I was a little girl I have been taught
to look nice and sexy and attractive but don't
let anyone touch. Look nice, but don't touch.
Now I am faced with a new freedom. Now I am
faced with sex. And every time I am faced with
sex, a little voice inside of me says "no,
this is wrong." Then another voice, this new
voice asks "why?" Goddamn it, I don't know
why! I just always believed what I was taught
and accepted it. But now I realize that there
must be a reason why not, but damned if I can
find it in my mind. And these two voices just
keep shouting at me and it is tearing me a-
part.

Jane Mather

Sex taken in the wrong respect can change a feeling of love into resentment and guilt. In less than seven minutes, the union of two people creates an expression of the beauty of life. In that short time, the fate of another life being conceived and brought into this world lies within the responsibility of two people. They might be willing to give each other those few minutes of their lives, but do they want to give all of their time to another life which they created together?

Pam Bourque

It was four a.m., my head was spinning and I couldn't go to sleep. As usual, when feeling intensely lonely and depressed, I decided to take a walk. In a few minutes I was sitting behind the Union next to the river. The campus was quiet. The world seemed dead.

Then, I noticed someone sitting across the river. Feeling really strange, I started walking across the bridge. When I was almost across I looked up and saw a girl standing about ten feet in front of me. I don't remember her face. I didn't notice if she was tall or short, black or white, young or old, or what. I only knew that she was crying. We sat down in the grass, held each other, and cried together as we watched the sun rise. Then we got up, she crossed the footbridge and disappeared, and I walked back to my room and fell asleep.

Now I know what nonverbal communication means.

Charles Townsend

being

For a week almost I have been trying to write something and it seems that nothing comes out of my head. Lots of questions, in complete disorder, are striving to find answers. Yet,

not even the questions are clear. It is like
all of them are intermingled . . . This has
happened before to my head. New experiences,
new ideas, new books. All need to be digested,
assimilated, so that they can come to be part
of the "permament" set of ideas that make me
what I am. Yet after they have been assimilated, I am becoming again a mixture of what
I am and what I will be--the beautiful process of being.

"To be" sounds so unshakable, yet it is so
ever-changing. To the world I am always the
same: the same face, the same figure, the
same name. That is what they see. That is
what I am, for them. But inside me, infinite,
almost inperceptible changes, even to me,
are going on all the time. My cells renew
themselves, my skin changes, my conception
of the world around me changes . . . What I
was the moment I started writing these lines
is gone forever, it cannot be recaptured.
But, what was I? who was I? how was I? I do
not know, I never knew, and I will never
know. What an enormous, beautiful enigma!

It is like when during a lazy summer afternoon I can hear the murmuring of water, so
pleasing to the senses, so refreshing. Yet,
from where I am, I am not able to see where
that water comes from. Then, I fill the time
imagining how and where the water is coming
from, and why it comes and sounds the way
it does . . . Maybe if we knew who we really
were, we would not need imagination . . .
If this is true, I wonder--while I still
can--what we will find in the place of imagination, the day we succeed in delving the
mystery of being.

                                    Beatriz Alonzo

enjoying the night

It's pretty late now so my mind isn't function-
ing. I just awoke from a nap which I didn't

really want to take, but I'm glad I did. It was so nice and now I can enjoy the night. I want to sit out on the back porch with my dad's shotgun and wait for the window peeker to come and make his nightly rounds. It seems such a waste for that man to live someone else's life instead of his own. That man has a problem, but I don't feel sorry for him, for he's intruding on my life.

It's a beautiful night. I'm glad that I can enjoy little things such as this and be able to remember them. Like the night I sat outside until 3:30 watching and listening to the wind. Did that ever make my dad mad! He thought I had really gone far off, even worried that I was insane. Once we sat on the back porch and talked for hours about our lives.

It's midnight so I'm going to turn off the lights and enjoy the darkness.

It's a beautiful night. As I sit in the dark, I can smell the cool, night breeze going past me, flushing away the pollution and heat of the day. Everything is serene. The only living things are me and the plants, breathing in the dark. The cars and the buildings and everything my eyes do not enjoy, especially the hassling, uncaring people, are gone.
Lost in the night.

It's like being set free. I can see myself more clearly now. There's no one to get in my way.

I'm glad that someone gave me life. For a long time I couldn't find anything worth living for, but now when I'm confused and lost with a problem, I find my therapy alone in the dark. Here I can think things out. I can get help from the stars. They're like omniscient guides. Up there in that dark sea of search lights, there's something looking for someone like me, someone who needs help or someone who can just enjoy the simple pleasures of the dark. I feel like the first and last person on earth. I'm the

first--alone--and the future of the earth depends on me. Yet I'm the last person. Everyone else has rushed to their graves because
they didn't take time out to enjoy life, so
I'm the only one left. Because I found the
way to know real living.

Now the night is beginning to recede. The
light is creeping up above the treetops, like
the Virgin Mary giving birth to the hope of a
new, peaceful, pure world. Then it happens
and it's not a miracle. Everything is shot to
hell before me. Lights going on, doors slam-
ming, milk trucks screeching to a stop, dogs
barking. Another busy day, full of rushing
and hassling.

If everyone could only enjoy the night perhaps
the days could be nights too.

Mary Eggenberg

one man's truth about grass

I've seen kids--good, strong, young Black
kids--turn to nothing and come out nothing
from the effects of smoking grass. Not from
grass alone, but I know grass was the starter
for the hard stuff. Not smack or heroin right
off, but the other drugs, like reds and bennies
and speed and coke. I have seen it firsthand,
and nothing any upper middle class doctor or
professor of pharmacy can say or write is going to make me believe otherwise. I know what
I have seen.

Lennie was heavy. No, Lennie *is* heavy. He is
a smart brother. Very smart. He works in the
library in the parish prison. He is doing two
to five years for possession of narcotics.

Lennie was the smartest blood in the ninth
grade. We called him names like Head, The
Thinker, The Brain. If there was a way to do
something, Len knew it or would find out how
to do it. All the teachers said he'd get a
scholarship at a good college. But still he
was one of the fellows. The cat could use his

hands with anyone, but he could rap, man, that cat could rap. I was afraid to fuss with him because he could cut you down, make you look like nothing, without using a four letter word. He was a hell of a brother. Lennie was hating white people long before any of us got in the black-white bag. He would always find a fight with some white boys, and he would fight like he was crazy. He really made me think. He said all white people, women and men, were rapists, that they had stolen this country from the stupid-ass Indians and had raped Africa of her black gold. Len was talking that in the ninth grade. He was one of us and he was not one of us, all at the same time.

Lennie started smoking grass in eighth grade. He said he smoked grass because then he was better able to understand the devil the white man was. And the better he understood that devil, the better he would be able to defend himself. He started dropping pills long before the rest of the fellows did. Smoking grass was a waste of time he said because the medical profession had devised a way for you to get a much faster high that would last much longer. By the time Len got out of high school, he made like he didn't know he had a scholarship. He just didn't give a damn. He was still heavy, he was still the main man on the block, but he didn't give a damn.

With dubious pride and inner hatred, Sammy lives with the distinction of being one of the few people on the block who has attended a University. Few of the streeters have even been to high school, but he's had a year at Southern on a basketball scholarship. With only a few weeks remaining in his freshman year, he was expelled for smoking grass. All he does now is smoke and drop pills and use coke.

In high school Sammy lettered in four sports—track, football, baseball, and basketball. Basketball was his main love and by far his best sport, but he could have won a scholarship for any of the others. To see Sammy on the court

was like watching a two hundred pound ballet
dancer. He moved with the grace and speed of
a jungle cat and he had the shooting eye of
an eagle and he could outrun a Ford.

Sammy started smoking grass midway through his
senior year in high school. The effects were
immediate and damaging. He no longer played
like there was no tomorrow; he played like he
was trying to make every second last. He no
longer outran Fords; he couldn't even keep up
with old Volkswagons. Sammy had lost his fire.
But he was still better than most of his oppo-
nents and he got his scholarship. He performed
well at Southern and we still thought he was
headed for the top. Then the roof fell in and
he was out on his ass. Just another street nigger, breaking heads, dropping pills and going
nowhere. All because of a reefer.

Walter is a caddie. When he sees his white
boss his smile is automatic. He yes sirs and
he no mams and he laughs if the sun shines.
Walter makes about ten or fifteen dollars a
day, caddying and finding and stealing balls.
This money he uses to buy dope with, to feed
the monkey that is riding his back and ruin-
ing his life.

As a freshman in high school Walter was the
Black state golf champion of Louisiana. When
he was fourteen, he could drive a ball 250
yards and he could putt with Casper. He had
learned the game, like nearly all Black players do, by caddying. He got his first club
from the man he works for to this day. He was,
if there is such a thing, a natural golfer.

Walter was in his sophomore year in high school
when he was picked up for shoplifting. He did
not finish that year in school. He had been
smoking grass for some time and was stealing
to get money to buy some jays. He was sent to
the state home for boys where he stayed two
weeks before he broke out and was sent back for
two years. While there, he started dropping
pills and using coke. His life was over at
seventeen.

Seventy-five per cent of the kids in my high
school smoked grass. I know because they didn't
give a good damn who knew what they were doing.
I do not know about the other 25 per cent; they
did not let what they were doing get out in
the streets. But every one of the 75 per cent
is using stronger drugs today. And their lives
are hopeless, each a little different, but
all like my three friends.

Murphy Anderson

one woman's truth about sororities

I came to school this fall very upset over my
recently broken home. I felt as if I no longer
had a place I could call my "home". Where did
I belong? In my father's home or my mother's?
I knew I was welcome in either, but I didn't
feel as if I could consider either "home".
"Home" from then on would be the place that I
made for myself.

I had no desire to make Burge Hall or any other
dorm my home. I'm sure none of you would re-
joice at such a thought either. So, I decided
to go "Greek".

After living in the house for a week, I felt
as if I had a home again. My sorority sisters
served as a family for me to identify with. I
no longer felt so alone. I felt and still do
feel that my pledging was the best move that
I could have made. So why is it that so many
people knock my decision?

Greek rush week ended in bitter disappointment for many girls. They had lived a week of
nervous frustration, only to be cut from the
houses in the end. No one wanted them as a
"sister". But yet, how is this one disappointment any different from many others that people
encounter all through their lives?

The athlete willingly over-exerted himself
during the strenuous practices only to be cut

from the team. The girls racked their brains
out, striving to memorize words and motions
to all the cheers in two or three cram sessions before tryouts. Only a few made the
squad. The rest were eliminated because of
their inferior skill. The students sang to
the best of their ability in hopes of making
the choir. They had worked on the strength
and tone of their voices for days in preparation for this decisive day. But for some,
all their efforts were in vain. The musician
had practiced for years, striving for per-
fection. He knew he wasn't perfect, but he
did feel that he was good. But he was cut
from the group because someone had more talent
and they didn't need him. The student studied
endlessly for four years seeking a grade point
that would enable him to be accepted into medical school. He was sure that was the profession for him. But they didn't accept him. He
wasn't smart enough. The girl tried her best
to make a good impression on her date. She
had been dying to go out with him for months
and here she was at last. As they parted at
the close of the evening, she felt as if she
were on cloud nine. But he never called again.

Life is full of disappointments. Everywhere
we go, we will always encounter them. To survive through life without letting these disappointments affect our mental state, we must
learn to forget and go on. Life is too full
of opportunities to let ourselves remain hung
up on one segment of it

                                    Rita Lorenzen

to say my father is middle class

I don't know, it's just not right. I mean he
has the fine makings for a "middle class negro."
He's smart, he has a master's degree, he has
a big car. An Olds 98. He's hard-working and
a good teacher. He's been teaching in the inner
city public school system seven years. Taught
the last two summers at a prestigious college
in New England.

But my father is a very complex person. He's about 5'10", 170 pounds, mean as hell, stronger than a bull, and uglier than sin. And he is crude. No polish. He's the kind of person you'll see eating downtown with both elbows on the table, eating with his hands, and his napkin's stuck in his collar. He's country. Walks around with his shoes off all the time. Never combs his hair. Extremely lazy.

Extremely kindhearted. Always giving money away to his friends and kids at school. One year at a typical "ghetto" school he bought his class approximately $600 worth of clothes. That's why we don't have any money now. I remember one Christmas he gave me a living room full of toys. Trains, planes, bicycles, boxing gloves--everything. Then that afternoon he made me give all my presents away to the kids in the building. That was the first time I remember wanting to kill my father. I can see his point, and now that I am older I understand, but till this day I still haven't forgiven him for that.

My childhood memories are not of baseball games with dad and Sunday afternoon picnics with the family. Instead I remember slappings and beatings and "cussing outs" and what little Black kids call "whoopin's." My father never beat me with a belt. He always beat me with his fists. Like I was a grown man. Many a time I plotted to kill him.

My father was born in the northern backwoods of Mississippi. Exactly where, I don't know because he doesn't have a birth certificate. His father was a professional gambler, who taught him and his brother how to mark cards with a razor blade at the age of five. His mother had to leave Mississippi with her family when she beat two white men with an ax handle.

These were the beginnings of my father

By the age of seven, living on the Southside, he had won $60 playing the numbers, been bit

by numerous dogs, hit by a car, hit on the
head with a brick, cut with a razor, shot at,
and stabbed with a knife by his brother. In
other words, he lived the average life of a
Black kid on the Southside.

As a teenager he went through the average
changes. He was in a street gang called the
Four-Corners, he went to dances, he hustled
watches, jewelry, men's colognes, and clothing
on Forty-seventh Street, and he met my mother.
Everybody called him Crazy Mo. Which is a good
name because he is crazy. At the same time
he is a warm and humane person.

And sometimes he's just plain stupid. We stayed at [a certain address] for years because he
refused to buy a house. The reason--he doesn't
like the type of people who buy houses.

This essay has no conclusion because I have
no words that will "sum up" what my father is.

                                    unsigned

monkey see what monkey do

There we were--surrounded by Burford's Circus.
The low roar of a caged lion penetrated the
rich and happy tones of the pipe-organ. A thousand shafts of light were dancing off a shiny
twirling ball above us, tracing endless patterns of light over us and the colorful awn-
ings. Burford's "extravaganza" seemed more
alive than the colossal realness of Barnum and
Bailey's "Greatest Show On Earth." But we were
in an art museum, looking at an artist's cardboard images of clowns and tigers and tightrope walkers.

We were the performers in the main arena. And
while looking at the cardboard images, we were
turning to look at the other people who were
looking at the cardboard images. And the people
we were looking at were turning away to look
at the cardboard images that made them want
to look at us. And so on and on and on.

Step right up folks. Get your cotton candy,
get your popcorn, get a look at yourself in
a mirror. Look around you. Look at that girl
wiggle her hips as she walks down the street
and look at that guy's eyes pop out. It's a
barrel of monkeys, my friends, and we're the
monkeys. A little more intelligent perhaps,
but what we see done, we do. It's all right
here, folks, in Burford's Circus.

Shocked, then indignant, and finally amused,
I realized that Burford is showing us that
we're all monkeys. Not the ones who hang from
trees (though some of us do) nor the ones who
gobble down a bunch of bananas (though I've
seen that too), but a monkey who meets a successful businessman and wants to be successful, or a monkey who sees a beautiful and
famous actress and knows what she wears is a
"must" for this season.

With a circus created out of cardboard and
canvas and light and sound and color, with an
"extravaganza" of art and truth, Burford is
abruptly awakening us to see ourselves. Burford is a genius. His circus is the work of
a genius. It is an artistic masterpiece which
I'm glad I experienced.

There is another aspect of Burford's Circus
that may or may not be valid. I think the
image you look at the longest is what you are
or what you are trying to be. I'm a mixture
of lion and tightrope walker.

John Posner

holden's crazy world

The Catcher in the Rye by J. D. Salinger is
a story of initiation. Its hero, Holden Caul-
field, **is** innocent but not completely naive;
he has some knowledge of evil, though he himself is not corrupted by it. His story is an
odyssey--a search and an escape. It begins on
a Saturday afternoon around Christmastime at

Pencey Prep and ends at the New York Zoo on Monday afternoon. Holden tells the story some months later in California, where he has been seeing a psychiatrist.

The central conflict in the novel is between innocence and experience. Holden can seem to find no fulfillment in an adult world, since all it can offer man is frustration or corruption; the only worthwhile job that he could see doing is that of a protector of children. Someone who stops them before they enter a world of phoniness, someone who keeps them in a state of innocence.

After leaving Pencey Prep, Holden sneaks into his home one night to see his younger sister, Phoebe, who, he says, is the only person who understands him. When Phoebe asks what he'd like to be when he grows up, he says he's always thinking about a lot of little kids playing a game in a big field of rye. He sees thousands of little kids with nobody big around except for him and he wants to be *the catcher in the rye*. He wants to stand on the edge of a big cliff and catch the kids who don't look where they are going.

As always, Holden says he knows it's *crazy*. He's always using the word *crazy*. This time because he realizes that his ambition is absurd. His Christ-like intention is opposed to the reality which children, like Phoebe, see when they are carted off to the Lister foundation to see movies on euthanasia and when they move along grimy school corridors which flaunt the words "fuck you" at them.

From the first page on, Holden sees a distorted, warped and cracked world. He views that world as being largely phony. Indeed, this is his most obvious aversion. Everyone in the book, except for his little sister Phoebe, is a phony, pretending to be someone he is not. At Pencey Prep, the school from which he fled, the phonies include the students themselves; old Thurmer, the headmaster; old Spencer, the history teacher; and the undertaker-alumnus, old Ossenburger, who is so grotesque that Holden describes him by telling how one student laid a terrific fart during his speech in chapel. Holden shows sympathy for the phonies who are obviously flawed, whose poses are defensive. Ackley, for example, is physically ugly, Sunny the prostitute is stupid, and Mr. Spencer is old and insecure.

Few areas of modern life escape Holden's scorn. The phonies of Hollywood and of religion are severely put down as he tells about the Christmas pageant at Radio City. Following the Rockettes and a man who rollerskated under tables, thousands of angels start coming out of boxes and a bunch of guys are carrying crucifixes all over the stage, and everybody's singing "Come All Ye Faithful." Holden can't see anything religious about what he knows is *supposed to be* religious. He feels so frustrated and alone after his experience with Radio City Christmas, he says he's glad they've got the atomic bomb invented. He says he's going to sit right on top of it if ever there's another war.

Wherever Holden turns, his search for truth seems to be frustrated by the phoniness of the world. From his hotel window, he looks upon the scenes of perversion and wierdness; in the bars and nightclubs he hears the shallow conversations of pseudo-sophisticates.

One reason Holden left Pencey was to search for a unity, to find something that would not change. He finds great comfort in the Museum of Natural History. No matter how many times he goes there, everything will still be the same, just the way he remembers seeing it when he was a kid--the Eskimo with the same two fish he's just caught, the same birds flying south, the pretty deer drinking out of that same water hole, and the squaw with the naked bosom weaving the same blanket. Nothing will have changed. Except *you.*

While waiting for his little sister in the
museum near the end of his New York odyssey,
he's thinking how she'll see the same exhibits
that he saw as a child. But when he climbs
down into the tomb, he finds the familiar
"fuck you" written under the glass case. It
is then that he comes to a very important
realization. No matter how long we look for
a nice and peaceful place, we'll never find
it. Even when we think we've found it, somebody will mess it up for us.

Holden realizes the conflict between innocence
and experience is inescapable and inevitable.
And later, watching his sister and the other
kids on the carousel, he realizes that the
real world is like the children grabbing for
the gold ring on the carousel. You have to
let them do what they want to do without saying anything to them. Even when they fall off,
you shouldn't say anything to them. Innocence
does not last forever. This truth has Holden
damn near bawling as Phoebe goes round and
round and the carousel plays "Smoke Gets in
Your Eyes."

At the end of the story, Holden's brother asks
what he thinks about all the "stuff" he had
been telling us about. And he realizes that he
does not know what he thinks. And now he starts
missing everybody he's told us about. I take
this to be a statement of Holden's reconcilia-
tion with society, because everybody includes
even that goddamn Maurice, the pimp who beat
him up. Holden, I think, is talking about for-
giveness. He misses even the phonies of the
world because his experience has taught him
something about the necessity of loving.

Randy Stein

farming and college, a comparison

Good weather on the farm means hot sunny days
when everybody pitches in and gets as much
work as possible done. In college it means
everybody gets up, goes to school and sits in
class and sweats. By the end of the day both
parties need a shower. The party engaged in
farming is filthy and smelly; the party engaged in sweating is just smelly. The farmer
is always somewhat worn out, but he has the
satisfaction of knowing his was a good honest
sweat. The student knows only that he is bored.
After he has showered, the farmer feels pleased
with himself and he's ready to enjoy the evening. The student showers but feels no different. He is just plain bored because he has had
no fulfilling physical or mental exertion.

Rainy weather to the student means the same
old grind with a slight variation--he's getting wet instead of sweaty and pissed off instead of bored. To a farmer rainy weather
means hurrying through the chores, changing
clothes, and heading for town or the neighbors to drink beer, play cards, or bullshit.
Everybody is happy. They all gather together
with a common interest.

In severe weather the student listens to the
radio reports on the blizzard or tornado,
hoping there will be no classes, but generally
hearing there will be. He goes stomping off to
class with nothing but anger in his heart. To
farmers severe weather means banding together
and fighting the elements as a team. It means
meeting all types of predicaments as a colony
of neighbors. Broken fences, loose cattle,
cars stuck in the ditch, fires, injuries to
people or farm animals. Whatever it is, everybody gathers to do the man's work for him
while he recuperates his losses. And when
things settle down, the colony settles down to
some hard drinking and general good times.

In essence, the factor which draws me to the
farming life is something I've never found
elsewhere. In a rural community there is an

uncommon amount of friendly togetherness which
could never materialize in the cold and drab
atmosphere of a college or a city.

John Kennedy

breaking the brains barrier

Teacher always tell you to come to their office and talk to them whenever you have a
problem. They sound sweet and understanding.
You feel as though you could spill your heart
out to them. When you go to talk to this person you're so confident in yourself. You know
everything you're going to say and just why
you're stopping in to visit. You're not going
to be tongue-tied.

As soon as you walk in the door you freeze,
you've forgotten everything you wanted to
say. Each step you take across the ice-tiled
floor sounds five times louder than ever before. All eyes are on you as you shyly look
around for something warm or familiar. Then,
like over a loud speaker, you hear your name
being called out. Your stomach tightens up
and you look around frantically for the person who called out your name. You know who it
is, it's that sympathetic, sweet person who
told you to come and see him any time you
have a problem. But that sweet person has
just turned into a TEACHER with the steel
case desk, papers with comments and F's written all over them, a coffee cup and pencils
strewn all over, and two chairs at his desk.
One has STUDENT written all over it. A
straight back chair with a hard seat uphol-
stered in cold leather. The TEACHER's chair
is even more obvious than yours. It rolls
around that ice-tiled floor, leans back so
he can sip his coffee comfortably and swirls
from side to side. So while he's leaning back
sipping on his coffee you sit uncomfortable
as hell and can't think of a damn thing to say.

No matter how much a teacher wants to be
accepted by the students as a person rather

than a teacher, there is still fear of the
superiority a teacher has. Now, if I were to
go to talk to a teacher about my problems say
in a relaxed, loud atmosphere like the Air-
liner, where I won't feel as though all eyes
are on me and everything I say is being broad-
cast, I think I could spill my heart out and
would definitely feel relaxed. That may not
be an ideal spot for talking about rhetoric,
but it sure as hell would help me get rid of
my teacher-student complex. Why would we even
have to talk about Rhetoric? We could just
sit and rap. Get to know each other just to
make things a little more easygoing. So that
when I do have to talk to him about rhetoric
I will feel as though he knows ME as a person
and I know him as a person, not the old
TEACHER-STUDENT type of know each other.

This may not work for anyone, it may not even
work for me. But the way it's set up now it
sure as hell ain't workin' for me!

Carol Garthwaite

dying

The room smelled of medication and disease.
The flowers on the table drooped pitifully,
the body on the bed did not stir. The sun
seemed reluctant to accept the invitation of
open curtains. I walked to the bed and paused.
The woman's eyes turned upward as if to greet
me. I was overwhelmed. If only I could comprehend what she held in her eyes, the mystery of life and death would be revealed, all
questions of why and how would be resolved.
But always, the answer to life written in the
eyes of strangers is illegible.

Jan Durlam

Knowledge, experiences
        Great minds, kind soul
Twisted and deformed
By the bitter truth that
        Today has pushed you in a corner
And forgotten where.

                                    Inga Wallize

What can you say about someone who is dying?
It grips the heart (maybe) and disturbs the
mind (sometimes). I have five dying relatives.
Three great aunts that we treat like china
dolls because this could (probably) be the
last time we shall ever see one of them or
all of them again. We've been doing this for
ten years now. Having special birthday and
holiday luncheons and suppers. Getting the
flock together one last time--because it would
be nice if they could have this one last memory. But though they be deaf and blind, though
they have had dozens of heart attacks and
strokes, laxatives have kept them going
through their eighties. My grandmother, the
youngest of the four sisters, was initiated
into their aging club with her first stroke
last year. On the other side of the family,
my father's mother has been playing the widow
role for six years. Now, for two months, she
is suddenly dying. A doped, drugged, senile
little lady without a care or interest in the
world, except to die. And she's *only* seventy-
six. They all have lived good lives. And now
we wait for the day when they shall die. Science, my friend, has kept these women LIVING.
And life is what counts. Not a purpose or a
desire, but LIFE! Thank you, science, for my
breath of air and misery. For protecting my
body and mind from the demands of natural
death.

I don't believe in euthanasia. Neither do I
believe in stretching out lives already lived.
Already fulfilled. I have no solution. But I
believe this cruel extension of useless life
has helped to create our insipid, cruel,
youth-worshipping culture. We see the loneli-

ness, the emptiness of old age. And we are
afraid of it happening to us. We want to feel
a worthiness that we can't find in our dying
friends at American resting homes. In other
lands the aged are respected for their wisdom.
No where else is there such drugging and beg-
ging for prolonged life.

Su King

Death was in the air. Soon as you left the
cabin you sensed it. The tarmac was hot.
Waves of heat bounced off the surface. Your
freshly pressed uniform suddenly becomes a
second skin, clinging tighter and tighter
with each second.

F-o-r-m ranks!

Move jeep!

No-o-o talking!

The silence closes in. You're a robot, with
thirty-four other robots Now you're moving
double-time. Heat all around. It's hard to
breath.

Halt!

Throw your gear by a bed!

O-u-tside! Move it!

F-o-r-m ranks!

Moving again, double-time, choking. The heat
is killing you. Where are you and your fellow
robots going? By now it looks like the jungle.
Down the path. Up the hill. I hope we stop
soon.

Halt! At ease!

That doesn't mean smoke, stupid!

No-o-o talking and L-i-i-i-sten!

Young Bloods, I'm here to give you some valuable information. So listen carefully. It may save your life. Everything and everybody here is dangerous. Any kid on the street could be Charlie.

A kid? Five years old? Why that's about two and a half feet. Why would he put poison in the bottle? Why would he want to kill me?

The green grass, open field, free clean air. That's for me. Free to be alone with nature and God . . . What?

> People in the grass . . . Mines in the grass . . . Booby traps in the grass . . .

Tunnels? Small round holes leading into the ground? Small graves for small men. Tunnel Rats exploring the tunnels in the grass. Their fatality rate is 80 per cent. 20 per cent come out alive. Some odds!

Hell! I'm only five feet, five and a half inches. If I were three more inches or weighed thirty more pounds--but I don't.

I'm twenty years old. When I go back this time I can drink. Wow! I don't want to be a Rat. I haven't seen all of the world. Or heard all of the sound in the world. I haven't lived enough. I don't want to die.

Roy Lee

My brother is in Viet Nam. And one of the worst things about that statement is that the people who sent him there don't even know what it means. In fact, they don't even know who my brother is.

They don't know about the time I had my head broken open with a baseball bat and he carried me up four flights of stairs and bandaged my head and took me to the hospital. And they don't know about the time he caught me smoking (cigarettes) and forced me to

stop smoking completely. When that happened
I was really mad at his interfering with my
life but without that interference my wind
could have been completely shot and what good
is a trumpet player with no breath support?

The people who sent my brother to Viet Nam
don't care that less than six months ago he
and his wife had their first child. Four
days later the baby died. I wonder what a
year's separation will do to my sister-in-law.
And what about *her* life if she loses her hus-
band too? And what about my mother who says
the same prayers every night that she said
twenty years ago when my father was in Europe
fighting another war? I wonder how my father
likes reliving all the hell he went through
every time he thinks of his son in Viet Nam.

My brother is one of the finest men I have
ever known. And his reward is to be promoted
to captain and given an option: one year in
hell or the death penalty.

Jim Gauthier

a commercial for living color tv

opening scene: twilight in a war zone that
looks remarkably like Vietnam. a platoon of
G.I.'s advancing up a hill. sounds and flashes
of rifle-fire, mortars exploding, etc.

the battle has been going on for several hours.
by the rocket's red glare, through the bombs
bursting in air, we can see that our boys are
still there. suddenly a rocket explodes in
their midst. arms, legs, heads--flesh and
blood go flying through the air.

a medic rushes onto the scene where bodies
and parts thereof are strewn and scattered.
dripping blood and guts all over the ground.

medic (shaking his head in dismay): this is
a hell of a mess.

voice (off stage): calling Man from Glad,
calling Man from Glad.

Man from Glad materializes in spiffy white
suit with his silver hair slicked down.

Man from Glad: medic, this is a job for Glad
Wrap Heavy Duty Plastic Bags. watch!

Man from Glad whips out a Heavy Duty Glad
Bag (garbage-pail-size), picks up a headless,
armless, legless bloody glob by the belt
buckle and drips it into Glad Bag.

Man from Glad: see--no muss, no fuss, no
bother. and Glad bags with Heavy Duty Double
Construction never drip or leak.

Man from Glad ties his Glad Bag, tosses it
over his shoulder, then turns and faces
camera.

Man from Glad: the next time you have a messy
job to wrap up, remember Glad Bags, the No
Drip, No Leak bag to dispose of all your
messy problems.

Lee Grover

the rhetoric of self

I'm only eighteen years old and sometimes
feel as if life has nothing to offer me. Is
life supposed to be where a man finds a job,
gets married, has kids, sends his kids to
college, then waits to die? Maybe this is a
good life for everybody in Jefferson, Iowa,
but I don't want it. Maybe later. But not
just yet.

I've learned one thing though. In one semester
I've found out that drugs aren't life. I've
taken drugs, not heavily, but enough to see
what they are--just one big cop out--a way to

lose reality. Just to be tripping or up all
the time is trying to lose something--possi-
bly life. But what is life? For me tonight
it's one huge question mark. I don't know
what I want out of life. But I won't cop out
by killing myself. I'm searching--searching
for something intangible--going crazy because
I can't grasp the handle.

Life to many is to be on top, to crush as
many as possible to get there. Blacks have
been the underdog for a century--and continue
to be. I made friends with Bill this summer--
probably a superficial friendship. But we
could horse around and have a hell of a time.

And in class Bill, Murph and Melvin talked
about the problems they've always faced because they are Blacks. So after summer school
I decided to read some books written by Black
authors. I read *Nigger* by Dick Gregory and
Native Son by Richard Wright. Then I looked
around me in Jefferson, Iowa, and just knotted
up inside and felt sick to my stomach.

In this peaceful little rural community of
five thousand middle class Christians we have
no hostility toward the Blacks. Because there
is not a single Black family living here. I
can never make these people aware of the op-
pressions and injustices the Black man suf-
fers. Even if I wrote about racial problems
in *The Jefferson Bee* it would have small influence on them. They will understand Blacks
only if they know them. True equality can be
established in Jefferson only if Blacks are
invited to live there. And that is impossible
unless the business community will provide
good jobs and suitable housing for them. But
there are no employers in town who would
think of hiring Blacks. I'd like to picket
every one of them.

I cringe to think of the police stopping Bill
or Murph or Melvin for doing nothing--except
being Black. And I get a sickening feeling
when I think of one of them getting in trouble
as Bigger did in *Native Son*. And I keep wonder-

ing if their childhood years in Davenport and
New Orleans were as harsh as Dick Gregory's
childhood was in St. Louis.

When I read some of their papers last summer
I thought I was beginning to see how the
Blacks feel. You wake up each morning, Bill
said, wondering how much hassling you will
get just because you are Black. And I saw a
parallel with the way some people love to
hassle me because I have long hair--because
I'm different. I really think that is it--
people like to bother others who aren't like
them.

One night I was standing on the bridge in
Cedar Rapids grooving on the river when a
mean and violent voice began shouting obscenities at me from the window of a muddy, red
and white pickup that was speeding by. I
didn't know what to do. There were two of
them and one of me and they sounded crazy
enough to kill me. I remembered all the
stories I'd heard about construction workers
and hippies. What if they circled around the
block and came after me? I couldn't run, my
knees gave out, my legs were rubbery, I
couldn't breathe.

I could almost feel their fists hitting my
face. They might even have a gun and BLAM. I
would see the flash and start to feel the
pain of the pellets hitting me and that would
be the end of me. Just because I have long hair.

So I walk into class one day just feeling
super cool. I had read these two books which
had really opened my eyes to Black problems.
And I had been hassled by people I didn't
even know. I thought I knew the Hell the
Blacks were going through. I really wanted
to help them, not only the ones in our class
but all of them. To start a conversation with
Murph, I asked what the yellow strand was
around the Black Panther on his button. As I
looked closer, I saw it was barbed wire. I
said to Murph, "What's that barbed wire
around the panther?"

He cut me down. I could see the anger in his
eyes and feel his strong body set to attack
before he lashed out at me with his voice.
All he said was that I didn't see the barbed
wire from across the room. I was afraid to
say any more lest he pounce on me. And I
couldn't understand why. I was really trying
to show him how much I felt for him and all
his Black brothers. But to him I was just a
white honkie.

Now I see I went at it in the wrong way.
Wanting to help the poor Blacks is all wrong.
I should wait for them to ask for my help. I
can see why they hate the people that oppress
them but they also dislike the liberals that
want to help them. That is just putting them
under the White boss again.

Murph's anger didn't stop me. I kept trying
and I think I have started to gain his confidence. We just started talking one day about
dope, and that really broke the ice. I know
a little something about dope and so does
Murph, so we just sort of put one and one together and are getting real close to equaling
two.

So I'm walking down the street the other day
just feeling great. It was a beautiful day,
blue sky and a nice big sun. "Wow," I thought,
"this should be a beautiful day for everyone."
Then, BANG, it hit me. I thought of the young
Blacks who had just been turned down for a
job after God-knows-how-many tries, and the
poor hungry children in the ghettoes. Would
it be such a beautiful day for them?

Bruce Myers

a child's game

When I'm tired and I walk around at
night, I have a strong urge to lie
down on the grass and go to sleep. I
don't care where I am or who's around.

I just want to lie down. It gives me
an open, loose and free feeling, but
at the same time it has a warm and
caressing effect on me. I could just
lie down in the grass and let my whole
life go by me.

With those words I made our second class
publication. They were mine and I was pleased.
Especially when the teacher asked me if I'd
like to write a longer paper about it. "We
respond," she said, "to the _feeling_ you express, but you haven't really shared the _ex-
perience_ with us." Trying to do that was not
easy. And when I read my first attempt to a
small group of my classmates, I was disappointed. It meant so much to me! I had tried
to write about my emotions and my responses.
But nobody responded to my writing, which
means nobody responded to me. I tried again,
this time determined to be heard:

When I lie down in the grass it's
more than grass to me. It is a lush,
green, comforting mattress. Each tall
blade is like the strong, supporting
coils inside the mattress, supporting
my weight, supporting me. As I lie
there I trail my fingers between the
blades of green beside me, building a
green dream city in my own back yard.
Or in the park, or down by the river,
or in someone's meadow way out in the
country. The little paths my fingers
make are the streets, and the blades
of grass still standing are the buildings. And the bugs I see are the people, traveling the streets I have made,
in cars and trains and buses. Then I
leave my body and walk through the
city. It's a beautiful city, with tall,
thin buildings in a million shades of
green. The only sound in the city is
the music. The music that everybody
likes. The music that you hear when
you "lie in the meadow and hear the
grass sing."

I was writing about a child's game that I
love to remember and still love to play. And
sometimes it helps me. To escape from my
worries, to put on a happy mood. And I suppose that's all it meant to me until someone
asked Why? Then I started wondering why.
Started analyzing my own reactions. Started
asking what I was reacting to. And I found
the answer. It had been here all the time,
but I just couldn't see it. Now it's obvious.
I was saying how I loved something in nature.
But I was also using nature to say something
inside of me. I didn't know what that something was. I didn't know what I was. But I
did know that looking very closely at nature
has helped me. I was trying to find myself
in nature.

When I would look down into the grass and see
all the bugs moving around, they seemed to be
more than bugs, they <u>represented</u> something.
Just something beautiful and happy. But when
I thought about my past life, it dawned on me
that I had always liked everything better than
I liked people. For my life, my relationship
with people is like a revolving ball of tangled
string. It's a funny thing though. When you
look at a ball of string you can not tell if
it is string that can be rolled out or if it
is string that is all knotted together.

When Ms. Kelly asked if I could clarify that
metaphor and I answered with my usual "I don't
know but I'll try," she said, "Read again
what you have already written." Here is what
I found, with some help from a "competent and
sympathetic editor-teacher":

Of all the writing I have ever done,
this is something I have wanted to do
for a long time. I am afraid to talk
to people. I have a feeling that when
I talk to someone what I say must be
of some important interest to them or
I am wasting their time. If I am talking and someone interrupts me, I get
the feeling that no one was listening
to me. Then I get embarrassed, not much,

but embarrassed, and shut up. When I
shut up it is hard for me to start talking again. My problem may be bigger. I
don't mind shutting up. It seems harder
to me sometimes to start talking than
just to sit and listen. I like to listen
to people talk. When people are talking,
I feel I can talk to them on what they're
saying without verbal communication. As
if I could just think of what I wanted
to tell them and they would understand.
This is why I should do this kind of
writing. When I think, I talk to myself.
Now I write what I think and talk on
paper.

. . . .

Did you ever feel, when you were a
little kid, that you were crazy? I
did. For a while I thought they were
going to realize it and lock me up
somewhere. This is the reason why, I
guess, I quit talking very much. I
figured the less I talked the less
they had to know I was crazy. I know
I'm not crazy, but I wonder if I know
if I like to talk or not.

Does talking and being crazy or worrying about it go together?

. . .

My father said to me, when he was bringing me down to school, that I shouldn't
become involved in anything. He said the
people who are going to make the changes
in the world will have to sacrifice and
even suffer. He said though that I was
not to become that kind of person and
that I should be greedy and secure my
education. Then later on in life I could
contribute my share.

. .

I would like to meet someone who can
help me change my life without creating more problems. Finding this person will be hard, if at all possible.
Because everything is so mixed up.
Though people say patterns of life are
based on something idealistic, like
Christianity and democracy, and they
say they want to live in an idealistic
world, when they are confronted with
idealism, they say it's bad to be
idealistic. My father is really saying don't be idealistic, be real. But
who knows what it is to be real, and
who can decide what should and shouldn't
be real?

Lying down in the grass as a child, building
my fantasy world, was just like sitting there
(at home, in class, wherever) saying nothing,
just watching and listening to people. The
whole thing made me wonder. Should I do nothing, or should I be involved? Involved in
what?

I can't sit down and write that I'm a
freak or a John Bircher. I'm not a
brain, a head, a conformist or a non-
conformist. I am me. Your everyday
run-of-the-mill guy. It isn't right
enough for me to have a name to say
clearly what I am. If I am going to be
something it is what I do the next
minute, the next hour, the next day.
I am what my brain tells me to be. My
brain is a collage of ideas and all of
them are related. I can not separate
any one idea. I am all of me. If you
don't take all of me you're missing
some. Not only am I my physical body
and my thoughts, I am also everything
I have ever seen and will see. I am
alive and I have to keep proving it to
myself. By getting my kicks out of
life. I am like a pawn in a chess
game. Either I am going to get busted

or I will be able to become whatever
player I want to become.

Whenever I get confused, I turn again to
nature to help me out. The best time is when
it rains. Especially at night. Everyone else
is inside, to keep from getting wet. So I go
out--alone--and let the rain fall on my face.
And it's like washing away all of my tensions.
Like walking through my own brain. And as I
walk I know how things stand. All I have to
do is look at the pictures on the walls and
I know all there is to know. The quiet world
of rain and darkness is not like the "real"
world where no one knows what he's doing or
where he's going. I once thought, wondered,
if the only way to live in peace in the human world would be to live in insanity. But
I know that isn't for me. Freaking out may
be fun, but not forever.

So I let mother nature help me get my head
together. Like when I went to Pike's Peak
Park. Standing down in the creek bed, looking up at the massive walls of smooth sand-
stone with all the weathered grooves--some
like enormous caves, some no wider than my
hand--I found the peace and contentment I
wanted to live in. It was really strange.
The enduring rock walls were certainly not
alive, yet somehow they seemed alive. Because a rock isn't just a rock. It is something constantly changing its shape--just
as we do--from the erosion of time and the
elements. And the rocks have a purpose to
fulfill--preventing erosion, holding back
the earth. The silent, empty park was teem-
ing with millions of individuals. Even the
tiny grains of sand under my feet seemed to
move with life. And everything was just itself. Alive and fresh. There were no hassles
about the canyon wall changing its shape,
no regret over the massive rocks being reduced to sand.

Nature has all the time in the world to do
what she wants. That's why Thoreau said,
"Let us spend one day as deliberately as

Nature." Life can be lived so that it can be
understood. Nature makes most sweet-smelling
flowers show off a bright color. Nature
makes complex things so very simple. If only
we could see that the hardest problems sometimes are the ones with the simplest answers.
Thoreau said, "Life is frittered away by detail. Why should one live with such hurry
and waste of life?" It took Thoreau two
years of living with nature before he found
the answer that he was looking for. But the
time he spent with nature, the time we spend
with nature, will stay with us for a lifetime.

Lying on my strong, soft mattress of green,
listening to the grass sing, I used to wish
my life was as simple, as natural, as the
lives of the little bugs I watched. For I was,
still am, like a half-developed human being--
I know some things, but not enough to know
what's going on. So I thought I had to conform to set ways of life. But now I think I
know a better way. It is to live life the way
I see it. No rules are worth having if you
don't know what they are for. I want to keep
my life simple so I can enjoy everyone I
know; I want to set no restrictions on the
growth of the other half of my humanness.

Mic Duggan

learning

I'm not completely sure what this class has
done for me or what grade I should receive,
but I have some ideas. First of all, I think
I have gained some respect for myself. Where
I used to shun my ideas, I have become more
outspoken. I've asked many philosophical
questions in my writing--about death and the
whole meaningless hassle called life and all
the phony acts I must put on so I will not
offend the adults I don't want to offend;
questions about how I can at the same time
reject and love my mother, then feel guilty
because I do not spend more time with her

now that she is alone; questions about my own identity and the wiped-out feeling my friend has because the girl he's known (and loved?) for years is marrying somebody else. I believe I have discovered how to cope with my own confusion with all these unanswerable questions. Just shrugging them off with an oh-well, I-can't-do-anything-about-them-so-don't-worry attitude is no longer enough. I can't say that I've come to any definitive answers, but I feel much more stability than when I started asking questions.

I've also come closer to a realization that everything is not just black and white. Some things cannot be (most things cannot be) categorized as good or bad, one extreme or the other. People's views are not perched on one end or the other of a teeter-totter. When people will discuss their ideas with each other, they may very well come to realize that while they don't completely agree, there are points where they do. I felt this over and over in class, and this summer, for the first time in my life, I communicated with my mother when I finally decided to go home for my birthday.

When I came into this class I guess you would or could say I had feelings of superiority about other people. But I have learned to have more respect for what others think or have to say. Whether I agree with what someone has to say or not, I can listen and consider his ideas. This resolves a lot of hassles and conflicts. I now feel so much better toward myself because I have learned to accept every human as my equal--no better and no worse than myself. I really feel wonderful.

Maybe I'm fooling myself, maybe I've donned a pair of rose colored glasses that possibly will fade. But now I feel so calm and tranquil about the troubling questions I have asked. Life just somehow seems different.

I also may be mistaken about calling these
few things learning. But if I have come to a
state of mind where I am able to cope with
my questions and to be satisfied in life
without being complacent, I think I have
earned the highest grade possible. Not a
grade indicative of academic progress or
accomplishment, but rather an accomplishment
in life. I have learned and I love it.

unsigned

What an experience it's been for me this
semester in English. I mean, I've learned so
much about myself and about others as well.
About myself I've learned all kinds of things,
like I know now to respect people's feelings
and opinions and to meet people halfway on
problems and ideas. Not to be stubborn and
stupid, but to be understanding and patient
in listening to what other people have to
say. I've learned to see who's afraid and
who's not afraid to share their opinions and
thoughts. I've learned that you can bring
out people's feelings and emotions by asking
a lot of questions. Like how, why, where,
when, how come and many other questions that
bring people out in the open.

I had another concept of people in general.
I thought everyone couldn't be heard, because
people try to feed you a lot of bullshit. But
that isn't so. There's a lot of truth in what
people say. All you have to do is give them
a chance to speak their piece.

Most important of all is that I've learned to
like to write, which I hated so much before.
Even though I haven't done much writing this
semester, I've learned to write what I feel
like writing, not what I thought it was right
to write about.

I still feel that a person who's afraid to
speak in class must have a real problem. Because to me it was kind of a good thing just
to sit in class and share people's thoughts

and opinions. I know now how much I've gained in this class, which I've never had in others. That's why to me this having an open class like this is such a good thing. I also think that it should be continued and should be supported by students.

Oh, and before I forget. You, the teacher, have been a great help to me.

Nelson Menendez

Yesterday, I sat down and tried to concentrate about the classes I'm going to take next semester and it struck me that I won't be taking Rhetoric, that is if I make it this semester. Even thinking about it left butterflies in my stomach. I know for sure I'm going to miss it even though I'll probably see everybody who was in the class again and again.

I know at the first of the year I said I dreaded to come to the class, that everyone seemed to reject me and feel superior to me; a few still do, but I know I would still miss them if I didn't have a class with them. Our class feels like a human body to me, like every one has a function and if something troubles one part it troubles every part. When Lee left the class I felt we lost more than just Lee. It was like a sore but it tended to heal without him coming back. Then when someone verbalizes one of their problems, we, or at least a few people in the class, tend to scratch at the problem until it becomes irritated, then it is medicated by concerned people and maybe cured. Wouldn't it be fabulous if we could cure writing problems or speaking problems like we do diseases? I suppose in a way we are curing them by talking about them, which parallels the experimenting they're doing for the diseases yet uncurable.

When second semester comes, our body will only exist as a ghost, never the same as it used to be. Its effect on us will probably

linger with us for awhile but die in the confusion ahead of us. In a way I wish there was
somehow we could stay together, but it's impossible. It'll be like saying goodbye to an
old friend, an old friend that opened up my
eyes to make me really aware of what's going
on, not only in my mind but in the minds of
others.

Ken Meisner

To be
Unknown is a
Way of life but
To be
Ignored is the
Sin of man.

Jeff Clark

to make your Voice stronger
and clearer

playing with Stylistic Possibilities

Here we find another way of saying what we've been saying all through this book: style is the total impact of your writing. The grammatical structures called sentences come to life only when they carry the sound of *your* voice and the substance of *your* ideas.

Perhaps nothing is more important to the development of competence and the release of creativity than the feeling of success—the feeling of fluency that talking on paper brings. But it's not just a feeling. The feeling is the real thing—the pouring out of words onto a page.

When you re-live, through your own words, an experience you have enjoyed or endured, you are quite sure your reader will share your feelings. When you re-create a humorous or tragic incident in writing, you can almost hear somebody laughing or crying with you. When you clearly and forcefully state an opinion already tested by your own experience, you don't see how anyone can disagree. You know what you want to say and the words seem *to flow*—from mind to pen to page. For others to read and respond to. Which they do.

And yet, on other days, we all know the frustration of not being able to say what we want to say. We can not fill a page because we seem to have no words for the thoughts and feelings inside us. That's when you must keep on trying to talk on paper. Day after day. With no concern about how it's going to sound. Week after week. Until your reluctance with words becomes competence with words. Until the fragmentary and unformed ideas that you want to express become clearly stated sentences on a piece of paper.

But forceful writing is more than clarity. There may be no question about what you mean, and yet your sentences may sound simplistic in content and form. Some of them may jerk and limp along in disjointed bits and pieces. Others may drone on through numerous connectives that hold your words but not your ideas together. And you long for the easy, impressive style that "good" writers have. You want your sentences to sound at least as sophisticated as you think your ideas are. Maybe, you hope, some old-fashioned grammar drills would help you eliminate your "bad" sentences.

But instead of drills, we ask you to keep on talking—on paper. We ask you to engage in what James Moffett calls *naturalistic* writing.

It's about time the sentence was put in its place. (187)

. . . proponents of grammar teaching (hope) that a knowledge of grammar will enable (you) to elaborate and diversify (your) sentence constructions . . . (But) evidence demonstrates very clearly that children's sentences grow in precisely this direction as a matter of normal development. That elaboration and complexity are developmental seems to be a well established fact . . . (162) The reasons children do not elaborate as much as adults do stem from causes other than ignorance of grammar. (163)

. . . let me give two examples from some trials of sensory writing. While watching some third-graders write down their observations of candle flames—deliberately this time, not merely in note form— I noticed that sentences beginning with *if*- and *when*- clauses were appearing frequently on their papers. Since such a construction is not common in third-grade writing, I became curious and then realized that these introductory subordinate clauses resulted directly from the children's *manipulation of what they were observing.* Thus: "If I place a glass over the candle, the flame goes out." And: "When you throw alum on the candle, the flame turns blue." Here we have a fine instance of a physical operation being reflected in a cognitive operation and hence in a linguistic structure. Consider also the following nominal clause, taken from a sixth-grade class where the pupils were dropping liquids of varying viscosity from varying heights onto papers of varying absorbency: "The drops it makes are almost indestructible." This embedding of one kernel sentence into another (*It makes drops. The drops are almost indestructible.*") resulted directly and organically, I feel, from the pupil's effort to render exactly what he saw, to specify *which* drops are indestructible, *it* referring obviously to one of the three liquids and his task being to discriminate among the three by testing for differences. Similarly, the cognitive task entailed in the candle tests *created a need* for subordinate clauses, because the pupils were not asked merely to describe a static object but to describe changes in the object brought about by changing conditions (*if* and *when*).

James Moffett
Teaching the Universe of Discourse

If you want to write sentences with all the complex and sophisticated grammatical structures that are a part of the language, don't think of the sentences you are trying to construct. Concentrate on the ideas and images you are trying to convey. And proceed with patience. Changing the way you think and talk and write may be as difficult—and slow—as changing your most firmly fixed personality traits.

But if the kind of discussion this book attempts to initiate becomes a significant part of your academic life, if writing becomes, for you, a self-involving experience, the simplistic form and content of your sentences will change. As you analyze and extend your own ideas, as you listen and learn from the ideas of others—in person and in your reading—you will find, within your natural thought processes, the grammatical structures you need to qualify and elaborate what you are trying to say. For they are all a part of your intuitive knowledge of your native language.

Which means, I'm quite sure, that your sentences will take care of themselves, that your language will keep up with your ideas—just as it always has.

But that does not mean you will never want to change what you have written. For filling a page with words is not our goal. What we want is a *reader's response.*

We have all felt the disappointment, the hurt that comes—sometimes to stay—because the pages we have filled do not get the response we anticipate. Sometimes, even before another person reads what we have written, we know we have failed to say what we were trying to say. Or, everything we wanted to say is there, but it sounds labored or juvenile. With none of the commitment we feel for the ideas we are trying to explain. With none of the excitement we feel in the experience we are trying to share.

Our failure to say what we are trying to say is sometimes as easy to explain as our success. Sometimes we do not get the response we want from the person who is our reader because we have not put our words together so that they *flow* into his ears. Our sentences do not move with ease and grace. They do not have the touch of sureness that engages and holds his attention, or the note of confidence that stirs his confidence in the person who is speaking from the page to him.

The flow of ideas and meanings you try to convey from your mind to mine may be obstructed by the very words you use to say what you mean or by the way you arrange those words in your sentences.

Visualize the problem as a little creek dammed up by fallen trees after a windstorm. Or slowed down by the dirt and rocks from a landslide. Obviously, if anybody wants that water to flow again, he's got a cleanup job to do. Developing a fluent style may involve work that is even more unpleasant. Some writing is like a foul and sluggish river channel, choked with debris and pollution.

But a hard-working writer and a competent and sympathetic editor can clear out the channel so that your sentences, your ideas, will move like a joyful woodland stream down a gentle slope. In other papers, your reader will feel the force of your sentences like the rush and pull of a river's deep current as you take him from line to line, from idea to idea.

As you talk with teacher or classmates about different pieces of your writing, you will become aware of the places where your style—*how* you say an idea—interferes with *what* you are saying. Think of the problem as linguistic habits that need to be changed so that your reader can hear your ideas—more easily, more clearly, more forcefully.

The *how* and the *what* cannot really be separated of course. The voice you create with your own perceptions (157-170) is an innate part of your writing style. I would say the most important part.

But your voice is muted, your perceptions obscured, if your sentences do not carry voice and perceptions to your reader—smoothly and convincingly.

Sometimes as you read what you have written you may think your words do not say what you are trying to say because your vocabulary is limited. You may be at least half right. That's why we must always be on the alert for new words. In this and other courses. And in all our encounters with new ideas. We must *assimilate* words—first in our thinking, then in our talking and writing.

But writing is not simply a matter of knowing the right words.

Ernest Hemingway once said he rewrote the ending to *Farewell to Arms*, the last page of it, thirty-nine times, before he was satisfied. And the interviewer said,

> "What was it that had you stumped?"

Hemingway's reply was not about finding the right words, but

> "Getting the words right."

Everyone who deals with complex ideas, everyone who refuses to settle for the easy generalization or the over-simplification, knows what Hemingway meant. Whoever would share his concepts with others—the scientist explaining the physical world, the philosopher analyzing the nature of man, the psychologist and sociologist exploring human behavior, the historian telling us how it was in the past, the newsman and the political analyst interpreting the present, the novelist and the poet recreating the joys and tragedies of the human condition, the teacher and his students trying to communicate with each other—we all share Hemingway's dilemma if we are concerned about reaching others with our words.

If you are intent on conveying your ideas to others, you will want to play around with different ways of saying the same thing. Some-Sometimes you will rearrange the words in a long sentence a dozen times or more while trying to say the complex relationships and meanings you see in a given situation.

For most of us, good writing usually means extensive rewriting.

For it is not enough to find the words that say what we want to say. We must put our words together in the combinations that give them the most clarity and force.

Sometimes we must consciously search for the best form, the best sentence structure for the thought we are trying to express. We write a sentence one way, reject it, then try another way. And another. And another. Until we find the way that sounds just right. Until we find the grammatical form that sets up the most precise relationships between the words we have put together to say what we mean.

Linguistic research clearly indicates that you are equipped to do that even though you may not know the names for all the grammatical structures you can understand and produce.

To anticipate a reader's reaction to your writing style, *read aloud* what you write.

Do you hear and feel some movement, some rhythm as you read? If not, what keeps your sentences from sounding easy and natural?

Are they stiff and awkward because you've put words together in combinations that are difficult to read, combinations you would not use when talking?

Is your style a discordant, self-conscious attempt to write the correct and impressive way you think teachers want you to write? an unhappy marriage between your talk and what you think is English-teacher talk? Are your sentences heavy with big words and cumbersome phrases?

Are they heavy with empty words, words that do not add any meaning? How many words could you cross out in each sentence without losing any meaning?

Have you tried to express complex thoughts and feelings in simplistic sentences? How can you re-structure your sentences so they will sound as sophisticated as your ideas?

To answer all those questions, you will, most likely, need some help—from a competent and sympathetic editor. So I hope the teacher-student ratio in your class and the number of classes your teacher is assigned will leave some time for individual conferences. For if your writing is "polluted" instead of fluent, you need specific, not general, suggestions. You need to learn to recognize and eliminate the kinds of "debris" that slow down the movement of your sentences—and your ideas.

But remember—in all our editing, there is choice. In all our playing with the possibilities, we are searching. For the best combination of words for a particular writer in a particular context. For the combination of words that is most nearly true to your vision of the world and to your purpose for writing about that world.

Classmates or teacher might suggest numerous ways of revising one of your sentences and never come up with the one way that would sound like you "writing-about-something-to-someone". (Wendell Johnson) But the suggestions that others make can help you see the possibilities. And seeing the possibilities can help you break through your limitations and become the writer you want to be.

In all your writing and rewriting, remember that talking on paper is, for most of us, the best way to begin.

Get it down. Take chances. It may be bad, but it's the only way you can do anything really good.

William Faulkner

Writing is just a [person] alone in the room with the English language, trying to make it come out right. The important thing is that your work be something no one else could do.

John Berryman

I can't understand how anyone can write without rewriting everything over and over again. I scarecely ever reread my published writings, but if by chance I come across a page, it always strikes me: all this must be rewritten; this is how I should have written it.

Leo Tolstoy

When you are ready—when you can *hear* and understand why you need to revise some of your sentences, build yourself a personal style book. The aim: to help you learn to recognize the linguistic habits that slow down the movement of your sentences and the ones that obscure the meaning of your ideas, and the ones that weaken the sound of your voice on paper.

Study your own sentences—as you first wrote them *and* as your teacher-editor suggests that you rewrite them. Read both sentences *aloud*. *Hear* the difference in the sound and the rhythm of your words. *Feel* the movement that makes the difference.

If you want your personal style to help you convey your ideas from your mind to the minds of others, *read aloud* all your talking on paper, listening for the linguistic habits that may come between you and your reader. Then revise your sentences to eliminate the interference.

I hope the student writing on pages 249-293 will help you see what I mean by playing with stylistic possibilities. I hope it will help you see that revising our talk on paper is, for most of us, essential to developing a personal style that will make our readers *hear* what we are saying.

But don't worry about rewriting until you can talk on paper with confidence and ease. And don't let any book or teacher or editor impose upon you a style or a voice that sounds or feels alien to your own personality.

In this book a sentence is not defined as a group of words expressing a complete thought or a group of words with a prescribed grammatical structure. A sentence is the word or the group of words a writer places between two periods.

hearing the writing of other students

Many people have many misconceptions about "good style."

We could talk for hours about why the pieces on the next three pages fail to engage and hold our minds or emotions as our eyes scan the words. But one question will get at each writer's basic problem—

Can you *hear* the voice of another human being speaking to you as you read?

This piece sounds like an attempt to impress the teacher with a bookish, academic tone and a few big words. But what *is* the man saying? about *what*?

With modern technology few will disclaim statistical findings as figures, and I am convinced that exception is usually a foolish exception. Yet when that technology is interpreted even on the success or failure of the data, there is immediate controversy. This controversy has become too great a part of our lives.

In a society so capable of producing facts there is no use for the middle-man, who in action has similarity to the pope, who interpreted out of the Bible that Galileo was a heretic. The middle-men today, however, don't seem to be as spiritually guided as were the popes. Today our lack of pure facts and the power given these middle-men have brought us things as complicated as the war and things as simple (statistically) as Vitamin C. Making these the speculative marvels they are today.

Now, in this time of working and applicative science it is not only ridiculous to have two sides of every human encounter but the sides having their differences have caused a lot of further trouble. It is not my intention to prove that there is indeed a left and a right sides view of most problems

today, rather that we are living too much of
this speculated conjecture and leaving it even
untested. We don't have enough hard and un-
speculated facts.

When you pick up a newspaper and just look
at the front page of it, generally four thousand words, you have not only stories of conjectures but conjecture of those conjectures!

Day by day people are exposed to sometimes as
many as three different newspapers and then,
the television braodcasts!

The television newscasters seldom agree on
what the conjecture is! Their accounts differ
from station to station! This may only be due
to lack of preparation time, but then, people
don't even get the proper account of the conjecture!

The author of the next essay says she never writes without a
thesaurus in hand. That's why she has put words together in combinations that sound strange and unnatural. That's why we hear
words, not ideas, as we read.

Jude Fawley had a dedication for education
all of his life. Jude was obsessed with the
motive of furthering his education, perhaps
to a professorship. Mr. Phillotson, in Mary-
green, was his first idol, connecting education to his life. His motive as a youngster,
was to be like Mr. Phillotson in furthering
his education.

Jude's first major block regarding his goal
into becoming a reality was Arabella Donn.
She possessed (at the time) a physical lust,
a beautiful and sensuous woman. Jude, at the
age of seventeen or eighteen, found this
aspect of physical attraction quite interesting. This, then in return, delayed his
motive concerning education. Which could be
expressed as an internal warfare between
flesh and spirit.

Another aspect withdrawing Jude from his education was his close and only relative in the novel, his aunt. She was always advocating to Jude that his meaning in life was to be laborer (a stonemason, etc.) for society and nothing more than that. Another psychological breakdown was the incident when Arabella threw his books (representing education) on the floor. She was insinuating that the study of furthering the capacity of a mind was not her earthlike way of living. Therefore, Jude returned to the conflict of education or leading a middle-class or lower-class life with Arabella.

The next consequence is Sue Bridehead, who represents the intellectual side of Jude's mind. Since Sue is a very educated person, she motivates Jude to strive for an educational background. Jude's environment of Sue makes him want to have the intellectual capacities of Sue. Her detainment of Jude's education is her confused mind of ascertaining who is her mate in life--Mr. Phillotson or Jude Fawley. Therein, Jude becomes overlighted with Sue's life and problems and therefore again delays any possible achievements of furthering his major goal--education.

When father-time enters Jude's life, Jude has (to a fair extent) decided that he can not obtain an honorable education (in his standing-of-mind). He therefore turns his motivations toward father-time. Jude becomes very anxious in the thought of his son carrying through his unsuccessful expectation--education.

Jude had many conflicts which flowed so close together that it seemingly appeared that Jude was destined *not* to further his education. Jude always had the conflicting struggle between education and relationships with people, all of his life. He seemed never to be able to coincide both existing problems. His life was constantly wrapped-up with physical and mental problems, which endlessly detained his motivations toward a desired education.

Ironically, it seemed that Jude never had the capacity of strong-enough-will to obtain education *first*. He always allowed himself to become over-involved with other problems, not as personally meaningful to his life as education.

Would you or anyone you know ever begin a conversation with the questions posed as an attention getting device by the next writer? Do you think he ever talks about his winter vacation as he writes about it here?

Have you ever yearned to partake in an activity? Have you ever longed to learn a sport, but have come across barriers of some sort making it impossible to fulfill that dream? The barriers not physical in human nature but geographical wise. The first experience flowing down a cotton colored mountain with the brisk winter wind refreshingly stinging one's face is an ultimate in recreation. To glide and soar down that mountain is by far the most graceful feat to spectate, but to perform is quite another story. From this illusion one has learned from experience.

While trying to be *really* descriptive, some writers dehumanize their own voices.

Velvety thick grass carpets the ground from tree to tree. The bulwark of each tree reaches skyward and the armlike branches bend over as if burdened by the infinite secrets they keep. The individual limbs separate themselves by the functions they serve as the guardians of life. On a lower limb after climbing out midway, one reaches a hornet's nest. The hustle and bustle of the bees as they buzz about their business adds to the rhythm of life growing in the tree. Above the hornet's nest and across a gap in the body of the mighty tree, young birds chirp incessantly while their parents flutter here and there trying in vain to satisfy their

tiny offspring's voracious appetites. A
worldly-wise old squirrel with its hollow
cheeks filled to bursting, climbs past the
bird's home as he takes advantage to clasp
his incisory feet into the rough thick bark!
The squirrel climbs higher to the branch
where he has made his private domain and
drops his bundle into the storage space for
winter food. He scampers out and down again
to reladen his cheeks with life-saving nour-
ishment. He too has a family to feed. Stretching lengthwise on the identical limb, leaves
fly like fingers over a piano as the breeze
blows the aromas of earthy smells through the
air. They crackle and jangle, adding to the
chorus of the birds, the squirrels, and the
buzzing bees as directed by God. This is life!

Here Wayne Herman is trying to deal with an assigned subject as
he thinks a college professor wants him to.

Humans often wonder just how and where the
universe, along with our planet, got its start
and why. Due to the enormous size and complexity of the universe there is no person
who can with any physical proof answer where
it began. Science has produced many theories
but can not produce an absolute answer or
even any fairly certain ones. There is the
idea that a superior power, a god, started
and controls the universe. Also there is the
compromise between a belief in god and in
scientific theories, combined to work out an
understandable beginning for creation. Understanding why man was created puzzles him. He
is concerned for what his purpose on earth
is and what is to happen after he dies. Each
person can create his own idea of creation,
which can not be proved wrong nor can he support it with hard facts. But his idea has to
be considered a valid thought.

I feel that certain scientific theories of
how the earth and its surroundings came about
are true to a certain extent. But I also have
to believe that there is a superior power,
God. I believe that God has always been, even
though I can not imagine in my own mind how
there can be something without a beginning
somewhere. But I also believe that after death
there will be an eternity. It is conceivable
to me that if something can exist without a
beginning then it will not have an end. Thinking that a superior power was the controlling
factor in developing the universe does away
with any proof by facts. It sounds more like
a fairy tale. But why a person would believe
such an idea must be understood.

A person does not feel that his life is over
after death. Since he can not understand his
creation he does not understand death. By believing in a superior power there is hope for
a life after death. If science had proof that

(continued on page 256)

Here Wayne is trying to speak with his own voice about his own
limited experience.

Sometimes when I'm home on the farm, I go to
the middle of an eighty acre hay field and
just sit down. Around the first of June the
alfalfa is about a foot high, a green carpet
with the freshest smell in the world. There I
lie back and stare into the clear bluish-white
sky. I never could understand where it ended
or just how big it was. As I walk home, I cut
across a cornfield. The corn plants are only
two or three inches high, tiny models with the
same shape they will have in October when they
will be over ten feet high. And I see hundreds
of living creatures in this field, from the
tiniest insect to the largest farm animal. I
see all these forms of creation and then I
know there has to be a god who created and
controls them.

Science has many fairly accurate theories on
creation, but behind them all I still have to
believe what I have been taught by parents,
relatives and teachers: God is the ultimate
power. And God created the earth, then the
sun, moon and stars, then all the living
animals and fish, and finally man. All in six
days. What a day is in the sight of God I am
not sure. The Bible says one day is the same
as a thousand years to God. Anyway, I do not
think that everything just popped into place.
The creative process took time, perhaps thousands of years. Which means the earth could
have slowly evolved in much the same manner
as the scientific theories say it did. But I
believe God was and is the controlling force.

A few years ago, while working on a space
program, some scientists at NASA ran a check
through the computer of all the time that
has elapsed since the beginnings of our solar
system. Somehow the computer calculations
came up 24 hours short. One scientist accounted for the lost hours by recalling two incidents from the Bible. When Joshua was leading
(continued on page 257)

continued from p. 254

the earth developed without the help of any
superior intelligence, then hope for something after death would be diminished. But
the idea that a god started the earth and
had a plan for humans satisfies many people's
fear of death.

There are people who know, or claim to know,
there is not a superior power and do not care
how creation started. They feel how creation
started and why it started does not apply to
how they should run their lives. Since death
is not understood, they really do not have
that much fear of it. Fear of death is overcome because as far as many people are concerned it will just be like a sleep or state
of unconsciousness. When life is over it is
over. You will not know or feel anything so
why worry about it. To some people creation
came and it will pass, but it was not designed for any specific purpose applying to them.

It is the thought that there is more to our
lives than we observe everyday that makes us
wonder about creation. Actually how or when
creation started is fairly irrelevant, but
if we are here for some purpose we would like
to know what it is. Most people have either
made up their mind how they believe we got
here, whether natural or by some other power.
It is not a question of worrying about why
they live but how should they live. The people that feel there is more than just this
life do what they feel must be done. The rest
just wonder but are not compelled to any
action. All people think about creation because something that escapes man's understanding causes thought. What is really the truth
is every person's own decision.

continued from p. 255

the Israelites in battle against the Amorites, he prayed to God for more daylight, and the sun stood in one spot for almost a day and night. In another incident a dying man asked God for a longer life and God promised him fifteen more years. When he asked for a sign, the sun stood still again. This time for ten degrees on the sun dial or about forty minutes. These two instances add up to the missing 24 hours.

This simplistic example from my hometown (Peoria, Illinois) newspaper does little if anything to help prove what I believe. But neither does science have *proof* of how our solar system started. And even if I could somehow prove to myself, with concrete physical evidence, that there actually is a god, I could not explain how he came into being. Personally, I believe that God has always been, even though I can not imagine how there can be something without a beginning. And I also believe that after death there will be an eternity. For if something can exist without a beginning, then it is conceivable that it will have no end.

Since I know I can not create something from nothing—or matter from a void—I believe it took more than human power to create the universe. I can not observe creation all around me and just take it for granted. Maybe a god is a crutch or a cop-out for not understanding creation. Or maybe someday, somewhere, I will find out I was taught the truth.

The differences in *what* Wayne says in these two pieces are even more impressive than the differences in *how* he says it. As we read the second piece, we are no longer scanning vague generalizations about science and religion that tell us nothing that we don't already know. Instead we are perceiving the concrete visual details of one man's particular internal experience. And we understand *what* and *why* he believes.

These examples show that the content of your sentences is an inherent part of style. If they are full of meaning, they flow from the page you have written to your reader's mind. If they are full of empty words, they may never move from page to eye to mind.

the writer talks with his teacher-editor

Wayne's second writing about creation is not printed here exactly as he talked it onto paper. For as he read aloud what he had written, as he heard the sound of his own voice speaking about his own ideas, he heard some changes that he wanted to make. And when his teacher-editor listened to the sound of that voice, she asked some questions and made some suggestions that led to other changes that make Wayne's writing more fluent and more forceful.

Because we both could hear some differences between the third paragraph and the rest of the paper—the sentences simply didn't flow the way the others did—that's where we started. There is no record of our conversation, but the following summary of the questions and answers that led to the final version of each sentence suggests the kind of editing that produces good results.

I believe that God has always been controlling and watching over his creation.

q: haven't you already said this?
a: **yes, so I'll delete it.**

A few years ago NASA was researching for some of their space programs. They ran a check through their computers of all the time that had elapsed since our solar system had begun

q: how can you make these sentences more concrete and visual? who is the *their* and *they?*
a: **scientists**

q: what is the relationship between these two statements? does this relationship suggest that they should be combined in one sentence? what word will express that relationship?
a: **the two acts described took place at the same time.** *while* or *as* **would say that relationship.**

Somehow their computer calculations came up 24 hours short. According to their report they had lost 24 hours somewhere which could not be accounted for

q: what new fact or idea does the second sentence add?
a: **none, so I'll delete it.**

One scientist came up with this solution. He had read in the Bible that when the Israelites were in battle against the Amorites, the Israelites needed more day-time to defeat them. According to the Bible the sun stood in one spot for about a whole day.

q: did he really come up with a *solution?*
a: no, he accounted for the lost hours.

q: how?
a: by recalling two incidents from the Bible.

q: what do your answers suggest that you can do with the first two sentences?
a: combine them.

q: how can you make the first incident sound as dramatic as the Bible makes it sound?
a: by giving more narrative details. name the leader. say he prayed to God.

q: can you delete any words that add nothing to meaning?
a: yes—*he had read in, that, to defeat them, according to the Bible.*

This scientist also said he remembered reading in the Bible where a certain man who was dying asked God for longer to live. He believed that God would give him fifteen more years to live, but he wanted a sign. For a sign the Bible says that the sun was set back ten degrees on the sun dial or about forty minutes.

q: how can you reduce the first 11 words to 3?
a: *in another incident.*

q: how can you reduce *a certain man who was dying?*
a: *a dying man*

q: can you restructure the second sentence to make it more concise and to make clearer the relationship between the groups of words connected by *but* and *and?*
a: the first part can be reduced and connected with an *and* to the preceding sentence. the relationship between the other 2 parts is best expressed by *when.* Then, *he believed that* and *for a sign the Bible says that* can be deleted.

q: I can't visualize *the sun was set back.* can you help me?
a: Instead of that I could say *the sun stood still.*

These two instances added up to 24 hours. These times were plugged into the computer and everything checked out.

q: are both these sentences needed? the second one sounds a bit simplistic to me.
a: I think you're right. I'll delete the second one.

To reproduce all the thinking and talking that went into the editing of Wayne's talking on paper about creation is impossible. But here are some of the other choices his teacher-editor suggested—by question or comment.

To give the reader a feeling of immediacy as he reads the first paragraph, you can change the verbs from past to present tense. In doing so, you'll eliminate 6 *would's* **that add more weight than life to your sentences.**

At the beginning of the last paragraph you emphatically summarize what you have been taught. But it sounds anticlimactic. Try moving that sentence to the second paragraph to take the place of the second sentence there.

How can you strengthen the concession you make at the beginning of the fourth paragraph?

Where did you hear the story about NASA?

Does this statement in your concluding paragraph sound logical?

> **I know I did not create the universe. Therefore I feel it took more than human power.**

Many readers may disagree with Wayne's beliefs about creation. But after reading the final version of his paper, they are not likely to ask him what he believes or why he believes it.

Talking on paper usually means your sentences say more than
they have ever said before. But if they don't flow smoothly and
forcefully from page to reader's mind, spend some time with your
teacher-editor, exploring some possibilities for revising, as the person quoted here did.

> From the time I was in the third grade, just
> in the stage of putting away the red fire
> trucks, green tractors and the shovel for the
> sandbox to throwing a basketball, football
> and baseball, I have wanted to be a profes-
> sional jock.

It didn't take long to discover an easy way "to fix" or "clean up"
that sentence. Just eliminate the words that say nothing (*just in
the stage of*), indicate the break in the smooth flow of words and
idea with dashes, and replace *to throwing* with *to play around
with* so that it will include catching, bouncing, and batting the
balls, plus shooting baskets.

> From the time I was in third grade--putting
> away my red fire trucks, green tractors, and
> the shovel for my sandbox to play around with
> baseballs, footballs and basketballs--I have
> wanted to be a professional jock.

That sounds smoother and clearer but no more forceful. The
change suggested: delete *was* and give the stronger verbs, *putting
away* and *started playing*, a more emphatic structural position in
the sentence.

> From the time I put away my red fire trucks,
> green tractors and the shovel for my sandbox
> and started playing around with baseballs,
> footballs and basketballs, I have wanted to
> be a professional jock.

The writer liked that but his teacher-editor didn't—"because we've
lost the lively touch that *putting away* gives the original version."
The final version grew from that comment. It's the best, not only
because it has rhythm, but because it gives us five concrete images.
It also goes beyond personal experience and suggests the implications such an experience may have for a wide group of "others."

I guess it's a stage every American male
goes through. Deserting the sandbox to play
catch with anybody who will throw a ball to
you. Putting away your red fire trucks and
green tractors to see how many times you can
bounce a ball. Forgetting all your toys to
watch the big kids play baseball. Trying
once more to throw that wobbly football. And
trying, endlessly, to put that heavy basketball through the high hoop. It's the stage
when we all start dreaming of growing up to
be professional jocks.

Here are some more examples from the piece just quoted. *Read aloud* each pair of sentences. *Hear* the smooth and forceful movement of the second one. Can you say how the original statement was changed to achieve the difference?

My class was always involved in playing baseball in the spring, football in the fall, and
basketball in the winter. From third grade
up until junior high, each class had a team.

    From third grade to junior high, each
    class at St. Ansgar's had its own teams--
    baseball in the spring, football in the
    fall, and basketball in the winter.

We had our own schedules worked out plus a
St. Ansgar world series for baseball, the St.
A's grade school bowl for football, and play-
offs for basketball.

    We worked out our own schedules, includ-
    ing a St. A's world series for baseball,
    St. A's bowl for football, and St. A's
    play-offs for basketball.

There was always a rivalry between my class
and the class two and three years ahead of
us because no one else could give us any competition.

    The fiercest rivalry was always between
    my class and the class two and three
    years ahead of us. No one else could
    give us any competition.

The piece ends on a wistful note—

Now being a jock is just a dream. In high
school I was good in sports but just good
enough to be a star. But only in a small
school. I realize I'm not big enough, quick
enough, or talented enough to play college
or professional sports.

What does each of the three changes in the revision below attempt
to convey to the reader?

Now being a jock is just a dream. In high
school I was good in sports--good enough to
be a star. But only in a small school. I'm
not big enough, quick enough, or talented
enough to play college sports. So, like
millions of other old high school athletes,
I dream away while watching the jocks on tv.

To end the piece with a satiric political note, we could add,

Just as our President does.

If your talking on paper does not come out in smoothly flowing sentences, read it aloud, listening for the verbs. If they are obscured by other words, play around with other possibilities, as the writer of the following sentences did.

Read aloud the original sentence and the revisions that follow it on this and the next page. *Hear* the differences.

Which of the suggested versions do you prefer? Why?

Will the versions you prefer for each sentence fit together in a smoothly flowing paragraph?

Do they all speak with the same tone of voice?

```
This stage I'm trapped in is far too perva-
sive, too deep-rooted, to be so easily out-
grown.
```

```
    This stage I'm trapped in, between ado-
    lescense and adulthood, is too deep-
    rooted, too pervasive, for me to outgrow
    quickly or easily.
```

or

```
    I'm trapped between adolescense and adult-
    hood, a deep-rooted, pervasive stage I
    may never outgrow. Certainly not quickly
    or easily.
```

Perhaps my unwillingness to accept the demands of my society is hindered by not being adequately prepared as I should be.

> Perhaps I am unwilling to accept the social demands placed on a freshman at this university because my family life has not prepared me to face such demands.

> or

> My unhappy family life is no doubt one of the main reasons I feel so inadequate as I try to mix with the strangers at this university.

I should have had some guidance from my parents and the rest of the family around me, but no help arose, not the help I really needed.

> When I needed guidance from my family, they did not help me. At least, no one gave me the help I really needed.

> or

> I suppose my parents tried to give their little boy the guidance they thought he needed. But nobody in my family came up with the help I really needed.

Sure, just people being around me helped a little, but none of the examples were that of which I envied, examples of how I didn't want to be were almost the only thing that arose.

> Sure, just people being around me helped a little, but no one in my family was a person I envied. They were all examples of how I didn't want to act (or of what I didn't want to be).

or

> No one in my family was the kind of person I wanted to become. Almost everything they ever did was something I would never want to do.

Taking my father for an example of what I'd like to be like when I grow older, no way possible.

> To take my father as the man I'd like to be--no way! impossible!

and/or

> "Like father, like son" sends a paralyzing shiver up and down my spine.

When you enjoy talking on paper, the words pour out—page after page about the state of the world inside you. Before sharing that world with an audience beyond the teacher who reads every page you fill, you will sometimes want to rewrite.

Read aloud the two versions of each paragraph on this and the next page. Listen for the verbs. Hear and feel the verbs in the second version.

The sun shone today. It warms my head and brightens my path. It's my own personal sun, because the ground I walk on is wet and muddy. While the storm raged, I smiled. It was a happy day. I love today and the warmth creates its own sun.

Today is stormy. My head was still warm and the path was clearly visible. No one sees my storm, except maybe when a tear slips out. Not outwardly for the kids are playing in the leaves of Indian summer, they think it's a beautiful day. Someone hurt me today. I can't understand why. I'm passing thru this stormy time.

Today is people. I want to meet people, be with people, and remember them. I'm friendly today, because I feel that way now. I need and want crowds around me. It is my own human need for today.

A night passed, now I want to be left alone. I need this solitude for my own sanity sake. I'm not mad at anyone. No person said anything to hurt me. It's just that I need to see myself without anyone's shadow casted over mine. I want to stand on a foot bridge watching the water travel underneath thinking.

Today is sunshine. It warms my head and brightens my path. It's my own personal sun. The ground I walk on is wet and muddy, the skies above me are stormy. I smile. I love. The warmth inside me creates its own sun.

Today is stormy. The kids are playing in the leaves of Indian summer. They see a beautiful day. They don't see my storm, except maybe when a tear slips out. Why did he want to hurt me? How can I get thru this stormy day?

Today is people. I want to meet people, be with people, remember people. I'm friendly because I feel friendly. I need and want crowds around me. It's my own human need for today.

Today is solitude. I want to be left alone. To feel my own sanity. I'm not mad at anyone and no one has hurt me. I just need to see myself without anyone's shadow cast over mine. I just want to stand on the foot bridge. Watching the river flowing below. Thinking.

cutting out the deadwood

If a word does not *add* to what you are trying to say, if it does not make an idea clearer or more emphatic, it's deadwood. Dead weight. Dead words that slow your writing down—so slow—that your sentences will not move at all. Dead words that turn your reader off—so fast—he will never hear what you are saying.

My relationship with my father is not the way a father and son relationship should be. Sure, like every father he is kind in many aspects, especially dealing with materialistic things he can offer, but when it comes to giving love a father can give to his family, he rates very low.

> My relationship with my father is not what it should be. Sure, he is often kind, and he is generous with materialistic things, but when it comes to giving love to his family, he rates very low.

The attitude I have gotten from him, is that he thinks he is the master of the household and the family are his servants, under him.

> He thinks he is the master of the household and we are his servants, under him.

The child is an innocent sufferer and usually has to suffer the consequences of the overbearing, overpowered father.

> The innocent child suffers the consequences of the overbearing, overpowering father.

This control is very evident dealing with the child and the rest of the family's time. He is very inconsiderate as far as any one else's feelings go.

> He is very inconsiderate of everyone's feelings. He tries to control everyone's time.

Why are fathers so bullheaded? Is it a bug that is in everyone of them? Many of the friends I have have the same problem of not being able to tell their fathers anything. My father, I believe, is one of the worse there can possibly be. He always has the attitude that he is always right and that no one can contradict him.

> Why are fathers so bullheaded? Is it a virulent bug in everyone of them? Many of my friends have the same problem. They cannot tell their fathers anything. My father, I believe, is one of the worst there can possibly be. He thinks he is always right. No one can contradict him.

Dealing with the social problems that face our world he uses many wild generalizations that would seem to be out of this world. Concerning the students gaining power over the campuses his solution would be to murder five hundred or so students which he thinks would make the rest sit up and take notice to what is happening and that there is a law to be enforced and they must abide by that law.

> He has a wild generalization for every social problem. Concerning the students gaining power over the campuses, he says, "murder five hundred or so and the rest will sit up and take notice. Then they'll know there is a law to be enforced and they must abide by that law."

When I was younger I always thought and
wished if there was a title or context for
the worst father of all, that mine would win
it because dear old dad was always setting
examples by the thousand for me not to follow.

> I used to wish there was a contest for
> the worst father of the year, so I could
> nominate dear old dad--the man who set a
> thousand examples for me not to follow.

Another writer finds a stronger voice by cutting out the deadwood.

The three candidates which were in class to
talk to us were ok, but only one in my opinion would qualify for mayor. I will give you
a brief opinion of each.

> The three candidates who talked to us
> were ok, but, in my opinion, only one
> would qualify for mayor.

First of all I will talk of the present mayor
of Muscatine, Mr. Barnes. Mr. Barnes I must
say is a good man in some of his ideas for I
agree upon his idea of a small annexation.

> The present mayor, Mr. Barnes, I must
> say, has some good ideas, especially
> about annexation.

Our town just wouldn't be able to afford econ-
omically the vast amount of expense the 17-
mile annexation would bring.

> Our town just can't afford the vast
> amount of expense the 17-mile annexation
> would bring.

If we were to add so much land we would tri-
ple the land surface of this town.

> To add that much land would triple the
> size of this town.

When our talk on paper comes out tedious and boring, as conversation sometimes does, we lose our readers. Usually we've used many words to say very little. But reducing three pages to two is easy—if you really want to hold your reader. For then you are willing *to consciously look for and strike out* every word that adds very little or nothing to what you are trying to say and *to consciously look for and delete* every sentence that merely repeats what you have already said.

On the following pages you'll find two versions of the same piece—before and after the writer cut out the deadwood and made other stylistic choices. (With some help from his editor-teacher, of course.)

Several sentences are marked with a *d* in the first version. Why did the writer delete them in the second version?

In the first version he often summarizes a particular incident (marked with a *g* in the margin) before sharing the details of the experience with us. In his rewrite he decided to delete these generalizations. Why?

Making your writing more concise usually means combining related ideas that you have expressed in separate sentences. The examples of this kind of editing are indicated with a *c*.

Other important stylistic changes are indicated with an *. Compare the revision of each sentence with the original version. Do you *hear* the difference? How would you describe the structural change the writer made?

Reading the first version is sometimes difficult because the punctuation does not give us the help we need. Compare the sentences marked with a *p* in the first version with the rewrite. Note the number of times the writer decided that merely changing the punctuation was not enough.

While deleting the words that did not help him share his experience, this writer found some places where more words were needed—words that would recreate the details of the week "I will never forget." For he had learned that only with graphic details could he make his reader *experience* what he wanted to share.

I would like to take a few months out of my brief   d
experience and try to relate to you some of my
feelings toward that experience.

First, a brief outline of my duties and locations   d
during my tour of duty in the United States Navy
as an enlisted man. Needless to say the first few   c
months were spent in bootcamp at Great Lakes,
Illinois. Bootcamp was all I heard it was it sep-   p
arated the ones that couldn't hack it in accordance to Navy standards. Here each enlistee took   c
exams and such to determine which billet he would
fill for the next three or four years to come. My
luck held through bootcamp, I received the billet   p
I requested which was aviation electronics. Next   *
I received ten months of concentrated electronics
theory at Memphis, Tennessee. After graduation I
was shipped to GTMO Bay, Cuba, my official desig-   *
nation being Aviation Antisubmarine Warfare Technician (AX). My duties in Cuba were to repair   d
antisubmarine electronic gear, but as it turned
out I repaired more radar and communications gear
than antisubmarine gear. One part of my qualifica-   c
tions as an AX was a secret clearance. A funny
thing happened while I was stationed in Cuba, a   p-g
piece of secret equipment arrived at the shop one
day, but no one could open it because they didn't
have the proper clearance as a result I was called
in to open it. Picture this, one division Lt., a   p
master chief (E-8), a senior chief (E-9), a couple
of chiefs (E-7), and me (E-3), gathered in an   *
office, and they had to let me open it because
they didn't have secret clearances. By the way,   c
Cuba was a boring place to be for one year without
liberty of any kind.

I guess after a year in Cuba they figured a guy   c
should be able to pick his next duty station,
within limits of course. So my next assignment
was to VP-26 Brunswick, Maine, notice that this   p-c
is on the east coast as far away from Vietnam as
possible. This is what I thought, but a couple   d-*
of months later VP-26 had orders to be in the
Philippines in November to fly support missions
over Viet Nam.

Bootcamp was all I had heard it was. It eliminated the ones that couldn't hack it in a accordance to Navy standards. But my luck held through boot camp. I didn't ace all the exams but I received the billet I requested-- aviation electronics. That meant ten months of concentrated electronics theory at Memphis, Tennessee. After graduation I was shipped to GTMO Bay, Cuba, where my official designation was Aviation Antisubmarine Warfare Technician with Secret Clearance.

A funny thing happened while I was stationed in Cuba. Picture this: a couple of chiefs (E-7), a master chief (E-8), a senior chief (E-9), a division lieutenant and me (E-3), all gathered in the same office because a piece of secret equipment had arrived. And they had to let me open it because they didn't have the proper clearance.

After a year in Cuba, without liberty of any kind, I guess they figured a guy should be able to pick his next duty station. So I chose VP-26 Brunswick, Maine--as far away from Vietnam as possible. But a couple of months later VP-26 had orders to be in the Philippines in November to fly support missions over Vietnam, and I was assigned to Combat Air Crew Nine.

While in Brunswick I satisfied the require-   d-c
ments for aircrew membership, so I was
assigned to combat air crew nine (CAC-9).
My primary position in our crew of fourteen   d
was ECM-MAD Julie, these are nick names
for various anti-submarine detection devices;
my secondary position was radar. ECM stands   d
for electronic counter measures, MAD stands
for magnetic air detection, and Julie
unfortunately is confidential.

Part of the preliminary requirements for air-
crew members who are assigned to a combat
zone is survival school. This is a two   g
week school consisting of two parts, the   p
first week is entirely classroom oriented,   p
the second week is a practice session
involving what was covered the previous
week, plus a few exciting extras. During
the first week they taught us how to read
maps, how to use a compass, how to determine eatable food and so on. The second
week is one I will never forget.

We were transported to a mountain area in
Maine, the first day was spent teaching us   p-*
how to preserve meat, how to trap animals and
so on. The second day we were told the speci-   *
fics of the mock survival, evasion, and
escape exercise that was to be conducted.   *
We were the survivors of a plane crash on   *
enemy territory, the objective was to reach   p-*
a friendly territory. We were given a com-   *
pass, one can of rations, a sleeping bag,
and our clothes. We were then instructed   *-c-d
to stay between a local road and the ridge
line of the mountains, and we were given
the direction of the friendly territory and started on our way. If we were
captured along the way we would be put in
a concentration camp, if we made it, we   p
were given something to eat and some rest,
then put into the concentration camp.
Regardless of whether you made it to friendly   d
territory or not, part of the requirements
of the school was to go through the concentration camp.

Part of the preliminary requirement for air-crew members who are assigned to a combat zone is a two-week survival school. During the first week they taught us how to read maps, how to use a compass, how to determine edible food and so on. The second week is the one I will never forget

We were transported to a mountain area in Maine. The first day they taught us how to preserve meat, how to trap animals and so on. The second day they described the mock survival, evasion, and escape exercise we must now go through. We would pretend we were the survivors of a plane crash on enemy territory. Our objective: to reach the friendly territory located some-where in a specified direction. Our instruc-tions: travel in pairs and stay between a local road and the ridge line of the mountains. Our possessions: a compass, one can of rations, a sleeping bag and our clothes. If we were captured along the way we would be put in a concentration camp. If we made it, we would eat and rest, then be put into the concentration camp.

Unfortunately my partner and I were captured   g
along the way. We arrived at a checkpoint and   *
a major was assigned to us who had torn his leg
open on a rock. The major slowed us down and   *
we couldn't get as high on the mountain as we
wanted, consequently we were captured. We were   *
knocked around a little and thrown into a truck,   p
our destination was the concentration camp.

If you have ever seen a concentration camp on   c-*
TV, this would be a good description of the one
in Maine. It had fences with barbed wire at   c-*
the top, also present were towers with flood
lights and machine guns, and run down barracks.

The temperature ranged between forty-five degrees   d-c
during the day to twenty-five degrees at night.
We arrived at about sundown, the first thing   *-c-p
they did was to take all our clothes, if you
wouldn't take off your clothes you were sprayed
with water and then your clothes were taken
from you and you were sprayed again. We were   c
left without any clothes for about an hour or
two. I have never before put my naked body
next to another naked male body, but I did then,   p
we all did as a matter of keeping warm. Finally
they gave us some clothes, naturally they weren't   p-*
our own, but we didn't care.

We were in the camp for about two days during   *
which they tried to get more out of us than our
name, rank and serial number. First they tried
the soft sell; cigarettes, food, promises of   p
release, warm clothes, this didn't work too well   p
so they spread the word that one of us had
accepted all these goodies to try to break up
our organization. Next came the hard sell; I   *
was knocked around by one interrogator, he spit
tobacco in my face, he stomped the American
flag into the ground, told me my sister was a
whore and many other things I can't remember.
I was put in a three foot cubic box, I got cramps   *
and charlie horses. Finally that phase was over.   d

At the first check point, a major who had torn his leg open on a rock was assigned to me and my partner. The major slowed us down so much that we couldn't get as high on the mountain as we wanted to. So we were captured, knocked around a little and thrown into a truck with other prisoners. Our destination was the concentration camp.

If you have ever seen a concentration camp on TV--fences with barbed wire at the top, towers with flood lights and machine guns, rundown barracks--you know where we arrived at sundown.

The first thing they did was to take all our clothes. If you wouldn't take off your clothes you were sprayed with water and then your clothes were taken from you and you were sprayed again. The temperature was about 25°. I have never before put my naked body next to another naked male body, but I did then. We all did. Finally (none of us could believe it had been only a couple of hours) they gave us some clothes. Not our own, but we didn't care.

For the next two days they tried to get more out of us than name, rank and serial number. First they tried the soft sell--cigarettes, food, warm clothes, promises of release. This didn't work too well so they spread the word that one of us had accepted all these goodies and would now try to break up our organization. Next came the hard sell. The interrogators started knocking us around. And we had to move very heavy rocks from one side of the camp to the other then back to the other side then back again over and over. One interrogator spit tobacco in my face, stomped the American flag into the ground, told me my sister was a whore and many other things I can't remember. At some point they threw me into a three-foot cubic box. I'm 6'3 1/2" tall, but I was so exhausted I fell asleep. And woke up with all-over cramps and charlie horses.

All the while they had this crazy oriental music *
playing and ever so often they would interrupt
it with remarks about the American government
and other such things, these were repeated over
and over. Toward the end of the second day I
began to question whether the whole thing was
really a mock affair or if this was actually *
happening.

Many other things happened during these two d
days, some of which I can't remember others
which are just little things like being pushed
around, and moving rocks from one side of the *
camp to the other, then back to the other side,
over and over. Finally the end came, one of p
our men came running out waving the American
flag shouting that we were free. p

This was one of the many experiences of my Navy d
tour of duty, one which I will never forget.
I actually began to wonder if I was ever going *
to get out of that concentration camp. Fortunately I never had to use the knowledge gained
at this school.

All the while they had this crazy oriental music playing. The same strange rhythm and melody. Over and over. And ever so often they would interrupt it with diatribes against democracy and the American government and our leaders. The same crazy talk. Over and over. Toward the end of the second day I began to question whether the whole thing was really a mock affair. Could it actually be happening? To me? I actually began to wonder if I was ever going to get out of that concentration camp.

Finally the end came. One of our men came running out waving the American flag, shouting that we were free.

Fortunately I never had to use the knowledge gained at this school

Here is a short but strong statement that is easy to read because the sentences move smoothly and easily.

Everytime I hear someone from a city say "dumb farmer," I want to tell them how inaccurate the expression is. Every good farmer must be businessman, salesman, wholesale buyer and broker. He must also have scientific knowledge of his soil and his cattle's diet and enough medical knowledge to take care of sick animals. Sometimes he must prove he is a competent carpenter or mechanic. And at all times he must be an expert on the weather. I would say he is not dumb but brilliant. A master of all trades.

Except for the last two sentences, the piece is easy to forget because it is too general to engage a reader's interest.

What has the writer done in the version on the next page to extend and strengthen her generalizations about a good farmer?

If my father is typical, a farmer is a master of all trades. 1

When he surveys his fields and lays plans 2
for contour plowing and the rotation of
crops, he is an engineer. When he analyzes 3
the soil and adds the fertilizer that will
produce huge ears of corn and lush fields of
oats, he is a scientist. When he diagnoses 4
a sick cow, applies ointment to a horse's
sore hoof, and helps a baby calf survive an
abnormal birth, he is a doctor.

But my father is a carpenter as he builds a 5
temporary lean-to to house the cattle through
a hard winter and repairs the wind-damaged
corn crib. The farm machinery also needs 6
repairs: the tractor with a broken hitch,
the elevator that just quit, and the corn-
picker that needs greasing after a year of
leisure; so my father is a mechanic. He is 7
the businessman who trades an elevator for
a horse, the salesman who sells his excess
corn and oats, and the wholesale buyer who
stocks up on baler twine, corn seed, and
fertilizer.

Just as a dietician plans the daily meals 8
for the students eating in university cafe-
terias, my father must plan, measure, mix and
grind all the correct nutrients in the proper
amounts to provide a balanced diet for the
hogs, the cows, and the sheep, each requiring
a special menu. Like the broker who watches 9
the stock market and sells and trades when
the prices are right, my father must watch
the farm market. He must have his cattle 10
ready to sell when the price is up and know
just how long to wait to get the most for
his corn.

But there would be nothing to sell if he 11
were not a weatherman, watching and knowing
the skies that tell him when to plant and
harvest his crops.

The two versions of the piece about "the master of all trades" demonstrate the best way, sometimes *the only way*, to add power to your writing. That is, by packing your sentences full of specific and concrete details; by making your voice your reader's eye. We know what one farmer's work day was like because his daughter has made her memories of childhood visual—in words, on a piece of paper. And her sentences are smooth and rhythmic because she wanted to perfect the piece she was writing to convey her admiration for her father.

Trying to imitate this piece, sentence by sentence, would, I think, be a mistake. But if you would like your writing to move as that person's writing does, take a closer look at the structure of her sentences. You may see some possibilities you hadn't thought of before.

Notice how she repeats the same sentence pattern in the first four sentences.

To avoid monotony, she changes the pattern in sentence 5. How?

Sentence 6 looks quite complicated. But if you look at the three parts separately, you'll see it really isn't. (The : and the ; mark off the parts.)

The basic word order followed in 6 is repeated in 7. How is that order elaborated in each sentence?

The next two sentences have a similar structure because each was written to express an analogy. Why is the analogy begun in 9 finished in the next sentence?

How is the last sentence structurally different from the first sentence?

In the next piece John Kennedy also talks about farming. Though you and I might have perceived no basic differences if we had actually visited the farms these two writers take us to, we hear differences as we read what each has written.

The sentence style and the overall form of each piece shows how what we want to say helps shape not only the structure of our sentences but also the way those sentences form a logical sequence of ideas that we call an essay.

I grew up on what could be called a farm. But not the kind most people envision when they hear the word. It was more like the specialized final step before the slaughter.

My Dad and Uncle Willie broke their backs to get things into this leisurely state. They started in 1937, the year of my grandfather's death, when they were 18 and 16, respectively. At that time the total worth of the family estate was estimated at $16,000. But the mortgage that was a part of their inheritance was so large that they were unable to pay off their two older sisters. They were therefore obligated to give them a free ride to the present value of more than .6 million dollars. It must be nice to increase your inheritance by over 150 times in 33 years.

Dad and Willie worked the nuclear farm of 350 acres mainly by themselves until 1956, when they bought out a failing neighbor (200 acres) and hired Fritz as their first fulltime hired hand. Fritz was an exceptional worker and Dad had developed into quite a financial manipulator. Together, with Willie as operations manager (president), Dad as finance manager (secretary-treasurer), and Fritz as the labor force (non-voting member of club), they extended their operations to 900 acres and over 1000 head of finished beef a year. They were extended to their limits and on shakey financial ground when falling prices made it seem as if the ground was about to crumble. That's when Dad had to take on the job of rural route mail carrier (which later caused his death).

Continuing their previous life style, taking only what was very necessary out of the farm account, they were able to straighten up the monster they had created by 1964. This was when the John Deere '4010' (twice the power of previous tractors) and I entered the picture. The effect was simple. They no longer needed Fritz, so he found an office job at the Co-op in a nearby town and made a $20,000 down payment on a 120 acre farm. Now he is assistant manager of a Co-op and plays farmer in his spare time.

Because I didn't experience the struggling years prior to 1964, I look upon farming as a matter of shrewd business manipulation and occasional good, honest, damn hard work. I didn't grow up learning about hogs, chickens, sheep, or milk cows. Instead of slopping the hogs, I merely turned on the automatic unloader on one of our six silos and scooped a few bushels of corn out of one of our ten corn cribs. I didn't grow up learning about all the different types of grasses, weeds, and other secondary crops. To me, farming was corn and beef and chores one hour every morning and night. It was working the fields spring and fall, baling hay three times a year, and, most of all, intense business proceedings. I didn't see farming as struggling with money and year round hard labor. I got in when the working capital was in excess of $100,000 and big tractors made for fewer field hours.

The system was on its feet, and nothing short of another tremendous depression could tear it down. But the farm officials were highly specialized and very interdependent. If one died, the other would have many years of depressed earnings while learning to do the dead partner's work. That is why I am in school. Willie is not too keen on learning the processes and transactions that were my father's responsibility. He can not teach me farm finance. I hope to learn enough here to establish my own system of money management so that I can add something to the partnership. I only hope I can get back in time to stop the undermining of my closest and least deserving rivals, the families of my two aunts. I hope to someday have my own partnership—Willie, my six year old brother Al, and me.

The pieces on the next several pages were composed by Lee Grover. Whether you can analyze the grammatical structure of a sentence or not, you can see and hear the grammatical differences Lee achieved by playing with the possibilities.

The first three pieces express the same general ideas. Each is based on the same experiences; the details presented vary very little. And yet you may first notice the obvious differences in the content of each piece. Try instead to concentrate on the sentences. For the sound, the tone of each piece, is partially determined by the kinds of sentences that Lee writes.

These pieces show how impossible it is to separate content from form. Sometimes our ideas and the details we choose seem to be determined by the patterns our sentences seem to be naturally following. The reverse, of course, is also true.

Read each piece *aloud*. Listen to the sound and movement of it.

Try to say how the sentences are different in each piece.

Try to say how the differences in sentence structure affect the sound, and the content, of the whole piece.

What can I say about prejudice except it is everywhere. At least everywhere I've been. Iowa, West Texas, Okinawa, and Maryland. Niggers, in-groups and out-groups stateside. Gooks, zips, chinks overseas.

If you wore a Gant shirt and drove a big new car at Roosevelt Hi in 1965 you were in. If you wore a J. C. Penney shirt and drove a beat-up '55 Chevy, they didn't know you existed. And you find out fast in west Texas that the local townies don't want to know you if you wear a uniform. They can always spot the outsider even if you don't wear a uniform. God-fearing, gun-toting, flag-waving Texans. They support our boys in Nam so long as they stay there. They don't want no GI messing around with their women.

On Okinawa whites and blacks had more or less divided up the GI villages, the bars, and the whores surrounding the various bases. My black friend and I could drink in one of the integrated bars. But the native barmaids, friendly when I was alone, never talked to the two of us. And I could not go down the road a few blocks to have a drink with my friend in a black bar without us both being beat up, knifed or shot.

On my final military post in Maryland, I was afraid to walk the streets of Baltimore without a black buddy. Local townies there don't like GI's any more or any less than West Texans do.

Lee Grover

No matter where I was stationed during my four years in the military, I encountered prejudice. In west Texas prejudice means gun-toting natives excluding GI's. So they won't mess around with their women. On Okinawa prejudice means white soldiers excluding black soldiers and black soldiers excluding white soldiers. It means a white soldier laughing half-heartedly at a black soldier's good-humored ridicule, then calling him a dumb nigger as soon as he walks away.

White soldiers and black soldiers both think the natives are dumb because they are different. And Okinawans hate black soldiers more than they hate white soldiers. And the Japanese feel superior to Okinawans. Okinawans have darker skin and coarser features than the Japanese and are still a rural and agrarian people while Japan is highly urban and industrialized.

When I came home again, first in Maryland, then in Iowa, I saw whites excluding Negroes. From old neighborhoods and new suburbs. From private clubs and public facilities. And I saw blacks fighting back. With violent words and violent acts.

Prejudice is judging anybody by external features, judging anybody by standards that cannot measure an individual human being. And nearly everybody seems to be doing that.

Lee Grover

Sometimes the way we say what we think is determined by the audience we are saying it for. Could that be the reason the next piece is so different from the two preceding ones?

If so, how does Lee Grover perceive the people he is here speaking to?

How much is the tone of this piece determined by the kinds of sentences the writer has chosen? Is Lee still talking on paper?

Does the voice of this piece sound as "honest" as the voice we hear in the other two pieces?

Though the Armed Forces were integrated by President Harry S. Truman, (Executive Order 9981, July 26, 1948) there is, solely on the basis of color, much racial prejudice among service personnel during off-duty hours. Racial prejudice on Okinawa is evident in the segregated villages, the segregated bars and the segregated houses of prostitution surrounding the various bases. However, to say that racial prejudice in the Military is the sole responsibility of white officers and enlisted men would be an oversimplification if not an unfair assessment of the situation. White soldiers not only say they are afraid of being beaten, knifed or shot if they go to the black sections, but their stories are more often than not verifiable even though there has been no official attempt to investigate any situation as an instance of reverse racial discrimination.

Many critics of the Military say that American prejudice has not left the native population unscathed. To support that criticism they cite examples such as the Okinawan women who work in integrated bars being noticeably less friendly with black Americans than they are with white Americans. Before condemning the Military, one must, in all fairness, consider some instances of Oriental prejudice. Any close observer of the native culture will verify, after only a few weeks on Okinawa, that all the Japanese who live there not only feel but express, very clearly and emphatically, their feeling of innate superiority to the Okinawans. The factors involved are as obvious as the factors that lead to American racial prejudice: the Okinawans have darker skin and coarser features than the Japanese. Other parallels can be drawn from the fact that the Okinawan economy and culture is still rural and agrarian while Japan is highly urban and industrialized. Therefore, it seems logical to assume, because it can be proven, that the Okinawans had their own prejudices before American military bases were established on the island.

Lee Grover

The final piece about Lee Grover's encounter with prejudice on Okinawa is very different from the other pieces.

The new details that he shares make the most obvious difference. But the focus on self and the reactions to what happened make the crucial stylistic difference. This writing sounds more like an excerpt from a story—a narrative—about Lee's experience than the other pieces do. Compare the use of *I* in this and the other pieces.

But in all our comparing, remember that one piece is not necessarily better than the others. They are different because Lee was playing with the possibilities that are indeed unlimited.

```
Four years in the military is a long time.
The prejudice you encounter makes it a
helluva lot longer.

The Okinawans I knew, though different from
me, were good and generous people. I met most
of my Okinawan friends through motorcycle
racing. They helped me learn to race, kept
my bike running and tuned up, and did a lot
of favors for me. And I did for them what I
could. They were more interesting to know
than most of my G.I. friends. And though I
was a G.I., and Okinawans are prejudiced
against G.I.'s, the family of one of my friends
welcomed me in their home, introduced me to
their friends, and took me to restaurants and
bars where Okinawans ate and drank. That's how
I got to know the Okinawan side of life rather
than just the G.I. side of Okinawan life.

But my G.I. friends called my Okinawan friends
gooks and considered them dumb because they
looked different. My G.I. friends who were
black were just as prejudiced against Okina-
wans as whites are against blacks. Getting
caught in the middle of racial conflicts--
the unexpressed ones I could always feel
smoldering just below the friendly surface
and the hostile, overt ones that I tried to
stop--became a part of my military day.
```

My best friend in the office was black. He was
arrogant but good natured, and made fun of
everybody. But it was good humored ridicule.
My best friend on the base was white. A white
racist, I have to say, who did not like being
ridiculed by a black. Whenever my black friend
was not around, he always called him a dumb
nigger. And yet, I knew, except for the color
of my skin, I was everything he didn't like
about my other friend.

Sometimes I think I should just give up, adopt
some conventional attitudes, make things black
and white, good or bad, instead of judging
each person individually. It would make my
life a whole lot easier.

                                        Lee Grover

Copyreading

Copyreading is not a part of writing, but a time to consider what you have already written, a time to ask if you have followed all the conventions that will make it easier for your readers to hear what you are saying.

If you are uptight about "bad grammar," spelling, punctuation and all the other conventions, you may be very anxious to read this section. Your concerns still rank first, of course. But please try to understand why, in this book, developing fluency is considered more important than developing correctness.

No matter how correct your writing is, it will not communicate ideas unless it engages the reader's mind—with words that are clear and with sentences that carry him smoothly from thought to thought. You can write good writing—writing that grabs and holds your reader—even though there are misspelled words, mixed-up verb tenses, or omitted commas on every line.

So talk on paper first. Without worrying about errors. Then, when you can fill a page—with clarity and coherence—without struggling to get the words out and onto paper—you will be ready to learn how to read and correct your own copy.

This book does not provide drills guaranteed to develop basic writing skills. If you are old enough and competent enough to enter college, you bring the basic skills with you. Otherwise you never could have survived as long as you have in a complex, highly verbal culture.

This book does not provide drills guaranteed to teach you how to write correct sentences or to eliminate your errors. It makes no attempt to label or describe all the errors that you must be on the lookout for as you write.

Here we consider errors only when they occur in your writing. Then we look at them only as obstacles that may prevent someone from hearing and responding to what you are saying.

This book asks you to think of "correct" grammar, punctuation, spelling, and other conventions as a combination of habits that you can develop—through carefully directed copyreading. It asks you to think of errors as habits you can break—through carefully directed copyreading.

The way you spell or misspell a word, the way you do or don't punctuate a group of words, the way you add or don't add the confusing *s* or *ed* to a verb is simply a habit. Not a good or a bad habit. Not a measure of your intelligence.

But developing *new* habits to take the place of the *old* ones may take a bit of effort. Like breaking any habit that has become an unconscious act. You smoke a cigarette without thinking how to do it. Without remembering the warning on the package. And what do you do with your hands during uneasy moments after you have stopped smoking?

To help you replace old writing habits with new ones, this book asks you to build a Copyreading Guide. From your own writing. With your own mistakes. To fit your own needs.

With your instructor's help, find the places in your writing where you deviate from the conventions and change the word or the group of words so that it will conform to an "acceptable" form. Then set up a page in your Guide for that kind of mistake.

After your instructor has helped you to find and to change a mistake, it is then *your* responsibility to find that particular kind of mistake whenever you make it again.

Learning to do that is learning to copyread. If you have a lot of writing habits that need to be changed, you cannot learn the changes you need to make by looking for errors in general. You must look for *specific* kinds of errors.

Before copyreading each new piece of writing, flip through all the pages of your Guide. Ask what kinds of mistakes you should look for as you read. Will you recognize the mistake when you *see* it?

Read the pages of your Guide aloud—so that you can *hear the difference* in your mistakes and your revisions.

If you continue to make the same mistakes, your instructor may not point them out. To help you learn to find them yourself, he may indicate the line, the half-page or the page on which they occur. Before the end of the semester he may merely tell you *how many* of your persistent mistakes to look for in a piece of writing. The reason: to give you more practice in finding your own mistakes. For that is what copyreading skill is.

Don't be discouraged if your progress seems slow. Remember you are trying to break firmly fixed habits. And that always takes time. And determination. And patience.

So forget about errors while composing your papers.

Don't let your agonizing or momentary concern about "correct" verbs and commas and capital letters interfere while you are trying to put your thoughts and feelings onto paper.

Your ideas have priority.

Never interrupt your thinking to recall a punctuation "rule" or to check on the spelling of a word or to choose between *me* and *I* or *he do* and *he does*.

All *that* belongs in a totally separate and final stage of the human behaviors that end in a paper for somebody to read. That final stage, called *copyreading*, is a combination of *looking and listening* for the mistakes you have previously made as you read a new piece of your writing.

If you habitually make several kinds of mistakes every time you write, don't try to tackle all of them at once. Read the pages that follow on grammar, punctuation, and spelling. And talk with your teacher about a plan to fit your needs.

On pages 336-345 there is a summary of a student-teacher dialogue that may help you decide where and how to begin.

If several of your classmates have similar problems, you may want to work together on them.

So how much grammar do you need to know in order to become a good writer?

You've heard this book's answer before—ever how much you bring with you.

The grammar that is a part of composition—oral or written—is not a collection of labels and rules in a textbook.

Grammar is what you were learning as you were learning to talk. You were not simply memorizing a list of words—not merely building up a vocabulary. You were learning how to arrange words in meaningful combinations. You were learning how to express the relationships between words by putting them together in certain patterns. You were learning the systematic arrangement of words that is basic to meaning.

And you knew it all before you went off to kindergarten. Almost.

Linguistic research clearly shows that preschoolers can produce or respond to nearly all the complex grammatical structures that are a part of our language. All the others you acquired by the time you were ten—whether or not you studied them in a book or a class.

So what is all that school book grammar for? Why all the drudging workbooks?

Why all the expensive multimedia equipment and systems for teaching basic grammar skills and usage?

I like Martin Joos' answer

English-usage guilt-feelings have not yet been noticeably eased by the work of linguistic scientists, parallel to the work done by the psychiatrists. It is still our custom unhesitatingly and unthinkingly to demand that the clocks of language all be set to Central Standard Time. And each normal American is taught thoroughly, if not to keep accurate time, at least to feel ashamed whenever he notices that a clock of his is out of step with the English Department's tower-clock. Naturally he avoids looking aloft when he can. Then his linguistic guilt hides deep in his subconscious mind and there secretly gnaws away at the underpinnings of his public personality. Freud or Kinsey may have strengthened his private self-respect, but in his social life he is still in uneasy bondage to the gospel according to Webster as expounded by Miss Fidditch.

. . . A community has a complex structure, with variously differing needs and occasions. How could it scrape alone with only one pattern of English usage? (Webster, of course!—Well. . . .)

It would be very little better served with a single range of usages, differing along the length of a single scale. And yet our public theory of English is all laid out along just such a single yardstick. (Webster is one Webster, and Miss Fidditch is his prophet.)

We have not yet learned to speak of English as we speak of the weather and agriculture, and as we are slowly learning to speak of sex and survival. In the school folklore called "grammar" . . . we are bound to speak of English usage only in a simplistic way, like a proper Victorian maiden lady speaking of Men.

Martin Joos
from The Five Clocks

But neither the Miss Fidditches of yesterday nor their more liberated successors get all the blame for our national attitudes toward "correct" English.

It's all a part of the American dream of upward mobility—get a good education so you can get a nice job so you can be somebody.

So English classes in all the schools that serve the children of the poor and uneducated are for teaching "good grammar"—to the children of sharecroppers, dirt farmers, and migrant workers; children of coal miners, factory hands and common laborers; children of domestics, janitors and garbage collectors; children of welfare recipients and the foreign born with their "funny" way of talking.

Nothing nullifies equality like a social dialect—except the combination of dialect and skin that's not lily white. Ask any American of Indian, Mexican, Puerto Rican or African ancestry if you don't know what I mean.

For a hundred years, if a "nigger" wanted to become a "Negro" who could make it in the white man's world, if he wanted to create for himself one grim possibility of escape from a hopeless existence, he had to reject his dialect, his language—his *self*. For your language is you whatever your skin color. When teachers reject your language they reject you. So you sit humiliated and degraded, silent and unresponsive, and they call you nonverbal.

The person who has never had to change his language can never imagine the despair and confusion of the child or the wrath and indignation of the young adult caught in that dehumanizing trap.

Teachers who cling to their obsession with grammar are not serving the child or the educational system; they are helping to preserve the notion that, though all men are created equal, the language you learn in the home and community where you are created stamps you inferior if it is not "correct."

But the open class would not be open if we did not respond to the students who have decided they *want* to learn Central Standard Usage. This book says that usage, too, can be learned by talking—in class and on paper. In your own language.

If you let your teacher know early in the term that you want help, you can learn how to revise what you have written so that it will have none of the "substandard" deviations from the "real or imagined standard speech."

The quotes are from Webster's III. What do they imply?

Follow the procedures already described for your Proofreading Guide. That is, with your instructor's help, set up a page for each kind of usage "error" that occurs frequently in your writing. When you are sure that you understand the difference between your usage and "standard" usage, rewrite your sentence as an example of the social convention you are attempting to master.

Try to fix that difference in your mind. Read your revised sentences aloud. *Hear* the sound of the difference. *See* the letters that make the difference. Use a tape recorder to help you make the new form a part of the vocabulary that you use when writing. You can do that even though you continue to use the old forms when talking. For many of your usage "errors" can simply be regarded as spelling mistakes. (See pages 319-335.)

And please keep on writing. Always work with sentences that *you* have composed. Sentences that say what *you* think and feel. Sentences that sound like *you* talking even after you have "corrected" them.

This book does not promise that mastering "standard" usage will be easy. You will be attempting to change habits fixed by a lifetime of daily use. You will be hampered by all the emotional hangups that you may have about the way you talk and all the resentment you may feel as you attempt to change your language to meet somebody else's standards. It will surely take a frequent realistic look at the alternatives and a cool and rational assessment of your opportunities.

Which means recognizing one fact even as you reject it: our country is now controlled by people who are beset by English-usage guilt feelings, people who can accept or reject us as they accept or reject our language.

No book can tell you what to do. But try to hang loose and talk your own language as you write. And make only the changes that you and your teacher consider absolutely necessary as you revise. Don't take all the life out of your writing as you try to make it "correct."

The composition of groups—and hence of classes—should be as varied as possible. Individuals would be in one group formed for one purpose and in another formed for another purpose. But for the sake of a rich multiplicity of dialects, vocabulary, styles, ideas, and points of view, the class should be heterogeneously sectioned from a diverse student population. It should constitute the most powerful multilingual assembly that can be brought together. This means mixing levels of ability and achievement, mixing sexes, mixing races, and mising socioeconomic classes. At times even ages should be temporarily mixed, and outside adults should come in and join discussion. Certainly the internalization process is severely curtailed if urban and suburban children, advantaged and disadvantaged, do not talk together. Not only will they have to "speak each other's language" in the future, for social and political reasons, but the language of each needs something from the other. Disadvantaged urban children can learn standard English only by speaking with people who use it. But, which is more important, they need to learn new *uses* of language—how to think by means of it, solve problems with it, influence others, and bring about action. Advantaged children living in suburban ghettos will not be sacrificed by mixing. They need to relearn constantly the emotive and communal uses of language that middle-class upbringing tends to destroy. And their language needs the mythic and metaphoric qualities of lower-class speech. But all this means breaking the socioeconomic gerrymandering of large cities and restructuring school districts along metropolitan rather than municipal lines. If the educational ideal is to expand to the fullest the verbal and cognitive repertory of students, then the biggest single obstacle is ingrouping of all sorts, from familial to cultural.

James Moffett
from *Teaching the Universe of Discourse*

If parsing sentences (that is, breaking them into parts, and explaining the grammatical form, function and interrelation of each part) was one of the joys of your life in fifth grade, if showing off in class for you meant filling the blackboard with diagrams that proved you were a parsing whizz, then you've probably spent some time playing around with punctuation marks. But if all that seemed like a waste of time then—and ever since—you probably find even less meaning in that kind of activity now. At least I hope so.

Though we must consider copyreading in this book and in your class, let's keep minor matters where they belong—at the bottom of our list of priorities.

In fact, if commas have been one of the bitter mysteries of school life for you, if you're always wondering whether to end a sentence or keep it going for a few more lines, never knowing when to use or not to use a semicolon, we now invite you to regress—about 400 years.

Go back to the days before all those punctuation rules were codified as the laws of "correct" writing. Take all the mystery and some of the confusion and boredom out of copyreading for violations of the punctuation ordinances. "Point" your writing to correspond to the pauses and the intonations of your natural speaking patterns.

Before the rules you couldn't or wouldn't learn were written and "standardized," the speaking voice—a person talking on paper—was the authority for the way he punctuated that record of his voice. With a few little symbols he punctuated (*punctuare*—to point) his writing. It was an attempt to tell the reader how the writer would read it.

The points still tell the reader when to pause; they still tell him when his voice should go up and when it should come down on the scale of vocal pitch and tone; they still tell him when to use his voice to stress a word or a group of words. And that's a lot of work for those little marks.

So much work and so many choices for each writer to make that the grammarians and printers thought we needed a system of punctuation—a rule for every instance that a writer might need to tell his reader how to read what he had written.

Some of the rules you can remember without trying. Like choosing between a period and a question mark. The sound of a question is a natural, easily recognizable vocal sound. So is the sound of an exclamation mark. But how many emphatic points (!) can you use before the reader starts ignoring them? Underlining as you write (italics in print) presents the same problem.

But that's an easy decision, too, compared with remembering all the rules that tell you whether you should use a comma or a dash or a semicolon or a colon or a period to divide what you are saying into parts that your reader can easily comprehend. The rules that attempted to clarify have instead confused you. They make the human behaviors we have called talking on paper seem like something quite different from your everyday language.

Perhaps that is why our system of punctuation did not become fixed and unchanging even though we have all those rules that are supposed to tell us quite precisely how to mark the grammatical structures of our written language. Many contemporary writers and publishers would insist that, within the basic patterns of the speech we share, the speech we hear and use everyday—naturally, with no need for rules—punctuation is still a matter of personal choice.

Recall for a moment the fastest talker, the most nonstop monop-
olizer of every conversation that you know. The glibbest, the
most compulsive monologist in this or any other class or in the
wider circle of your acquaintances, the person who never stops to
let you have your say, who never stops for a long breath.

And yet, there's always some intonation of voice, some slight
pause that indicates he'd use an occasional period or maybe a lot
of commas and dashes if he were talking on paper.

And when he decides that he wants you to hear *what* he is saying
(not just to thrill to the sound of his voice), when he wants you
to respond to his ideas so he will know what you think about
what he is saying, he will "point" his words with pauses that
vary, though ever so slightly, and with subtle or obvious variations
in the pitch and tone of his voice.

And unless he has completely lost his intuitive sense of the drama
that is inherent in his language, he knows that a monotonous,
endless stream of written words never gets through to a reader
unless the flow of speech (on paper) is segmented. He knows that
what he is saying must be said in little parts—with varying lengths
and patterns—if he wants his words to catch a reader's eye and
mind as they would catch a listener's ear and mind.

Read aloud the pieces of writing your teacher has returned with a comment about punctuation. Can you *feel* yourself talking— *hear* yourself talking?

How much are you asking your reader to take in between the capital letter that begins your sentences and the period that ends them?

Have you used all the commas you need to use to designate some shorter-than-period pauses within the sentence?

Would it be better to designate some of those pauses with a period?

Do some of your periods stop the reader too soon, cutting him off before he reads to the end of a group of words that obviously needs to be read without a pause?

Are some of your periods used primarily to separate a group of words that you want the reader to hear with extra force? Would a dash or an exclamation point be a better way of telling your reader that he must not miss that group of words?

What is the difference in the tone of voice suggested by a dash and the tone we hear for a period? a comma?

How many commas do you use to separate the groups of words that sound like interruptions as you read a sentence? Do you always put in the second comma that's needed—the one that tells your reader the interruption is over? (Double-or-nothing in commas, we say.)

Do you hear any groups of words that function like introductory remarks at the beginning of your sentences? When do you need a comma after such a group of words?

Of course, the talking on paper you have done in response to this book has not been an actual transcription of words you have spoken out loud. It is, instead, a record of the silent voice that only you can hear. While talking to yourself about a pleasant memory or a baffling problem, you are not aware of any pattern of pauses and intonations. The same is also true of your silent composing voice. In both instances your mind is engaged with ideas, not punctuation marks. But when your inner talk becomes written talk, your ideas must be "pointed" for the reader—to help create the sound and movement of your speaking voice and to help clarify the meaning of what you are saying.

For punctuation is simply a means of making it easier for your reader to *hear* and *respond* to what you are saying.

Try reading the next three pages *aloud*—without stopping for a breath until you come to a punctuation mark. I'm betting you'll not only miss the air but a lot of the meaning. In fact, the writing may have very little meaning, make no sense at all unless you hear the *natural* word groups as you read, unless you pause for the periods and commas that are not there.

Don't try to figure out the grammatical structures that need to be marked off by punctuation. Don't try to remember the rules that might apply on each line. Instead, listen for the groups of words that seem to go together—naturally—just as they would if you were talking.

First, my thanks to the writers who gave me permission to quote the following pieces without the punctuation marks they used as they talked their thoughts and feelings onto paper. And if you don't hear the pauses necessary to restore the coherence now missing, I'll have to send them my apologies. For what they say is certainly worth reading.

I feel like I'll be able to make it in this class everyone has been friendly and not uptight cause of my skin tone I came into the classroom afraid and nervous my first day in that monstrous institution COLLEGE it wasn't bad at all the people made me feel at ease the teacher made me feel at ease and all was well I feel as if I'm *in* the class already a friend a classmate whatever

the way the class is being taught is beautiful kids come to college scared out of their minds and to have a class like this where you're able to rap half of the period is really relaxing it demolishes the scaredness of college and makes it joyful at first it doesn't freak or panic you before you get a good start everybody starts off all tensed up and you can't do good work all tensed up you have to be right in the middle of it everyone not just the smart ones or the teachers' pets I know all classes won't be like this but what a beautiful beginning after one day I feel like I can go on and handle the problems that I know I'll have later on

                        Billy Williams

since I was not in the upper half of my class which would have meant I had to have a grade point average of 3.2 I was allowed into the university on probation if I had graduated at one of the other Iowa City high schools I would not be on probation so I have come to think of the administration as a bunch of strict bastards set on their little rules and not looking deeper into each person's situation I am very nervous and so afraid I'm

going to fail this really hasn't made me try
harder instead I compare myself to the others
in class which is just the opposite of what
Ms. Kelly wants this class to be like rather
than taking a person's ideas and listening
to them and respecting them I'm trying to compete or maybe I'm trying to write what the
teacher wants and not what I feel because I
want to impress the teacher I feel very inferior to my classmates because they are most
likely not on probation even though no one
knows you're on prob you feel as though everyone is staring at you and thinking inside boy
are you stupid I'm afraid to open up my inner
self in class because then someone would know
for sure that I am dumb and on probation.

Carol Garthwaite

of all the kinds of writing I have done this
is something I have wanted to do for a long
time I am afraid to talk to people I have a
feeling that when I talk to someone what I
say must be of some important interest to
them or I am wasting their time if I am talking and someone interrupts me I get the feeling that no one was listening to me then I
get embarrassed not much but embarrassed and
shut up if I shut up it is hard for me to
start talking again my problem may be bigger
I don't mind shutting up when people are
talking I feel I can talk to them about what
they are saying without verbal communication
as if I could just think of what I wanted to
tell them and they would understand this is
why I should do this kind of writing when I
think I talk to myself now I write what I
think and talk on paper

Micky Duggan

the world I know is small but as I grow the
less I know and the world begins to grow I
don't know why but I can't see eye to eye
with dad but the older I get the fussier he
gets as if he tries to rule my world even

though it is small and here today I step into
a bigger world but alas my father never gives
up

I love but yet I hate why

LOVE
under dirt filth and disease people walk they
see they hear they feel they talk but still
reject our human brothers how long will it
last why does it continue they're blind
they're blind they're insensitive they're
silent of one another's problems and agonies

Ron Conatser

I'm confused I wonder at what stage of a person's life he stops asking the questions and
starts receiving the answers at the present
time I'm trying to establish the values that
are really important and relevant to me but
about the time I decide what is more important things change I meet new people and experience new situations then I change my mind
not complete or drastic changes all of the
time but gradual no matter what the change it
always or usually always seems relevant

you ask if anyone can write honestly well the
best way I can answer is to say that you cannot write any more honestly than you can talk
many times the things I say and really feel
that I mean can change in only a matter of
weeks or days or hours so I suppose I'm saying or you can probably detect from my writing
that I don't know how long I can stand behind
the things I write or say

Dennis Young

fake that makes me mad

I was walking past Old Capitol Saturday night
and this chick was sitting up on the steps
leaning against the pillars reading a book

I said to my self Bill what are you doing
tonight and I answered not a damn thing my
mind said how about reading a good book with
a good looking girl and I said sure man why
didn't I think of that you're dumb

I advanced and she smiled oh-oh Bill take it
easy what are you reading *Demian* by Hermann
Hesse good I love Hesse mind if I read along
no be my guest

she scooted over and man this girl reads a
thousand words a minute while I was finishing
the first page she was turning the second page
she politely waited for me to finish the page

all the while we're leaning against the pillars of Old Capitol and I'm tapping and rapping on them like I'm always doing something
with my hands but my mind was wrapped up in
the book (ha ha ha ha ha) I am now an ambitious university student sitting with a pretty
girl reading a good book leaning on the solid
granite pillars that stand at the center of
the campus a hippie came by carrying his flute
how nice I thought a free concert so I asked
him to play us a song or two he said sure I'm
so stoned I could play all night he played
one long jam and left and all the time I'm
tapping on a pillar of Old Capitol then sud-
dently it hit me

man this thing's a fake I tapped and tapped
all over trying to find one solid spot which
is nowhere to be found I tapped all four of
those damn granite pillars and dig they are
all fakes they all sent out that sick hollow
sound

then I thought of all the people who cherish
Old Capitol who look upon it as a symbol of
education or a beautiful historic monument
they'd be surprised to find out the graceful
pillars are fake they've walked past them
many times and maybe just admired them or
maybe thought of their parents who went to
school here or remembered the pictures they've
taken in front of Old Captiol or felt proud

of their own college degrees and swelled up
with self-importance

what a letdown their monument is just a fake
like everything else people look up to

I couldn't get back to the book or to the girl
we talked awhile and I smoked a cigarette she
was a very nice girl but I decided to let her
finish her book

Billy Williams

I hope you'll read this piece by John Kennedy. First, because it conveys some truth about one man's experience. But if punctuation is your interest or your problem, read it again to ask a few questions about how John "points" his sentences.

Home for vacation. Quite the deal. Rolfe's   1
only hippie arrives to upset the weak minds
of the most respected citizens. All eyes are
turned toward "Little John," one time the
town's most-likely-to-succeed.

"What a dismal failure."   2

"Why does he have to look like that?"   3

Let me use just one dramatic situation to ex- 4
plicate the social chaos I aroused by going
back to my childhood stomping grounds. But
first I must admit one fact which had some
bearing on my homecoming; I did egg the in-
habitants on by wearing my most outlandish
clothing.

I arrived on Friday night. It was cold and   5
very wet. Knowing there would not be any
field work for a few days, I made plans to
start my terrorization of the townspeoples'
minds at the local pub the following afternoon during the card-playing time. I arose
early the next morning and did a few odd jobs
around the house for mother. The way any hippie freak would. Afterwards I cleaned up,
combed my hair neatly, put on my blue-flowered
bells, ate dinner and drove up to the pub.

As I walked in I knew I was early. Although   6
there were a dozen or more men there, only
the meek talk-behind-your-back type had
arrived. I walked up to the bar and ordered
my usual Bud. Then I went over to one of the
tables where a card game was going on. Straddling a chair near the corner of the table,
I leaned over the top of the chair and started guzzling my booze. As I exchanged a few
choice obscenities with one of the players
who was once a close friend of mine, I could

sense that I had command of every mind in that pub. Everyone was full of objections to my appearance, but they could not force out any words about the way I looked.

I acted in my normal way: arrogant, bold and, to some extent, over-confident. This upset them no end. How dare I look so different from them, yet come in and not cower in the corner was beyond their comprehension.   7

Then in came Steve, the town mouth.   8

"Kennedy what are you trying to prove? You   9
not only act like a girl, now you look like
one."

I immediately had this vision of all the   10
little men in the pub staring out from behind
Steve's back. Spiritually, though not physically or verbally, they were rallying behind
him. But after his absurb opening statement,
I felt as if I was momentarily struck by fits
of laughter. There I sat wearing a full beard,
old work boots, and a half-buttoned shirt
that revealed my breastless chest. I was still
straddling my chair, guzzling my seventh or
eighth beer, and spicing my talk with the
words that prove you're a man in Rolfe. Obviously Steve's remark did not merit an answer
so I merely said hello.

Since it was clear to me by now that I would   11
not be asked into a card game as I normally
was, I did not object to Steve taking a chair
close to me and continuing his illiterate
attempt at harrassment.

"Why don't you cut your hair?"   12

"Why does it need to be cut if it does not   13
bother me?"

"What pleasure do you get out of wearing   14
long hair?"

"Why do you wear a silly green Co-op cap?"   15

Steve inferred that to be a man you must wear 16
short hair, I explained at length how absurd
his test of a real man is. He lectured me on
the need to conform in order to get along in
the world, I pointed out how he would still
be using horses to work his field if all
earlier farmers had thought like that.

The conversation grew more ridiculous as we 17
continued, and when Steve saw no way to win
me over, he finally gave up and left. I left
shortly thereafter, gaining nothing, losing
nothing. Merely a waste of time. But I respect Steve far more than I respect the men
who were too weak to speak out for their convictions. Whether I am right and Steve is
wrong, or vice versa, is not for me to judge.
At least we both spoke up for our beliefs
which is more than I can say for the rest.

Rolfe--what a colossal letdown! Why does it 18
have to be the way it is?

Here are some questions to help you talk about the choices John made as he punctuated this piece of writing—

Why does he begin with two very short, "grammatically incomplete" sentences? If you find them offensive, ask why.

Three other sentences in this piece demonstrate how stylistically wrong the old rule about fragments is. "Correcting" them would add neither meaning nor more sophisticated grammatical structures to John's writing.

The 31 commas John uses here illustrate what many texts would call seven "rules" about the use of the comma. But John can not cite those rules. He uses a comma when he hears a pause shorter than the pause he hears for a period.

What length pause and what kind of relationship between ideas is he indicating with the semicolon he uses in paragraph 4?

Why did he choose to use a comma instead of a semicolon or period in paragraph 9?

Does John make his meaning less clear to us by choosing commas instead of semicolons in the long sentences in paragraph 16? What stylistic effect is he trying to achieve with the commas?

Why is the colon in paragraph 7 a better choice than a dash would be?

Why is the dash better for paragraph 18?

If you do not know the "rules" for using a hyphen, learn four of them by analyzing the ways John uses the hyphen in this paper.

If you are not able to hear all the places where your teacher says you need a punctuation mark, let's hope someone else in class has the same problem. Then you can work together. Read each other's writing *aloud*, and agree or compromise on the punctuation that generally seems essential to meaning.

If you continue to omit marks that are really needed or to use unnecessary marks, set up pages in your Copyreading Guide for the particular kinds of word patterns that you are not recognizing as you read aloud what you have written.

Read the sentences *aloud*, trying to hear the places where other readers have felt the need for a punctuation mark.

Master the conventions that will make it easier for your readers to hear and respond to what you are saying to them.

Becoming a good speller in one or two semesters is too much to expect if you have a serious spelling problem.

The way you spell a word when you are writing is a habit. Usually a habit firmly fixed by years of repetition. In fact, it is a *motor response.* Your hand writes the word with no direct help from your mind because your mind is busy with the ideas you are trying to express.

And that is the way it *should* be.

When you misspell a word, it means your hand did not learn the correct response in grades two through six. And you have been reinforcing the incorrect response ever since. To ask you to break such a long standing habit by "just memorizing" the correct spelling is unrealistic if you habitually misspell many words. But *finding misspelled words* can become part of your proofreading skill.

When your instructor spots a misspelled word, he is making a *visual response.* The word doesn't "look right" because somewhere in the memory storehouse that is a part of his mind there is a definite *visual image* of the correct spelling.

Before you can recognize an incorrect spelling, you, too, must have the correct spelling *in* your mind. You must fix a *visual image* of the correct spelling in your memory so that the word will not "look right" when you see it spelled incorrectly.

The procedures recommended here will help you build up that kind of response to the words that you habitually write incorrectly. Which means you can become a competent copyreader.

Instead of providing various lists of frequently misspelled words for you to learn to spell, this book asks you to build your own list—to provide *visual reinforcement* of the correct spelling of the words you misspell in your own writing *and* to serve you as a Guide to Correct Spelling *while you are copyreading.*

Instead of repeating the usual spelling "rules" for you to memorize and apply, this book asks you to add a second column to your Spelling Guide. Record there *the reason the word confuses you.* Sometimes that will be easy to do; other times, not so easy. Pages 325-335 offer examples, comments and questions about a few of the many reasons learning to spell can be so frustrating. I hope they will help you understand your spelling errors. Ask your teacher for help whenever you cannot figure out why a word is easier to misspell than to spell.

Set up a third column on your Spelling Guide for any other nota-
tion that may help you *fix the sight and the sound of a word in
your mind*.

GUIDE TO CORRECT SPELLING

Correct spelling of word I misspelled	Some indication of why word confuses me	Other helps for fixing correct spelling in my mind

The first column of your Guide to Correct Spelling should include:

words you look up while copyreading

(even though you discover your spelling is correct)

words your writing instructor points out

words your other instructors point out

(copyread all your papers, not just those written for
your composition class)

Because you need to see the word on your list as you will see it
while copyreading, write each word as you usually write when
talking on paper—that is, by hand or by typewriter.

To make each word stand out as a *distinct object* on the page,
skip 5 or 6 lines between words.

To help you *see* and remember the correction, underline the part
of the word you misspelled.

If you misspelled only one syllable or if your error seems to be
related to the way the word divides into syllables, write the word
in syllables in the second column. If your error seems to be related
to the way one or a combination of letters is pronounced, write
the symbol for that sound in the second column.

If others in your class have spelling problems, you may wish to
work together in small groups, sharing the information you already
have on your Spelling Guides and helping each other analyze
words you are ready to add to your lists.

See examples on pages 323 and 342.

Always use your Spelling Guide while copyreading. First, so you don't waste time looking up words already on your list. Also to make sure that you have spelled correctly any word on your list that you have used in the paper you are copyreading.

When you find a misspelled word that you have already added to your Spelling Guide, try to fix a visual image of that word in your mind. Concentrate on the way it looks in your handwriting or when typed. Stare at it for several seconds. Close your eyes and *see* it inside your head.

Some people find it helpful to cover all the other words on the page so that the word they are trying to learn will stand out more sharply. Don't worry about learning to spell words that you never use in your writing.

And don't ever decide not to use a word because you don't know how to spell it. Spell it any old way while composing, or leave a blank space for it. Then, while copyreading, look it up.

If there's no time for copyreading, write *sp* in the margin so your reader will know that you are aware of your need to look for your spelling errors.

GUIDE TO CORRECT SPELLING

Correct spelling of words I misspelled	Some indication of why word confuses me	Other helps for fixing correct spelling in my mind
perform	per as in person who performs perfectly in spelling.	performance, percent, perhaps, perception, perfection, percussion, permission
prefer	pre as in preference and pretzel.	pretend, prevail, prevent, preview, previous
conscience	moral sense — a little voice inside me — conscientious	
conscious	To be aware of that little voice or anything else — consciousness	My conscience is clear — especially when I'm unconscious.

advantageous	don't drop _e_ _ge_ spells _j_	just keep the _j_ (_ge_) in advantageous.
families	plural form	not to be confused with possessive form: family's or plural possessive: families'
committed	committing committee commitment	The committee cannot double its commitment without committing twice the number of errors they committed before. That's doubling man!
bulletin	bul le tin	The bulletin was full of bull.
genius	The _i_ sounds like the _y_ in yes.	yes, I'm a spelling genius.

spelling the sounds we don't say

Sometimes we misspell a word because of the difference in the
correct spelling and the way we pronounce the word. When that
is the reason for your error, the first two columns of your Guide
should clearly show the difference.

athlete

    ath lete--I put an unac-
cented vowel sound (ə)
between h and l when I
say athlete.

candidate

    I omit the first d sound.
So do a lot of other peo-
ple. The dictionary shows
our pronunciation like
this--kan(d)ədāt.

government

    Like most people, I omit
the n when writing because
I omit it when speaking.
Dictionary says ok for
talking, not for writing.

aspirin

    Like many other people,
I say aspirin without the
first i. Dictionary says
ok for talking, not for
writing.

misery

    Again, I don't say the
second vowel, so I make
misery a two-syllable
word. Dictionary disagrees
with me. Yet it gives my
pronunciation for the first
part of miserable. A later
one may say the way I say
misery is ok.

going to

    I pronounce this as a con-
traction--gonna.

want to

    I pronounce this as a con-
traction--wanna.

though	ugh is silent. The same silent letters are in thought and through. Tho and thru are listed as variant spellings. Why not tho't? Looks a helluva lot better without the ugly ugh!
thorough	Nobody's wised up and dropped the ugh that nobody says.
running	I drop all my final g's.
rhythm	h is silent in rhythm and in rhyme. But rime is a variant spelling of rhyme. Why can't we drop the h in rhythm?
listened	I never sound the ed when I'm talking. Gotta (got to) add it in writing tho (though).
asked	I've been spelling asked with a t instead of ed because I say it that way.
a lot	I write a lot as one word because I'm generalizing from aloud, along, alone. Like everybody did for all right which is now right as alright. Just like already and almost.

Most texts consider the verbs listed on the previous page as usage or grammatical errors. But dropping the final *d* and *g* sounds in speech is a linguistic characteristic of a geographical region—not "bad grammar," not "substandard" dialect.

If you are from the South that's how you talk even though you may be a lawyer or doctor or professor from one of the oldest and most respectable families. Southerners also use many contractions, like *gonna* and *gotta*. (As do a lot of other educated people of relatively secure social standing.) They learn to spell the written forms they see in spelling and reading texts but go on talking with a Southern Accent. Unless they decide to exchange it for Central Standard Usage (see page 301).

With a whole geographical region for supporting evidence, it seems quite logical and feasible to have you work with all *ed*-verbs simply as spelling mistakes.

But as you proofread for the *ed's* you have not added, you'll discover that's not the way to change all verbs from present to past tense. *Bringed* and *doed* don't sound right if most of the people we talk with say *brought* and *did*. But "he brung it" or "he done it" sounds ok if that's what we hear more frequently than we hear *brought* and *did*.

These so-called irregular verbs, and all the others like them, can be mighty confusing. Maybe you'll need to memorize the "socially acceptable" combinations (called conjugations) whenever you use a verb that doesn't become respectable when you add an *ed*.

The forms of the verb *to be* may cause even more confusion if you consistently use *be* instead of *am, is, are, was, were,* and *been*. In fact, you may discover that teacher and classmates do not understand all the distinctions you make, all the meaning you convey by using *be* as it is systematically used in your speech community. Give them some examples. Try to explain this distinctive characteristic of your dialect. Help them realize how difficult it is for anyone to change his language.

Adding or not adding an *s* to a verb is sometimes more exasperating than choosing the "correct" form for tense. But that, too, is a decision to make while proofreading, not while composing. If you consistently omit the *s* when talking—in person or on paper —ask someone who doesn't—either classmate or teacher—to read aloud to you the sentences where you deviate from "standard" usage. Listen for the differences in their verbs and yours. You can learn to spell verbs "correctly" (that is, learn to add or not to add the *s*) while copyreading, even though you continue to talk in your own social or geographic dialect.

making similar sounds look different

If you misspell a word because it is similar to another word, list all the words involved and write a sentence that illustrates the differences in meaning.

two
too
to

If you think <u>two</u> thousand is <u>too</u> much <u>to</u> send <u>to</u> me, I disagree, <u>too</u>.

they'<u>re</u>
th<u>ere</u>
th<u>eir</u>

They'<u>re</u> going in th<u>ere</u> without th<u>eir</u> boots on?

<u>ac</u>cept
<u>ex</u>cept

Everybody was willing to <u>ac</u>cept my proposal <u>ex</u>cept the man who thought he had a better idea.

ad<u>o</u>pt
ad<u>a</u>pt

If you ad<u>o</u>pt a baby, you'll have to ad<u>a</u>pt to many new routines.

l<u>ea</u>d
l<u>e</u>d

"<u>Lea</u>d me to your <u>lea</u>der or I will turn you into a little <u>lea</u>d pencil," this ugly critter cried. "So I have l<u>ed</u> him to you."

<u>here</u>
<u>hear</u>

"<u>Here</u> he is. Now you can <u>hear</u> him with your own <u>ears</u>."

If that is the problem that plagues you, you may be thinking that neither dictionary nor Spelling Guide will ever fix in your mind the visual images of all the words that may or may not have a doubled consonant.

You may be right about what the spelling books call "terminal doubling before adding a suffix."

The "rules" certainly seem more complicated and confusing than helpful. And every book adds a list of exceptions that add to the confusion. Other words have been "misspelled" so many times the error is now an accepted variant spelling.

But the insoluble problem can be controlled. Add to your Spelling Guide all the words in this confusing category that you look up while copyreading and all the ones your instructor points out. And look for each word as you copyread your next piece of writing.

If you notice some recurring pattern in the words in your Guide, you may have enough examples to make a generalization about that group of words. Let your teacher know if you need help stating the spelling pattern you have observed.

But don't take time from your writing to try to memorize and apply somebody else's spelling "rules."

Analyzing a word that has a doubled consonant near the beginning or in the middle is usually easier.

Why are there two *s*'s in misspelled and only one in mistake?

How do you spell the word that means *not* legal? the word that means *not* mature?

Why is there a doubled consonant in the middle of with<u>h</u>eld and roo<u>mm</u>ate?

Break the following words into syllables:

    para<u>ll</u>el
    ac<u>comm</u>odate
    a<u>ss</u>ignment
    stu<u>bb</u>orn
    o<u>ff</u>ensive

What happens to the sound of one of the doubled letters when we say the word?

What is the vowel sound of the syllable that letter is in?

Now make your own generalization about the cause of your confusion with words that follow this pattern.

As your spelling list grows, you will frequently discover that the cause for confusion in one word applies to many other words. Whenever you do, you will not only be learning to spell the words on your list but also learning to be aware of the same kind of confusion in other words.

Assume these words are on your list:

```
fallacy          agency                origin
        dragon           auditorium
```

What symbol would you write in the second column to indicate why the underlined letter in each word confuses you?

What symbol would you use to explain why these words may be confusing?

```
liar             deserter          flirt
      instructor           pursue
```

Here are some more words with the same kind of confusion:

```
tolerant and diligent

elegance and violence
```

What other words do you use that sound as if they end with ant or ent? ance or ence?

Durable and flexible present another pair of confusing suffixes that spelling books give many "rules" for. One is easy to remember: when in doubt, use able because more words are spelled with able than with ible.

This book says the odds are better if you build yourself a Spelling Guide. And use it.

Here are some examples of the kinds of notations you can make in the third column of your Guide.

List and say other words that present the same confusion. Hear the sound you misspelled.

whether	what, why, when, whisper, whiskers, whip, whim.

List other forms of the word that sound more like the correct spelling.

grammar	We pronounce the a in grammatical and grammarian.
rhetoric	We pronounce the to in rhetorical but rhetorician sounds more like rhetoric.
environment	I can hear the ron when I say environs (en vi rons). The syllable becomes weaker, gets less accent, when suffix is added.

List other forms of the word that has confused you.

definition	define, defined, defining, definitive, definite
different	differ, differing. difference, differentiate, differential

Think of something "cute" or "witty" to help you remember the correct spelling. It's called a mnemonic (memory) trick.

privilege	Grooving on pretty legs is a privilege.
knowledge	He didn't know the ledge was loaded. She had no knowledge of his ledger.

All the other common spelling problems can be analyzed *as they occur in your writing*. Don't worry about them until they do.

You will never be a perfect speller. Nobody I know is. But you can become a competent copyreader—if you look for your own ways of fixing the correct visual image of a word in your mind instead of trying to memorize and apply rules.

One young man, while struggling with his visual uncertainty about the first vowel and the single or double *f* in *definition* and *different*, discovered that none of the *def* words in his dictionary had a "double f" and that all of the *dif* words did have a "double f."

The same young man convinced me the *ie-ei* jingle should be banned. He found thirteen exceptions (not single words but groups of words that he could make a generalization about) in addition to the "except after *c* when sounding like *a* as in n*ei*ghbor and w*ei*gh."

He also convinced me that no case of misspelling is hopeless. In his first page of writing (by hand) in the fall, he misspelled 27 words. Before Christmas he found all his errors while proofreading the first draft of a 17-page (typed) term paper for a course called Religion and Human Culture.

letting your hand learn it for you

If spelling seems important enough to you and if you can find the extra time necessary, you can replace your incorrect motor responses (misspelled words) with the correct ones by setting up and following a practice routine.

As often as possible, once a day or several times a week, use the words on your list. Not in isolated sentences. That would be too much like filling the blanks in a workbook and too unlike getting your ideas on paper.

Simply write whatever thoughts occur to you as you read your list, copying the correct spelling of the words you are trying to learn. Most likely what you write will make more nonsense than sense. But don't worry about that.

Your eye and hand will be spelling (copying) the words from the list while your mind is engaged with your thoughts. Which means you will be establishing the correct motor responses. That is, learning to spell the words correctly.

To further strengthen your correct motor responses, use a tape recorder to dictate to yourself the pieces you write that include all the words on your spelling list.

In the piece of writing that is the subject of the dialogue summarized on pages 338-341 a young man talks in his own language about his particular experience. And the reader who responds to the human voice he hears is not deterred by the many deviations from "standard" usage and other conventions.

But the writer knows that in some situations some people may not accept him because he cannot write "correctly." So he wants his editor-teacher to help him identify and change all the errors that some readers will *see* before they *hear* a word he is saying.

But first he must realize how futile it would be to try to eliminate all his problems by correcting one paper. He must accept the very slow, sometimes painful, process of looking at one kind of deviation from the conventions or one small part of one paper today and going on to other deviations, one by one, on other days in other papers.

And he must keep on writing—every day—without worrying about the errors he knows he is making. And after writing, he must copy-read—*consciously* looking for the specific kinds of problems his editor-teacher has already helped him identify.

The student-teacher talk shared on the following pages is a very thorough analysis of one paper. But don't get the idea that every paper you write must be criticized line by line. Instead try to learn to identify and start working to change one or two specific habits in each paper.

Here we talk at great length about one piece of writing to help the writer make the changes that will make what he wants to say clearer and more convincing to the people he wants to reach with his words. I hope you, too, will frequently write something that you want teacher or classmate to help you perfect before sharing it with a wider audience.

When you do, ask the person you are working with to read your writing aloud to you. Then you can *see* and *hear* the places where the way you put words together makes it difficult for your reader to hear what you are trying to say. Ask him to stop reading and ask questions whenever he cannot grasp, whenever he cannot visualize, what you are trying to say. Then you can think and talk together until you find the answers that will add clearness and force to what you are trying to say.

I feel because of my natural race of Mexican
brith. I can wrote how it would feel to a   √√
negro in America.

I myself have felt the hate and dislike of   5
the so call white race which I'm part of. I √
feel as a negro I would feel this hate and
dislike even more. I've seem and hear people √√
talk about the negro race. How all they do
is cause trouble. Then I ask myself, how   10
would they like it if the shoes is on the
other foot. How would they like it if they
lived in a black world. A world when almost √
everything is in favor of the black and not
the white. Where something go wrong and the √ 15
first thing people say is well it was that
dirty White guy down the street, he did it.

My self, I know this because it happen to   √√
me. Place where I'd gone into to get some-   20
thing eat and been ask to leave because I'm √
a Mexican. One event toke place in West   √
Branch and another toke place in Marshall-   √
town. I ask the person why I couldn't eat
there.   25

He gave me a very simple and straight
answer: I don't like Mexicans in my place.
They just aren't any good. I felt very
up-set and hate ran down my veins. Here is √ 30
a man telling me that because his skin why √
ligher then mine in color. He though he   √√√
why better. If I can receive this kind of   √
treatment and I'm not a negro. Well I can
just imgane how hard they feel toward the   √ 35
white race.

I been around many negroes and some are   √
good, some are bad. I feel that if I was
a negro. I would not be ashame of what race √ 40
I am. I'm black and I'm pround. This is   √
how I feel now about my race. I feel no
better then anyone but, I feel no less.
Some day will understand that the color of √
skin is so little a thing to judge people.   45
They will learn that people with this kind
of out look in life are the best and happy √
people of the world. I think Negro people

of the world some day. Maybe not for a
long but it will come. Will walk with they ✓ 50
faces high. They will walk along side the
next person no matter what color his skin
is.

The student-teacher talk here and on the next few pages is an
attempt to help the writer reach the reader.

Read aloud the sentences on lines 1-3, 30-33, 33-36, 39-41, 48-51.

q: do the periods tell your reader the best place to pause? do
      they say this is the end of a group of closely related words?
a: no. the period interrupts ideas that go together. the 2 or 3
      sentences should be one sentence. I should change the
      periods to commas.

q: how is the last one (lines 48-51) different from the others?
a: there are three sentences that should be combined. the
      second one interrupts the other two.
a: a dash or parentheses would set off the thought that inter-
      rupts better than a comma would.

Lines 19-25 make up the most moving, the most convincing part of your paper. But they do not flow as smoothly or as forcefully as the previous part does. Probably because you were trying to condense two "events" into one telling. You may also have tensed up while recalling experiences that upset and angered you. Whatever the reason, it does not make easy reading.

Try reading the whole paragraph aloud.

q: what does *this* in line 19 refer to?
a: **the thing I'm about to tell about.**
a: **then say** *one thing* **instead of** *this.*

q: do you hear the gap between the first two sentences? what causes it? how can you smooth it out for your reader?
a: **add** *in a* **before** *place.*

q: does the sentence that begins on line 22 sound like you talking?
a: **no, I'd probably say, it happened once in West Branch and another time in Marshalltown.**

I know it's true, but it's hard for me to believe what happened to you. I can't imagine a person doing that to you. Help me see and feel what you are telling me. On line 21 change *been ask to leave* to *the man ask me to leave*. Make it even more graphic by telling me what he said. And how he said it.

Now read the whole paper aloud, listening for words that you have omitted and for the points where you need a punctuation mark.

We won't stop to talk about them now, but let's also check any place where your words don't convey an idea or an incident or an image as clearly or as precisely as we think you can.

the omissions found:

> *be* on line 2
>
> *people* on line 44
>
> *by* on line 45 (it's alright to end a sentence with a preposition)
>
> *time* on line 50

I hear a different kind of omission on line 41. You'll hear it, too, if you ask who all the *I's* on lines 39-42 refer to. Try changing *what race I am* to *my race*. Then add, *I would say* at beginning of next sentence.

the punctuation added or deleted to "mark" the natural pauses:

> ⌐ after *feel* on line 1
>
> a *?* on line 12
>
> a *?* on line 13
>
> 2 ,'s and " 's on line 16
>
> a " on line 17
>
> a " on line 27
>
> a " on line 28
>
> a , after *well* on line 34
>
> no comma after *but* on line 43

Now let's look at the places where the idea or incident or image you are trying to convey is fuzzy or confusing.

q: do you mean to suggest on line 1 that Mexicans are a separate race?

a: **no. I should say** *because I am Mexican* **or** *a native born Mexican.*

q: and how can you change line 42?

a: *about being a Mexican.*

q: does *foot* mean your left foot or your right foot or both of them?

a: **for both I'd say** *feet*.

a: **so would I. that's why, on line 11, I can't visualize a** *pair* **of shoes on a** *single* **foot.**

a: **ok, I'll strike the** *s.*

q: want another picky-proper one?

a: **go ahead. pick on me.**

a: **on line 11 you say, if the shoe** *is*; **on line 12 you say, if they** liv*ed*. **The shift from present to past tense would bother, even though it wouldn't really confuse, many readers.**

a: **please, don't gimme a choice.** *is* **should be** *was*. **right?**

a: **right! and if somebody says you should use the subjunctive, tell 'em next year maybe but not now. and if they ask about the sentence fragments we haven't touched, tell 'em that's how we talk. and so do they unless they are hypercorrect.**

Your spelling errors would keep some readers from hearing what you are saying. Look for them on the lines checked in the margin of your paper.

Are some of them already on your spelling list? Can you correct some of the others without a dictionary? Since looking them up would take time that might be more profitably spent writing another paper, don't! Let me give you the correct spelling for your Copyreading Guide.

GUIDE TO CORRECT SPELLING

Correct spelling of words I misspelled	Some indication of why word confuses me	Other helps for fixing correct spelling in my mind
birth	I reversed ir	maybe because my mind jumped ahead to write while my hand was still writing birth.
write	wrote is past tense	
so-called	past tense	hyphen turns 2 words into 1 word
seen	not seem	
heard	past tense of hear	
where	not when	the where in next sentence could be when
goes	I say, something go, just as I say, he go. must remember to add es.	it goes, he goes, she goes, something goes, anything goes

myself	one word	
happen_ed_	past tense	
ask_ed_	past tense	
t_oo_k	I say toke instead of took.	took rimes with book, look, cook
upset	one word, no hyphen	
was	not why	why was he so confused?
ligh_ter_		My eyes must not miss what my hand misses
th_an_	not then	I would rather go th_an_ stay because th_en_ I won't be bored.
though_t_	not though	Though I though_t_ I knew...
imagine	i ma gine	i ma gi na tion
I've been	I leave out the _re_ when I'm talking	I have been — if it's o.k. to leave out the _ha_, why not the _re_?
ashame_d_	past tense	
proud	Can't say why I put the _n_ in	I'm prou_d_ of every poun_d_.
outlook	one word	
their	not they	They have th_eir_ own ideas.

Notice how many of the words you misspelled present the same kind of confusion.

past tense:	so-call<u>ed</u>
	hear<u>d</u>
	happen<u>ed</u>
	ask<u>ed</u>
	asham<u>ed</u>
similar words:	see<u>n</u> / see<u>m</u>
	where / when
	th<u>an</u> / th<u>en</u>
	though<u>t</u> / though
	their / they
compound words:	myself
	upset
	outlook

Now put together all the little pieces you're rewritten as we've talked and you'll have one big beautiful piece—to distribute to the class if you want to. But if you never let anyone else read it, I'd like a revised copy to keep. If you please. Putting it all together may also help you learn more about the changes you've made. And help you remember what to look and listen for next time you copyread. It's called *reinforcing* what you've learned.

I feel, because I am a native born Mexican, I can write about how it would feel to be a negro in America.

I myself have felt the hate and dislike of the so-called white race which I'm part of. I feel as a negro I would feel this hate and dislike even more. I've seen and heard people talk about the negro race. How all they do is cause trouble. Then I ask myself, how would they like it if the shoe was on the other foot? How would they like it if they lived in a black world? A world where almost everything is in favor of the black and not the white. Where something goes wrong and the first thing people say is, "Well, it was that dirty White guy down the street, he did it."

Myself, I know one thing because it happened to me. In places where I'd gone to get something to eat, they asked me to leave. It happened once in West Branch and another time in Marshalltown. Their voices sounded mean and hard. And they looked mean and hard.

"I'm asking you to leave, young man. Get out. Right now!"

I asked the person why I couldn't eat there. He gave me a very simple and straight answer: "I don't like Mexicans in my place. They just aren't any good."

I felt very upset and hate ran down my veins. Here is a man telling me that because his skin was lighter than mine in color, he thought he was better. If I can receive this kind of treatment and I'm not a negro, well, I can just imagine how hard they feel toward the white race. I've been around many negroes and some are good, some are bad. I feel that if I was a negro, I would not be ashamed of my race. I would say I'm black and I'm proud. This is how I feel now about being a Mexican. I feel no better than anyone but I feel no less. Some day people will understand that the color of skin is so little a thing to judge people by. They will learn that people with this kind of outlook in life are the best and happy people of the world. I think negro people of the world some day--maybe not for a long time but it will come--will walk with their faces high. They will walk along side the next person no matter what color his skin is.

from Teacher to Teacher

I hope you never publish your book. Mimeo-
graph millions of loose pages just as you now
have and send them to every freshman in high
school and college. But please don't make it
into an authoritarian book. The teachers who
use it will say, "Now students, open the book
to page 27 and answer the questions at the end
of the chapter."

The students will all sit there stiff and cold,
wondering what kind of response the teacher
wants. And no good will come from the beautiful new book.

from a Student-Teacher dialogue

This book grew out of an experience where I was trapped—between all the old ways of teaching composition and all my despairing, sometimes hostile, students.

For them the old ways meant failure. The freshmen were getting D's and F's on every theme they wrote for Rhetoric. Most of the sophomores had already flunked the departmental theme exam after completing one or two semesters of Rhetoric; the others were failing their first literature course because they were writing failing papers. The upper classmen were failing a course because they had encountered a professor who not only required but graded papers. And the graduate students were living with the threat of failure as they struggled with their dissertations.

For all these students, learning to write meant getting through a teacher's drudging assignments so they could turn out a finished product that would pass somebody's inspection. They rarely, if ever, thought of writing as human communication. For them it was just a phony game, played for the chips called grades.

Working with these students changed my concept of myself as teacher, changed my concept of teaching composition. To put a little joy and a lot of reality into *my* teaching, into *their* learning—into *our* hours together gradually became the goals that dominated the dittoed pages that have grown up to be this book.

You'll find no prescriptive rhetoric or grammar here. No collection of readings to serve as models of organization or to provide a content for the course. I believe the student's own language and the experiences—external and internal—that he shares with the class make the best content for composition. Or to say it another way: the content of composition is the writer—as he reveals his *self*, thoughtfully and feelingly, in his own language, with his own voice. And while he's doing that for an audience that responds to and questions what he says, he'll learn to analyze, limit, organize, and support whatever he writes.

So this book, based on my own experiential learning, is for composition teachers who share the conviction that real learning—self-involving, pervasive, meaningful learning—does not come in scholarly or groovy packages from publisher or teacher. Real learning happens *inside* the learner. But if you are trying to create a place, an atmosphere, the relationships and situations—the *context* where real learning will happen, maybe the guidelines suggested here will help. I certainly hope so. I hope your classes will never be textbook-oriented, assignment-centered, or teacher-dominated. I hope you and your students can turn sterile academic classrooms into places where everybody will enjoy sharing his knowledge and skills and opinions with other human beings.

After reading all or part of this book, some teachers want to know if I'm talking to teachers or students or both. They think much of what I say should be for teachers only. And they feel ignored when I speak directly to the student about what should happen, about what he should do, in the classroom. These reactions may suggest some of the fundamental differences between the usual class and the kind this book attempts to describe. There are no pedagogical secrets in the open class because the pedagogical process is not the exclusive responsibility of the teacher. The distinctions between teaching and learning that are clear to everyone in the traditional classroom are not so clear, in fact, they gradually disappear, as a class develops its own direction, its own structure and content. For the teacher also learns and each learner also teaches. We never lose our teacher-identity, we never become "just another student," but we see ourselves, and our students perceive us, as a participating member of the group, not the voice of authority that controls the group.

So this book is addressed neither to the teacher nor to the students. Instead it speaks to the *community of learners* the class is or hopes to become. It asks that the teacher, like all other members of the group, give of his ideas, his knowledge, his competence —his self. It asks that he give by responding—to each person and to the group. What we say and do on a particular day develops not from our past teaching experience but from whatever is happening in class on that day. Instead of following the sequence of assignments that worked *last* year, we respond to the experiences —external and internal—that students talk about, in class and on paper, day by day, *this* year. We respond by sharing a bit of our experience that seems relevant or by asking questions that will help each person better understand his own ideas and the ideas of others, questions that will help each person express his ideas more clearly and more forcefully.

In this book you will find more questions asked than answered, more issues raised than resolved, less explication and fewer examples than you might expect in a textbook. The intent: to leave as much as possible *un*said, to place as much responsibility as possible on the class, to let them find clarity and completeness as they discuss the concepts and practices briefly or barely mentioned here. For each person can make the general and abstract suggestion specific and concrete when we ask him to look to his own experience (including reading) for supporting or refuting evidence. And as each shares his point of view and his experiences with the class, they will ask new questions and raise new issues for discussion.

While giving whatever we can to our students, while responding as best we can to the needs they express and to their verbal and nonverbal appeals for help, we must let them find their own answers if we want them to experience the kind of learning this book attempts to promote.

But the open class is not an extended rap session without form or subject matter. For the dialogues, the interaction described here will lead the class to its own unique structure and content as teacher and students work together to understand and respond to the linguistic and rhetorical needs of the group and of each person in the group. While you're trying to do that, you'll be bombarded with many disturbing questions—from skeptical and condescending colleagues, from apathetic and overanxious students, and from your own sense of obligation to the human beings you are encountering in your classes.

> What takes the place of the required 500-word theme
> in the open class?

The student-student dialogue (talking in class) and the student-teacher dialogue (talking on paper outside of class) are both essential to the open approach of this book. Both must go on—day by day—from beginning to end of term.

And that is *not* the easy way out of the frustration and boredom you may have known in English 101. An open class is not achieved by casually deciding to try something new you've heard about. To turn their students on to what sounds like a terrific concept of learning, a great innovation in teaching, some teachers walk in the first day, read Jerry Farber's "The Student As Nigger," or an excerpt from John Holt's *Why Children Fail*, then simply announce that they're making no assignments and setting no requirements. Then they sit down and wait for something exciting and impressive to happen, and when it doesn't, they decide that students can't be trusted because they don't want to learn. Then they write articles, denouncing the open classroom as another romantic educational myth, never assuming their rightful share of responsibility for what doesn't happen. Perhaps they will never know that they invite their students *not* to learn. Perhaps they don't want to know that it is teacher—not students who fail. Why? Because they plunge into their little experiments with no self-examination, no clear notion of what a teacher must give when he asks students to create something to replace the old ways he has discarded.

In response to the requests of young teachers who have used an earlier version of this book, the first part now includes many suggestions to help get the dialogues started and to help keep them going for several weeks at the beginning of the term. The present arrangement attempts to indicate how you may at first wish to help the class coordinate their out-of-class writing and their in-class talking. You will also find some recommended classroom procedures, including a very strong recommendation for the small "task" group.

But on every page I offer possibilities *not* required assignments. That's why, I think, each person and the group can retain their freedom while reading and responding to the first part of this book. Just remember that extending the class discussions and searching for answers to everyone's questions are always more important than "covering" the text or "getting to" an important chapter or "finishing up" a well-planned unit or project on a given day.

> Is the student free to do nothing—free *not* to learn,
> free *not* to respond to classmates and teacher?

This book says no. If the dialogues do not develop, if there is no ongoing interchange of ideas, the class is not open. Instead it is a collection of closed mouths, closed ears, closed minds, and closed hearts.

If as teachers we cannot accept Erik Erikson's assessment of the young people in our classes (p. 56), then an open class is beyond our reach. But if we believe our students possess the youthful virtue he calls fidelity, then we can assume, with confidence, that they will respond to our faith in them and our concern for them. Not every day, of course. Some will not respond on many days. Sometimes it may take several weeks, perhaps a whole term, to break through the walls that some people bring with them. But if we bring with us a full commitment to the concept of an open class, and patience—from a source that never runs dry; if we can live with the recurring frustration that closes in on the days when nothing's happening for nobody, the recurring feeling of impotence that could be dispelled in an instant by simply asserting our authority; if our egos can stand the persistent, uncomforting feeling that we have not yet achieved what we hope to achieve; then we can keep on responding to the unresponsive ones. And eventually we will reach them. But until and after we do, the trusting teacher must also be a demanding teacher.

> What happens to departmental goals and expectations
> in the open class?

We discuss them—in relation to the goals and expectations of each person in the class. And if they seem unreasonable or useless, we question them. To passively accept what we do not understand or to grudgingly submit to what we reject, can destroy every possibility for meaningful learning. But if the general purpose of the course is to help students extend the knowledge and experience they already have in sending and receiving messages—spoken or written—the guidelines of this book can be adapted to your class. The group and each person in the group can develop specific objectives early in the term and work, together and individually, to achieve them.

How does a class move beyond social chatter and superficial exchanges to significant ideas?

Not by listening to lectures full of the teacher's ideas. Not by reading essays to support the teacher's ideas. Not by discussing the teacher's ideas. The student's knowledge, though not as extensive as ours, is equally valid. And though he may not be able to understand and analyze all that he knows, his experience is just as human and complex, it is just as full of implications, as ours is.

In the open class the teacher must stifle every impulse to agree with those who say their students have no ideas. Instead, we must ask if our students trust us enough to share what they really think. And in discussions that may sound trivial, in chatter that could become boring, we must listen for insights into what they really think. If we are intent on *learning our students* instead of teaching them, if we want to know what's going on inside their heads instead of wanting to fill their heads with what we know, we never tune them out. Someone's frequent or occasional comment and all the nonverbal signals everyone is always sending out become tiny pieces of a human jigsaw puzzle. And day after day, we try to fit it all together. So we can see and respond to the whole person. So we can hear and respond to the ideas he is trying to express.

We can't do that, of course, without asking questions—questions that will help teacher and class understand what each person has experienced, questions that will help all of us see significance in what appears to be trivia. Usually the class hour ends before we can consider all the questions raised. And just as often it's obvious that nobody has the quick and easy answer. That's the time to form small 'task" groups. The task: to explore some aspect of the situation being discussed, to search together for some answers to some of our questions. Next day, or a week or two later, the group can report their findings to the class and the class can ask more questions. We may never decide on the *right* answers, but shallow conversation becomes serious discussion as we explore the possibilities. But I hope your class will not attempt subjects that require close analysis and extensive reading until most students can talk freely and easily in small groups and are no longer afraid of speaking out in full class discussions. For they cannot effectively handle questions about conflicting issues and values when they are tied up in emotional knots. Most classes are over that by midsemester, but please don't push anyone to perform for the class if he is obviously not ready to.

> How do you get them to turn the corner from talking
> on paper, that is, from free and spontaneous writing,
> to writing (or speaking) that is thematic, analytical,
> tightly organized, and fully substantiated?

By hearing what each person is saying and by asking questions. First, the questions that will convince him that you want to hear more. Then, the ones that will lead him to a competent and creative telling of his own thoughts and feelings.

The guidelines offered here are called "turning Dialogue into Discourse" (129-194). The focus moves from the writer's own "Voice" and "Perceptions" and the "Values" he lives by, to "Questions" that help him see that the rhetorical structures many texts and syllabi prescribe are not unlike his own natural thought processes. But please don't ask anyone to read a single page of that section until you have engaged each other in the dialogues described in the first section.

Much of the talking on paper that students do provides examples of the traditional patterns of organization. They relate experiences or describe processes that can be classified as narration or time sequences; they describe people and places; they explain the causes of their joy or despair; they compare and contrast what's happening to them now with what happened to them last year. For some, of course, everything comes out hazy and confused. But for almost all of them, if it's something they are *ready* to share, what they say is forceful and coherent. When they *know* what they want to say, there is no hassle about organization or content, each is part of their *knowing*.

To make the students' writing a part of the dialogue going on in class, I like to begin "publishing" excerpts or whole pieces as soon as possible. But I never share a person's writing with the class without his consent. And I never discuss a piece of writing as if I am grading it. I do not ask What do you think of the Introduction? or Does the writer include a sufficient number of representative examples to establish his credibility? or What's wrong with this paper? Those questions and many others may be considered in personal conferences or in small groups later in the term, but we do not talk in class about published writing unless someone, including the teacher, wants to respond to something somebody has said. Like, I know what you mean because this is what happened to me . . . or No, man, that's *not* the way it is because . . .

To ditto the lone A paper to show everybody else what the teacher wants, or to distribute inadequate papers so one student can tell another what he did wrong or how he can improve his paper is asking students to talk to each other as teachers have always talked to them. It is asking them to evaluate each other as they think we would. It is asking them to compete with each other as they try to meet prescribed academic standards, as they try to fulfill teacher-imposed requirements. They learn far more, I think, by responding to each other's ideas as they would in a non-threatening situation outside of class.

All students—the brilliant and the slow, the enthusiastic and the indifferent, the aggressive and the meek—need to be assured that they know something that teacher and class will value. So this book asks them to write and talk first about what they know best, what they enjoy most. I have never known a student who could not choose something that class and teacher knew very little about. Which means each student becomes a teacher. Explaining his special knowledge and skill. Answering the questions asked as he talks or as he reads something he has written. Restating sentences that are not clear. Seeing the need for logical order if his audience cannot follow what he is saying. And when someone says, "But I don't see what you mean," he adds some concrete details or visual images that help us see what he is trying to explain. And when someone says, "But I just don't get it. What is it really like?" he tries to think of an analogy that will help us understand. And sometimes, even the ones labeled slow, come up with a striking metaphor any writer would be proud of. When convinced that somebody wants to learn what *they know*, they learn what we want to teach them.

Opening up the rhetoric class is not an exercise in empty idealism. It is, instead, a practical and realistic approach to helping people develop more competence in sending and receiving messages, oral and written. The help the teacher offers a student, the feedback students give each other, is always part of someone's effort to convey whatever he wants to convey to the class that is his audience. Whenever a message does not come through clearly and forcefully, the open class becomes a questioning class.

Wha'd'y'mean may be the question your students will ask each other most frequently if their writing is full of vague and ambiguous words or if their opinions are always stated in meaningless generalizations. When the person challenged cannot come up with a satisfactory answer, a classmate may be able to help. Or the teacher can respond with a quick and easy lesson on definition or supporting evidence. Or we can cite books, periodicals or people who might be helpful in the search for answers that will help one person or the whole class extend and develop their ideas in well-supported essays.

When a student makes a generalization, in class or on paper, that is obviously a strong conviction, an attitude fixed in and by his own experience, our natural response is Why? And his natural response to that question is an attempt to analyze what he has said. Which means he will either state some supporting reasons for his opinion or he will begin to question it. Whichever, he will be going beyond his easy generalization. He will be analyzing what he thinks. He will be organizing his thoughts. In the natural give and take of conversation, he will be setting up a plan for an essay.

Instead of trying to teach everybody how to make outlines or giving them assignments that designate the way they must order their ideas, instead of giving them external forms to fill, this book raises questions that we hope will help our students analyze and understand their own lives, their own beliefs, their own values. Questions that only they can answer. And with their answers they can build coherent verbal structures; out of the meanings and the relationships they find, they can learn to analyze, organize and substantiate their ideas.

Perhaps "turning Dialogue into Discourse" can best be described as an attempt to show the student—through his own writing—that his attitude toward self, subject, and audience can control (that is, help him, sometimes quite unconsciously, to organize) whatever he wants to say; that he can create the sound of his own voice on paper by recreating his experiences—external and internal—with details so graphic and images so visual that readers will *see* what he means.

But this book holds nothing for students who merely read it. They must learn—experientially—through the small task groups suggested through the ongoing interaction with teacher and classmates without which an open class cannot be.

Some of the student writing in this book is published here exactly as the person talked it out onto paper—forceful, coherent, spontaneous responses to what a teacher was saying on a dittoed page to him. Other pieces have been extensively revised after one or several student-teacher conferences. The pieces on pages 203-208 best illustrate how a single response from teacher or classmate can turn a bit of talk (written) into a short essay. The ones on pages 223-232 show what a writer (with a little help from his editor-teacher) can do with the pages he has filled by talking on paper every day or so for several weeks. All the "Voices from the open classroom" are evidence that a free and easy response to teacher or class or text, sometimes as it sparkles out, sometimes after we work to make it stronger and clearer, is worth reading.

How do you get them to read without always requiring everybody to read the same selection on a fixed date?

Though this book rejects the notion that students cannot produce college level writing unless we feed them college level ideas from anthologies of nonfiction, fiction or poetry, the importance of reading in the open class is clarified and emphasized on pages 89-104. Whenever it seems relevant, preferably early on in the term, the class can read and discuss the opinions expressed there. On page 99 I suggest one way students can let you know what and how they are reading.

Perhaps they will talk about reading while first discussing class objectives and expectations, or while looking together at the organization of this book and reading aloud some of the quotes on the title pages. I hope they will use the notes on pages 363-367 frequently—whenever they want to hear more from the person who speaks to them from poem, story, or essay. The quotations are here not only to support my ideas but to introduce writers I think they might enjoy.

You can add to the *un*required reading list for your class throughout the term by sharing whatever you recall from your reading as you listen to their discussions. But never make it a little or a big lecture. Just a casual, though forceful, comment. A part of the conversation that's going on. Whenever you come to class excited or angry about something you have just read, share your reactions just as you would with a group of your friends. But remember that students get bored more quickly than anyone else. Unless they ask for more, we should always shut up before they shut us off.

Sometimes we can help someone discover reading as we respond to the bits of experience he shares with us in writing. Maybe the feeling he expresses recalls a poem that expresses a similar feeling. Or what has happened to him parallels the experience of a character from a short story or novel or play. Or we know a book or essay or an anthology that deals with the problem he is facing.

The aim: to help all our students see reading as an extension of, or another kind of, personal experience instead of a drudging academic requirement; to let reading become meaningful and involving, an integral part of what's happening in a community of learners.

When class talk peters out because no one can answer the questions they are asking each other, or because no one can support or refute the generalizations and opinions they are tossing about, the teacher again becomes a resource person, citing periodicals and books they can turn to for the information they need. That usually leads to small task groups that assume the responsibility of finding what they or the whole class wants to know.

Again, just as in class talk and writing, students move toward the kind of reading performance we hope for when the small group work becomes a self-involving, pervasive experience. For now they are dealing with the realities of a human situation. They are a group of people brought together to look for answers to human questions, to look for solutions to human problems. So they read with a purpose. And they try to read critically. And they try to synthesize what they read with all their other experiences.

And the teacher, listening to them talk on paper and in class about their reading, responds not only to *what* but also to *how* they are reading. He responds by setting up individual conferences or small task groups for those who can not comprehend the basic meaning of a selection and for those who are ready for close analysis or critical appraisal of what they read.

How does a student improve his sentences? his style?

Because the teacher in the open class no longer prepares lectures that tell the students how or what to write and no longer plans daily activities to stimulate and motivate them to write, we have more time for responding to each person's writing. So as soon as we break through the student's concept of English teacher as corrector-grader-judge of writing, as soon as a person perceives us as a fellow human being who can help him learn to say what he wants to say more clearly and more forcefully, we are ready for the kind of student-teacher talk summarized in "playing with Stylistic Possibilities" (238-293).

That section is based on the strong conviction that trying to help a person rewrite all the sentences in a piece like the ones on pages 249-253 would be a hopeless waste of time. That's why this book begins with the invitation to talk on paper. Talking on paper eliminates most of the phoniness that sets the tone for many academic papers. It also exposes stuffy and pompous writing. Though some students may sometimes talk like that, most of them will admit that they usually speak with a more honest and natural style. And they can hear the difference between their lifeless attempts to imitate what they think good writing is and the sound of their own voices on paper.

When a person talks on paper about what is going on inside him, he is no longer hacking out an assignment but composing. He is attempting to make his own internal experience visible, in words, on a piece of paper. And in his own unique way, within the limits of his own linguistic competence, he is developing a personal style.

I hope your classes will work in small groups with the questions asked and the possibilities suggested in "Voice" and "Perceptions" (143-170). I hope the examples of student writing included in "Stylistic Possibilities" will help you show your students, individually or in small groups, some of the ways to achieve a smoother flow of words and ideas and a clearer, stronger voice.

But this book insists that we learn to write graceful instead of cumbersome prose, we learn to write with clarity and force, only by working with our own writing. If students read aloud what they have written, in a student-teacher conference or in a small non-threatening group of classmates, they become sensitive to the patterns and the rhythms of their sentences. They also learn to spot the generalization that weakens, the repetition that bores, and the vagueness and ambiguity that confuses.

As a student covers a wide range of thought and feeling in his dialogues with teacher and classmates, he discovers, if he does not already know, that he has many voices. He hears them as he reads aloud what he has written. And he sees that the voice that "comes naturally" in a given situation controls what and how he writes about that situation. He learns from his own writing that he can define and enlarge his resources of self-expression by exploring and expanding all the possibilities that lie within the *self* that he is or is becoming.

Because I do not separate style and content as I write or as I try to help students become better writers, I make no attempt to do so in this book. If pressed to define style, I would say it is the total impact of a piece of writing. And I would say playing with stylistic possibilities includes the whole complex process of putting words together to say what we think and feel.

What about correctness?

This book has not thrown out spelling and punctuation and "good grammar." It does put those matters where they belong. That is, in a totally separate and final stage of the human (or academic) activity that ends in a paper for somebody to read. That final stage is here called "Copyreading." (295). This approach assumes that the student writer learns "correctness" *not* from a book of rules but by building his own Copyreading Guide with examples from his own writing.

I hope no one using this book will ever have students spend a lot of time working on copyreading until they can fill a page with some ease and with much pride in the sound of their own voices on paper. I hope no one will ever ditto and distribute writing with glaring errors that might diminish the writer or his ideas in the eyes of his classmates. If someone decides he wants to share with the class a piece that is full of spelling and punctuation errors before we have decided to start his Copyreading Guide, I introduce myself in a new role. I become his copy editor, the person who corrects errors *without changing* the form or content of what he is saying and *without changing* the sound of his voice. Seeing and hearing the difference in his copy and the "published" one often means he sees a reason for learning something he has for years rejected, and he begins his Guide with some enthusiasm and determination.

On pages 336-346 I try to show how I work with a person who has serious copyreading problems.

What do you do about grades?

The concept of learning this book is based on and the open class it advocates make grades irrelevant. But they aren't. Because we still have deans and executive officers and legislators who measure the quality of instruction in a department, and judge the reputation of a whole school by the number of low grades we give; and vice presidents in charge of personnel in the public and private sectors, and policy makers in graduate colleges who accept and reject applicants by comparing their cumulative grade averages; and students who equate getting an education with getting grades in courses leading to degrees; and students and teachers who doubt that any learning would take place if the reward of high grades, the threat of low grades, were eliminated; and teachers who think students should be flunked out if they cannot achieve prescribed levels of competence in one semester; and teachers who judge student writing by criteria that other teachers would call vague and questionable; and teachers who judge students by some preconceived notion of how grades should be distributed instead of asking *what* and *how* and *how much* each person has learned or *why* he has not learned.

I have spent most of my teaching life working in one-to-one conferences with students, helping them plan, write and rewrite papers assigned and graded by other teachers, or helping them get ready for a departmental theme exam to be given and graded by other teachers. Perhaps that is why grading a piece of writing that shares a bit of a person's experience, a bit of himself, seems such an *unnatural* act. Perhaps that is why I do not grade any piece of writing (or speaking) in my classes.

After trying to let the writer know that I am receiving the message he is sending me, that I want to understand the meaning that message has for him, I try to ask the kinds of questions asked in this book, and I try to engage him in the kind of student-teacher talk summarized in "Stylistic Possibilities" and "Copyreading." For me and my students that kind of feedback leads to far better writing than any grading system ever could.

The teacher using this book will have to find his own alternatives if he decides traditional grading is no longer the answer. But whatever we consider or decide on, the grade sheets from the registrar arrive. And each grade we report is supposed to indicate that a person has fulfilled certain academic requirements, that he is ready for certain future requirements, that he belongs where we have placed him on the bell-shaped curve.

So we're caught again. Between what is and what ought to be. And we hassle on. Determined to change the things which, they say, cannot be changed.

At the end of the semester I ask each person I am working with (whether in a class he is taking for credit or in the non-credit lab) to evaluate the course in relation to what he has learned. If I must report a grade for him, I ask him to tell me the grade he thinks he should have and to explain why he thinks he should have that grade. If I cannot see the relationship between the grade he suggests and his explanation, or between the grade he has chosen as a measure of his learning and what I think he has or has not learned, or between the grade he now wants and his response to the class and to me throughout the semester, we talk our way to an agreement.

And I keep on talking about the proposal to make rhetoric at our school a *pass-no record* option for all students. And I keep on hoping for the beautiful day when what they learn will be more important than what they get, the day when we will not be told that a certain percent of the class should get D's and F's, when we will not be told that no more than half of the class should get A's and B's.

Can this book be used in developmental classes?

I certainly hope so. If not, I must live with the sad irony that here I contribute nothing to students like the ones who changed my teaching life.

If you are free to let each person begin with his own language and to let him talk and write about what he already knows, then, I believe, developmental students will respond—and learn—in an open class. Whatever level of competence they have, whatever "track" the entrance exams place them in, they can engage in the student-student dialogue and the student-teacher dialogue of this book.

The least competent may need to try to talk on paper two or three times a week for a full semester before they can fill a page with ease and confidence. But when teacher or classmate asks why or what do you mean, they, too, can give clear and forceful answers—if they believe we really want to hear their answers. If answering the questions raised about the experiences and opinions shared with the class becomes everybody's main concern during the second semester, you will not have *to teach* them how to organize and support their ideas. They will learn to—experientially— in their dialogues with you and each other.

If, as the second semester gets underway, someone still cannot extend a statement of opinion or attitude into a longer piece that analyzes and supports that statement, have him work with page 187 or 104 of this book. The questions there will help him see how he must question his generalizations and how his questions can lead him to a plan that will help him turn his free and easy talk into an essay.

If students are ready to start working on copyreading by midterm or a little later during their first semester, they are usually able to find most of their deviations from the conventions by the end of two semesters.

But changing the way we think and talk and write is a slow, sometimes painful, process. Every developmental student probably needs a third semester of talking and writing in an open class. In. fact, I believe we should provide the opportunities for them to continue the dialogues begun in English 101 in every course we offer. If we don't, college, like high school, will be little more than a place where they collect credits toward graduation, a place where they will again be denied the experiences that are essential to everyone's development as a thinking, feeling *literate* human being.

I like to think—perhaps only hope—that this book offers a new direction—a new hope—for the thousands of persons in open door colleges who every year fail the subfreshman English course or drop out in frustration and despair because what they are being "taught" has little or no meaning for them. For I believe they will never learn what they need to know by sitting through mass lectures or class discussions dominated by the teacher and a few of their classmates; they will never learn to put their thoughts and feelings onto paper by filling blanks in workbooks and programmed texts; they will never know the joy of writing for others if they spend their class hours with learning systems and learning machines that provide "individualized" instruction in lonely carrels.

We must reject all the software and hardware that offer us new or old ways of *pouring* grammar or rhetoric or great ideas into the student's head. We must permit, we must help *all* our students bring the reality of their own lives, their own language, into the classroom.

No book can tell us how to do it. Nobody can answer all our questions about the open class.

With the human resources our students bring with them, with the human situations that develop within the group, we make whatever we can. For teaching is a creative act.

notes

When you wish to hear more from the writers who help me say what I am trying to say in this book, use the notes that follow here. Some quotes are not documented here because I am including no secondary source.

page the quote is on	author and title the quote is from	book or other source you'll find it in	publisher you can order it from
1	Gerard Manley Hopkins "Spring"	*Poems and Prose of Gerard Manley Hopkins*, p. 28 (ed. by W. H. Gardner)	Penguin Books, Inc., Baltimore (1967)
7	Carl R. Rogers "Learning: What Kind?"	*Freedom to Learn*, p. 5	Charles E. Merrill Publishing Co., Columbus, Ohio (1969)
9	William C. Schul† "Interpersonal Relations"	*Joy: Expanding Human Awareness*, pp. 131-132	Grove Press, Inc., New York (1969)
17	Percival Hunt "Disciplined Writing"	*The Gift of the Unicorn*, p. 60	University of Pittsburgh Press, Pittsburgh (1965)
27	Charles E. Silberman	*Crisis in the Class Classroom*, p. 155	Vintage Books, New York (1970)
38	Paul Goodman "Jobs"	*Growing Up Absurd*, p. 17	Vintage Books, New York (1960)
49	Robert Penn Warren	*Meet Me in the Green Glen*, pp. 369-370	Random House, Inc. New York (1971)
50	Kenneth Koch "Teaching Children to Write Poetry"	*Wishes, Lies and Dreams*, p. 6. Excerpt in *New York Review of Books*, April 9, 1971, p. 17	Chelsea House Publishers, New York (1970)
51, 54-55	Hermann Hesse	*Siddhartha*, pp. 30-34	New Directions Publishing Corp., New York (1951)
56	Erik Erikson "Toward Contemporary Issues: Youth"	*Identity, Youth and Crisis*, pp. 233, 235-236	W. W. Norton and Company, Inc., New York (1968)
56	Erik Erikson	*Insight and Responsibility*, p. 125	W. W. Norton and Company, Inc., New York (1964)
57	Robert Frost "Letter to *The Amherst Student*"	*Selected Prose of Robert Frost*, pp. 105-106 (ed. by Hyde Cox and E. C. Lathem)	Holt, Rinehart and Winston, Inc., New York (1966)

60	Ralph Ellison "Prologue"	*Invisible Man*, p. 7	Signet Books, New York (1952)
70, 71	Mark Twain (Samuel Clemens) "Corn-Pone Opinions"	*Europe and Elsewhere*, pp. 399-401, 404-405. Also *The Portable Mark Twain*, pp. 572-573, 576-578	Harper and Row, Publishers, New York (1923); The Viking Press, Inc., New York (1966)
72	Erik Erikson "Toward Contemporary Issues: Youth"	*Identity, Youth and Crisis*, p. 258	W. W. Norton and Company, Inc., New York (1968)
73	J. D. Salinger	*The Catcher in the Rye*, p. 211	Bantam Books, Inc., New York (1964)
73	Charles A. Reich	*The Greening of America*, pp. 148-149	Bantam Books, Inc., New York (1971)
74	Kahlil Gibran "On Children"	*The Prophet*, pp. 18-19	Alfred A. Knopf, Inc., New York (1936)
75	Joseph Stein	*Fiddler on the Roof*, p. 103	Crown Publishers, Inc., New York (1964)
75	The O. M. Collective "Other Groups"	*The Organizer's Manual*, p. 293	Bantam Books, Inc., New York (1971)
77	James Moffett "Drama: What is Happening"	*Teaching the Universe of Discourse*, p. 92	Houghton Mifflin Company, Boston (1968)
105	Wallace Stevens "The Idea of Order at Key West"	*The Collected Poems of Wallace Stevens*, pp. 129-130	Alfred A. Knopf, Inc., New York (1968)
111	Geoffrey Summerfield "A Short Dialogue on Some Aspects of That Which We Call Creative English"	*Creativity in English*, p. 44	National Council of Teachers of English, Champaign, Ill. (1968)
113, 115	Erich Fromm "The Theory of Love"	*The Art of Loving*, p. 33, 23	Bantam Books, Inc., New York (1963)
115	Carl Rogers "The Interpersonal Relationships in the Facilitation of Learning"	*Freedom to Learn*, p. 109	Charles E. Merrill Publishing Company, Columbus, Ohio (1969)
127	Walker Gibson "Style and the Limits of Language"	*The Limits of Language*, p. 113 (ed. by Walker Gibson)	Hill and Wang, Inc., New York (1962)

136	Robert Frost "Letter to *The Amherst Student"*	*Selected Prose of Robert Frost,* p. 106 (ed. by Hyde Cox and E. C. Lathem)	Holt, Rinehart and Winston, Inc., New York (1966)
136	Alfred North Whitehead "The Organization of Thought"	*The Limits of Language,* p. 12 (ed. by Walker Gibson)	Hill and Wang, Inc., New York (1962)
137	Robert Frost "Letter to *The Amherst Student"*	*Selected Prose of Robert Frost,* pp. 105-106 (ed. by Hyde Cox and E. C. Lathem)	Holt, Rinehart and Winston, Inc., New York (1966)
143	Norman O. Brown	"Apocalypse" *Harper's Magazine,* p. 47, May, 1961	
149	Gertrude Stein "Poetry and Grammar"	*Lectures in America,* p. 209	Random House, Inc., New York (1935)
150	Emily Dickinson "Letter to T. W. Higginson"	*The Letters of Emily Dickinson,* p. 548 (ed. by Thomas H. Johnson)	Belknap Press of Harvard University Press, Cambridge, Mass. (1958)
150-152	Emily Dickinson Poems	*The Complete Poems of Emily Dickinson,* pp. 115, 318, 381-382, 110, 209 (ed. by Thomas H. Johnson)	Little, Brown and Company, Boston (1960)
154	Theodore Dreiser "Foreword"	*Bibliography of the Writings of Theodore Dreiser,* p. 12 (compiled by Edward D. McDonald)	Centaur Bookshop, Philadelphia (1927)
154	Percival Hunt "Disciplined Writing"	*The Gift of the Unicorn,* p. 62	University of Pittsburgh Press, Pittsburgh (1965)
157	Elizabeth Bowen	*Afterthought,* p. 208	Longmans, London (1962)
171	Kimball Wiles "Foreword"	*Values and Teaching,* p. vii (Louis E. Rath, Merrill Harmin, and Sidney B. Simon)	Charles E. Merrill Publishing Co., Columbus, Ohio (1966)
181, 194	Wendell Johnson "You Can't Write Writing"	*Language, Meaning, and Maturity,* p. 108 (ed. by S. I. Hayakawa)	Harper and Row, Publishers, New York (1954)
195	Buckminster Fuller	*I Seem to be a Verb,* p. 1	Bantam Books, New York (1970)

241	James Moffett "Grammar and the Sentence"	*Teaching the Universe of Discourse*, pp. 187, 162, 163, 180	Houghton Mifflin Company, Boston (1968)
244	Ernest Hemingway	*Writers at Work: The Paris Review Interview*, p. 222 (2nd Series)	The Viking Press, Inc., New York (1963)
247	Leo Tolstoy	*Talks with Tolstoy*, p. 26 (A. B. Goldenweizer)	Hogarth Press, Richmond, England (1933)
300	Martin Joos "Too Many Clocks"	*The Five Clocks*, pp. 4-5	Harcourt Brace Jovanovich, New York (1961)
303	James Moffett "Drama: What is Happening"	*Teaching the Universe of Discourse*, pp. 93, 94	Houghton Mifflin Company, Boston (1968)

contents